A Faith for Today

E. Flesseman-Van Leer

Translated by John E. Steely

Association of Baptist Professors of Religion
Box A
Mercer University
Macon, GA 31207

Printed in the United States of America
for
The Association of Baptist Professors of Religion

Box A, Mercer University   Macon, GA. 31207

ISBN 0-932180-06-X

Library of Congress No. 79-56514

Special Studies Series No. 7
Cover Logo by Joe Chris Robertson, Mars Hill College
First printed....1980

First printed....1980

TABLE OF CONTENTS

FOREWORD TO THE SECOND EDITION

I did not write a foreword to the first printing of this book. It was my opinion that the book would have to speak for itself. The decision to provide such a foreword now for this new edition is prompted by conversations and reviews that have called my attention to some points that are not fully clear.

1. I have been asked several times what is the intention of the indented sections. In the writing of my book I was thinking primarily of those readers who were brought up in a Christian environment but who now are no longer comfortable with it all and have become uncertain. I also had in mind those who have the desire to think through their faith more thoroughly. In the part of the text that is indented I try frequently to make a connection between what I have written and what has been taught previously. Sometimes particular data from the Bible also are treated. In both cases the indented sections often have a somewhat technical theological character. In reading the book one can skip over these sections without breaking the train of thought.

2. It seems that it is not always clear what I intend when I say that something is "unbelievable," or that it "does not justify belief." If I were writing the book again, I would be more cautious with the use of that kind of expression. Ordinarily I mean by this that a certain idea in my opinion is not in harmony with the thinking of faith as it is gained on the basis of the Bible. Sometimes I use the term also for an idea that is in conflict with what I think I know about the world. My faith indeed transcends my understanding, but it may not be in conflict with it. I am, after all, called to worship God and to love him with my mind.

3. From the reviews of the book it has appeared to me that chapter XI, "God in Christ," has given occasion for some misunderstanding. Naturally I still hold to the ideas that are brought forward in that chapter. Otherwise I would not have allowed the chapter to be reprinted; and I have changed only one sentence, which could easily be misunderstood. But if it had not been difficult for technical reasons I would have arranged the chapter differently, on the basis of the criticisms it received. I would have explicitly repeated what is said in earlier chapters, that the covenant relationship between God and man, as well as the maintenance and the re-establishment of the covenant, came from God's initiative and not from man's (see specifically what is said about the covenant, about election, and about Israel). I would also have emphasized the point that Jesus, this totally obedient man, was given by God and equipped with his Spirit for

his particular special task. It remains true that because of Jesus Christ's perfect, free obedience, God is one with him; but it must not be forgotten that this obedience is based upon God's election and gracious provision. Here too the initiative rests with God. All this is already said—see, for example, what is said on page 86 about the Spirit in Jesus Christ—but it should have been brought out more forcefully in this chapter. A part of the criticism is based on a misunderstanding of what I intended to say, and for this I myself am partly responsible.

Finally, I wish to express my gratitude for the many affirmative reactions that I have received. I have been impressed by the fact that these came chiefly from the side of those people for whom I wrote the book in the first place. I hope that in its second printing the book will also find the same response. I shall continue to place high value on the comments and observations it receives. I am constantly discovering that on a great many points I am far from finished with thinking about them.

TO THE THIRD EDITION

Since the publisher has given me the opportunity, in connection with this new printing, to revise the text, it almost goes without saying that I now have changed those points of obscurity that I mentioned in the foreword to the second edition. Further, as an outgrowth of observations in conversations, I have partially rewritten the part about the appearances of Jesus (pp. 59-60.), although the thrust of this section remains the same. I should like also to point to the insertion of a new line on page 64. The other changes, often no more than a couple of words or a single sentence, have been introduced for the sake of clarification or on the basis of the ongoing theological discussion.

TO THE FOURTH EDITION

Again in this republication I have introduced a few minor changes. More important, however, is the fact that an entirely new chapter (XV) is added. When the book first appeared I was already aware of the lacuna created by the absence of anything on prayer. But at that time I felt that I had nothing meaningful that I could say about it. I think that I have arrived at fuller clarity, to the extent that I now have ventured to devote a chapter to this subject. I hope that the readers will find something worthwhile in it.

TRANSLATOR'S PREFACE

It is gratifying to have a part in bringing before the English-reading public this book by Dr. E. Flessman-van Leer. The task of transposing such carefully wrought-out reflections from one language to another is a delicate one. I am indebted to the author for her gracious help in reviewing the translation and in making suggestions for improvement. Of course I must accept the responsibility for any failure to give proper expression to her ideas.

A word of gratitude should be expressed to my colleagues in the faculty of Southeastern Baptist Theological Seminary for their kind encouragement and generous support of this work. They have taught me the necessity of listening to views that differ from my own and the value of reexamination of ancient and treasured truths. What they have contributed, though it may not be evident to them, is visible to me in almost every page of this translation, where I have drawn upon their resources in seeking to give adequate expression to Dr. Flesseman's thoughts.

The most extensive and intensive obligation is owed to my wife Donnie for her support and for many hours of labor in preparing this work for publication.

John E. Steely

Wake Forest, North Carolina
February 1979

Editor's Preface

In 1974 the Association of Baptist Professors of Religion inaugurated the publication of *Perspectives in Religious Studies*, a scholarly journal containing articles and reviews of the widest interest for the professional scholar-teacher. This bold undertaking marked a significant departure for the Association. With only limited funds available it was truly a venture in faith. The journal has been well received and its contribution to the study of religion has been widely acclaimed. It appears three times yearly (Spring, Summer, and Fall).

Early in 1977 the Association began the second phase of its publishing program. This volume marks the seventh offering in the "Special Studies Series." We believe that, together with *Perspectives,* the Special Studies Series will make available the very best scholarly materials to the teacher of religion.

Watson E. Mills
Series Editor

I. ADDRESSED BY GOD

God as not self-evident

How is it possible for rational men and women still to be able to believe in God and to venture to speak about him? There was a time when this question could not arise in our Western cultural setting. It was taken for granted that a civilized person was a Christian and naturally believed in "the existence of God." Then there came a time when the question was posed by people outside the church. But in our time Christians themselves are posing this question; for many of them their own faith has become a problematical thing and they no longer know how they can speak intelligently about it.

It has always been difficult to talk about faith with outsiders. Yet in this respect our parents had an easier time than we have. The outsiders then were often deliberate and committed opponents. Their militant attitude usually was based in part on misunderstandings which one could set straight, and in part on faults of the church in which one had to concede that their criticism was just, but which did not affect what was essential to the faith. We, on the other hand, find ourselves in general confronted with a wall of indifference, of unconcern. Christianity is no longer being disputed, but is denied; people are not actually against it, but it has come to lie completely outside the field of vision.

Yet this is not where the greatest problem lies. Instead, it now lies in the fact that in recent years it has become difficult to talk about God even in the church. A growing number of believers no longer know what content they can give to the word "God," and they are asking what they actually mean when they say that they believe in God. They know that God is not some sort of wise old man somewhere up there in the clouds. The remark of one of the first Russian space-travelers that he had not met God anywhere in space either testifies to an inconceivable naïveté or, as appears to me more probable, was not meant to be taken seriously. The difficulty, however, is not so much in our inability to point to a place somewhere in space where God is, nor in the fact that we cannot picture him, but in the fact that we do not see what necessary and identifiable role he fills in the world. A god who is only an explanation of where everything comes from is no more than an unknown quantity, a kind of X, to fill a gap in our knowledge. A god who intervenes in nature and history from without is for us unbelievable. Nature has become too much subject to our calculations and control for that. For example, how can we still seriously believe that it is God who gives a poor harvest or causes a flood, when man can in increasing measure forestall such disasters? And as for history, to our way of thinking it is formed by people and by human decisions, while the element of happenstance and incalculability that it continues to include is given with the freedom of man. For this the concept of "god" does not need to be introduced. And even the god of our inner life will no longer do; we are suspicious of a god for whom we have a "need," who comforts us in our grief and comes to help our feeling of weakness and dependence. We all know too much of psychology not to see therein a projection of our own yearning.

The "self-evidentness" of God

Through the problematic indicated above, which in greater or lesser measure is the experience of all of us, God has become for us "un-self-evident." Alongside this, however, I wish also still to speak of the "self-evidentness" of God. That is to say, at the moment when we meet him in our lives and he addresses us, our rational difficulties are not solved, but we do, as it were, leave them behind us. God then has granted us in our lives to know him in such a way that we can no longer deny him; we cannot help believing. For believing is not the acceptance of "supernatural" truths, but a standing-in-relation, the knowing and experiencing that God is confronting us and that we stand before him. We cannot persuade someone else that God is. But if we experience him in our lives, then that is an experience which carries its truth within itself and which is utterly convincing for us.

The experience of being addressed by God is in the nature of the case subjective. It is a phenomenon of our inner life. Hence we shall never be able to show convincingly to an outsider that it is not "merely" subjective. But for one who experiences it, this inward, of course also psychologically determined experience points away from what is private, inward, to the other, who is not ourselves. It will however not be only the so-called outsider who skeptically asks whether this experience of God is not only a matter of subjective imagination. This is also the peculiar affliction of faith, to which perhaps no one is entirely immune. This being addressed by God, this encounter with him—or however else we may wish to describe it—is however not a constant experience. It is something that comes over us each time it happens. In the moments or times in our lives when God is present for us, he is self-evident to us, he speaks for himself. Afterward, then, often comes doubt, and we ourselves are inclined to explain away these moments as merely subjective imagination. But then there still is also something like trust—trust not in our own experience, but trust in God, who has come to meet us in our earlier experience. It is like friendship or love for another person. We do not consciously experience or feel such friendship or love continuously, and this can lead, particularly at the beginning of a relationship of friendship or love, to doubt. Later on then there develops something like a "habitual" love or friendship, just as there can also be "habitual" faith. This is fortunate, because otherwise life would become burdened with excessive tension which would make it intolerable. But even our trust must be based on an experience of God. Without this experience no faith is possible and we can at best speak of God only "by hearsay."

Experience and recognition

When in the foregoing I spoke so emphatically about the experience of faith, I was not thinking of mystical experiences and raptures, of which most people, with a certain healthy sobriety, are usually suspicious. But there also are only a few who ever have that kind of experiences. And when I spoke of being addressed, I was not thinking of an inward voice which a person hears. But it is easier to say what I do not mean than to give a positive description. Indeed, experiencing God has this feature in common then with other experiences which touch a person in the very depths of his being. It is difficult also to describe the human experience of love, and it is even impossible to describe it to someone who does not know what love is. Moreover, just as the experience of love between persons is unique and cannot be captured in one fixed, universally valid pattern, so also is the experience of God different for each person. Yet in order to describe this experience, words will first be set forth which are borrowed from the relationship of man and his fellowman: to be addressed, to be seized, to encounter. All these are images, and not an adequate description. Obviously not. For God is different from and more than all else that we know; therefore even the encounter with him is a unique experience.

We also must not speak solely in images of encountering and of being addressed, regardless of how indispensable these are for me. But if these are the only figures which are used, then the life of faith appears to break apart into nothing but momentary experiences, in which any continuity is lacking. There is, however, also such a thing as fellowship with God, a walking with him, as the Bible puts it. But these images also are once again borrowed from interpersonal relations.

We are addressed. In that respect an encounter with God is something that comes over a person. Yet it is not such that the person can be merely passive. He can also open himself and can himself set out in search for God. And again we can refer to human love. It too comes over a person. But he can indeed prepare himself inwardly for it or, on the contrary, so armor himself against it that it has practically no chance of conquering him.

If it is possible to speak of setting out in search of God, this includes the idea that even without this experience of encounter, and prior to it, we can already know something of God. And, in fact, this being addressed by God, personal as it is, does not take place in a vacuum and does not come to a person as an individual detached from all history. We are not the first who have had this experience. Before us there were many others who in their time and in their own way knew themselves to be addressed by him. God has not come into our lives alone, but he has also done this for people and generations before us. There is not only a communion of God with us, but also a communion of God with other believers besides ourselves and before us.

This being addressed by God has a dynamic of its own in the life of a person; it prompts him to speak about it and to bear witness. In this connection I am thinking in the first place of the biblical writers. They tell, each in his own way, how God has made himself known to them in a particular event. And time and again later generations and later writers have recognized in the testimony of the earlier ones the same God who now has come anew to them in a new event. The Bible is rightly called the story of the mighty acts of God. It can be stated thus if one only remembers that this, too—of course, like all speaking about God—is symbolic language, an attempt to give expression to the fact that for certain people an event became as it were transparent, so that in and through this event they experienced God's presence and that in this event God interpreted himself to them and addressed them. This holds true for the Old Testament as well as for the New, with this difference: in the Old Testament many different events are discussed, while the New Testament treats the one event of Jesus Christ. But in both what is involved is a recognition, time and again renewed, of the same God.

Thus the note of recognition is of fundamental importance for faith. For the experience of being addressed by God occurs, as a rule, through the means of earlier testimonies. Apart from these, the experience evaporates into a vague mysticism in which he who addresses us does not become known. On the other hand, however, the God of whom the earlier testimonies speak must also now be recognized in our own experience. Apart from this, those testimonies are for us splendid or not-so-splendid religious monuments from the past.

The revelation in Israel and Jesus Christ

The question which is posed in almost every conversation with non-Christians is whether for our faith we are dependent on the testimonies of the Bible or, what is in essence the same, on those who interpret these testimonies. Now in any case it is a fact that in very specific, decisive events, culminating in the person of Jesus Christ, people have come to know God and the life of fellowship with him; that the biblical writings are the resulting deposit; and that as is proved in experience, other people also, down to our own time, have time and again had the experience with these writings that they meet God therein. However, we do not have the right to deny that God could also address a person and reveal himself to that person in an event in his own life or in the history of his own time. But if it actually is *God* whom he encounters therein, then it is the selfsame God as that of the Bible, or, better said, the same as the one who has communicated himself to men in the history of Israel and in Jesus Christ. For there is no other God. Therefore a person who has encountered him elsewhere will also be able to recognize him in the biblical testimonies.

Very closely related to this is the question whether people of other religions cannot know God just as well as can Christians. I think that it is not fitting for us to pass judgment here and that indeed we must leave open this possibility. But again it must be added that if they actually know *God*, they will recognize him in the God of the Bible.

> 1. In theology one speaks of "special revelation" and "general revelation." By the former we mean that God has actually made himself known only on the narrow line of the history of the biblical Israel and of Jesus Christ, while by the latter we suggest that he can be discerned everywhere, at least partially. I consider these terms unfortunate. For if revelation is a category of encounter, then revelation is always special, particular. God is not present always and everywhere; he is not just "at hand." Although he communicates himself elsewhere than only in and through the biblical history, that is not a general or common phenomenon, but a special occurrence, a special act of God. Hence it would perhaps be better for us to speak of universal revelation rather than of general revelation. But the term "special" revelation too can evoke misunderstanding. The idea of exclusiveness must not be bound up with it. When God discloses himself, this is not for the sole benefit of the recipient(s), but this self-disclosure of himself is for the sake of all.

2. Still more confusing is the pair of concepts "supernatural" and "natural" revelation. The expression "supernatural" suggests the idea that something is added to the ordinary, natural event, whereby it becomes revelatory, or indeed that God intervenes in nature or history in a "supernatural" fashion. But God wishes to be experienced and acknowledged in the natural event itself when and where he gives himself to be known. Hence the idea of a "natural" revelation too is rejected. History, the world, and nature are not in themselves, by nature, revelatory. God is not identical with these, although he does let himself be encountered in them.

3. Nor do I have much use for the alternative of a completed or a still continuing revelation. For this presupposes the understanding of revelation as the imparting of all sorts of truths, so that one can pose the question whether at a given moment all truths have or have not been made known. But if revelation signifies that God gives himself to be known to a person, then this happens again and again where a person meets God and comes to faith. This does not deny that a person in the course of his life or the believers in the course of history can come to know God better and better, just as a person can get better and better acquainted with friend or beloved and can more and more establish a relationship of trust and confidence with him or her.

A new orientation

A person who knows himself to have been addressed and laid hold upon by God comes thereby to have a particular standing in life. One can speak here of conversion or rebirth, if one does not therewith necessarily connect the idea with an inward experience at a particular, demonstrable moment. Although this cannot be excluded, with most people it comes much more gradually. Just as it can happen that a person knows suddenly, as in a stroke of lightning, that he is in love, so also can the encounter with God be a sudden, overwhelming experience. But people can also fall in love very gradually, so that they cannot tell precisely when it began. In the same way, many people, especially if they have had a Christian upbringing, realize slowly, or only afterward, that they have been laid hold on by God. But this does not minimize the fact that when one once becomes conscious of this, it brings with it a feeling of gratitude and reverence, and often also of surprise and amazement. Thereby his life also comes to stand in a particular light. He senses himself to be standing in the presence of God, addressed by him, and hence called upon to give answer to him with his life. And the world too comes to stand in a particular light. Of all that is or happens, nothing can carry absolute meaning within itself, not because it has become unimportant, but because it has become relative in the literal sense of the word, that is, standing in relation to God. Thus the recognition of the great Other signifies a particular orientation, a particular way of looking at the world and at one's own existence.

II. THE GOD OF THE COVENANT

God in his revelation

There is discussion in our time of atheists' faith and an atheistic idea of God, a use of words that seems at first glance to be unintelligible and a contradiction within itself. But it must not be forgotten that the connotation of the word "atheism" has changed. Originally it was understood to mean the denial of God; in that case indeed one cannot speak of an atheist's God. At present, however, people often use the term not to reject the very existence of God, but to reject a particular "theistic" view of him. By this is meant then that conception which views God as a Superior Being who omnipotently intervenes in what happens here from a world above or outside our world. In our time, however, many people can no longer believe in such a God; they cannot accept the idea of another world above the world known to us or the idea that people's lives and history on earth should be governed from outside and, as it were, manipulated. By this they do not intend to attack belief in God, but they are firmly convinced that we must speak of him in a new way. The great difficulty, however, is then to find words which give expression to him and which can find a responsive echo in our time. For one can share the objections to the all-too-assured and objectifying talk about the existence of an omnipotent Supreme Being in heaven and yet not be satisfied with the proposed alternative figures, in which, for example, God is identified as the "Reality which sets us free," or as "That which gives direction to our lives," or as "Him whom we cannot name but have in view in the deepest ground of our being," or as the "Transcendence which we experience in real fellow-feeling with humanity." Certainly there can be a thread of truth in these descriptions. Nevertheless for many believers they are no adequate way of referring to the reality to which these believers point when they say "God."

It may also be asked whether it is not better then to be silent about him. This is suggested not only because our human words are inadequate, but primarily because God is too lofty and exalted for us wretched little men to be able to know him. Now that does sound pious and reverent, but in reality we would thereby wrong God. For this so high and exalted God has made a point of becoming known to men. The entire Old and New Testaments are in fact nothing other than God's great self-explanation, broken by the prism of human experiences.

Christians do not believe in an unknown God—about such a God we would indeed be able only to be silent—but in a God who has granted to men the power to know him. That is to say that we believe in a God who has willed to reveal himself to us; therefore it is not allowed us to keep silent about him.

God with man

That God has made himself knowable to men includes the affirmation that revelation is a two-sided event. It is something that takes place between God and man. If God explains himself, this does not take place in a vacuum. To say it another way, divine revelation and the faith that accepts this revelation belong together, so that we cannot speak of the one without the other.

> For this reason, in my opinion, the terminology of objective and subjective revelation is untenable. In dogmatics, objective revelation is understood to mean God's "objective" revelatory actions, apart from man and his faith, while subjective revelation refers to God's action in man whereby this man understands "subjectively" also the revelation that has taken place. This distinction is meant to see to it that the divine revelation is not made dependent on human belief. I think however that it makes sense to speak of revelation only where something also becomes revealed, evident, to man. God does not make himself known "objectively" in a vacuum, but to persons. To use a comparison on the human plane: an "objective" declaration of love that is not addressed to the beloved, so that the latter can recognize the declaration of love as such, is no *declaration* of love.

The God whom we know is not a God-by-himself, but a God who has entered into relationship with us human beings. About him as he is in himself, apart from his revelation, we can say no meaningful word. This does not mean that he is totally comprehended in his revelation. He cannot be communicated in his fulness to man with his earthly, humanly limited capacity for comprehension. We know only in part and imperfectly, says Paul, and this is preeminently true of our knowledge of God. But if God is more and greater than he has communicated to us, still he is not *different* from what he has revealed to us. As surely as it is God himself who has entered into contact with us and as surely as he is trustworthy and does not make sport of us, he himself *is* in all eternity as he has made himself known. We know him as the God who wills to be with us. But this then is what he is, this is his nature. Therefore it is a denial of the real God to speak of a God-by-himself. To put it in the form of a paradox: God-in-himself is God who turns to man and wills to be with him.

In this connection something must be said about the transcendence and the immanence of God. If one understands transcendence to mean that God is more than the world and is superior to it, one can indeed speak of God as transcendent. But if one takes transcendence to mean that God "exists" outside the world, one moves into a climate of thinking that is alien to faith. As we have said, God is essentially together with man, together with the world, and he is not found by us anywhere other than in this world. This is not meant to say, however, that he therefore is immanent in the world, for he is not simply at hand in the world. He *comes* to the world. This "coming" gives expression to the experience of faith that knows that he also can be absent. He comes when he chooses to do so. And if one should pose the question of whence then he "comes," this would only indicate that one does not understand the language of faith. Perhaps we should therefore be able to speak of God's immanent transcendence or his transcendent immanence, unless we prefer to let this entire philosophical terminology drop.

The covenant

Following the example set by the Bible, we can best summarize the relationship of God and man with the concept of the covenant. In this the heaviest emphasis must not be given to the static motif, but to the action in which God has bound himself to men. The covenant is, so to speak, God's declaration of love for Israel and through Israel for all men, that he will be their God, the God of all men. Then the more static side of the covenant-concept must also be voiced as an expression of the divine faithfulness and trustworthiness. Through the covenant, one could say, God's declaration of love is ratified and acquires this extension in time. The most unbelievable and most tremendous thing that we can say of God is that the great, ineffable God is a covenant God, a God who has a compact with us.

Included in the concept of the covenant is a certain reciprocity. Yet this need not involve an agreement between two equal parties. This certainly is true if we wish to use the word in its biblical sense. When a covenant between men is spoken of in the Old Testament, it can for example refer to the confirmation of the relationship between conqueror and conquered, or between king and subjects. And when it is the covenant between God and man, then we cannot at all speak of a two-sided agreement. Here the covenant issues from God alone. In the New Testament this comes to the fore almost more strongly, all the more when one considers the fact that the basic meaning of the New Testament word for covenant is "last will and testament." It is God who gives the covenant. Therein he pledges—one could almost say, he binds himself—to man. And therewith he also binds man to himself. Thus the two-sided character also is preserved, for through the covenant which God gives, man becomes an ally, a participant in covenantal bonds. The covenant says something not only about God, but also about man. Just as there is no God-in-himself, but only a God who is the great covenant-partner of man, so also there is no man-in-himself, but only man together with God, the man who may be his covenant-man.

> When the emphasis is laid so heavily upon the point that God is essentially the God who is Covenant-ally, the question can arise as to whether he could have been otherwise. In general this question is answered in the affirmative, because otherwise the conclusion appears inescapable that God is bound to man, that is to say, is dependent on man. However, I reject this entire question, because in my opinion it belongs to a thought-world in which one practices an objectifying speculation about God-in-himself. Under the guise of modesty and respect for God's freedom, man places himself in a position where he may not and cannot stand, outside the relationship with God and in fact above him; from this position then he undertakes to judge God. Indeed, the question is already in itself an impossible question, because in the last analysis it means to ask whether God can be other than he is. Here what was said earlier still applies: God

is indeed more than, but not other than he has disclosed himself to be—and he has revealed himself as Covenant-God.

The personal God

Words declaring that God is a covenant God who meets man as the great "Thou" and who can be addressed by him as "Thou" point to a personal relationship. And this means once again that we are in line with the Bible. It speaks of God in a very human way. The biblical image of God is man-shaped, or anthropomorphic. Originally this most likely extended even to the figure or form of God; from the oldest strata of the Old Testament it still can be discerned that people conceived of God in the form of a man. But even the later biblical writers, who have abandoned such a realistic conception, still speak without embarrassment about God who hears, sees, speaks, stretches out his hand, loves, is wrathful, repents and so forth. Now of course one can attribute that to the so-called primitive, unreflective naïveté of the biblical writers, but I am of the opinion that to do so is to do them an injustice. Rather, they were so deeply permeated by God's awe-inspiring majesty, his being wholly other than man, that without danger of being misunderstood and without hesitation they dared to write about him in such human terms. But this is not the foremost thing. The deepest reason for their speaking anthropomorphically of God is that God indeed comes to meet man thus, in anthropomorphic fashion, or perhaps better said, in personal fashion. Man experiences him as the one who acts with and for him personally. I prefer not to speak of God as person, and even less as personality. This sounds too spare and too static, and moreover too much reminds me of the God-to-himself. Martin Buber somewhere writes that God himself is not a person, but that he has become a person for the sake of us men. I am also afraid of this idea because it suggests a God who stands behind the God whom we know, and who in his essence is other than he presents himself to us. But in my opinion we may and even must continue to speak of a personal God, and that not as an abstract description of his being, but much more relationally and functionally. The point is not that he has ears, but that he hears man; not that he has eyes, but that he sees us; and when we say that the world is in his hand, in this we speak of his dealing with the world. All these words are meaningful because and insofar as they point to God's connection with us and indicate that he is the Covenant-God who addresses us and loves us.

Does this mean then that I come out again with the traditional, "theistic" conception of God? I do not know. I do know that I have no need at all to conceive of God in any sort of form, nor to believe in a God who exists "somewhere."

But we can speak of God only in human words. This cannot be otherwise, because for us men these are the only words we have. The question is only which words are the most adequate, the most in agreement with the way in which we have come to know God. In harmony with the Bible, we have opted for the words which lie in the sphere of a personal standing-in-relationship: God is the Thou who calls us, he is covenant-God, man's ally, king who leads and protects his people. And then above all: he is our Father, the one who loves us, our lover. It is true that with this last expression the Bible is very cautious, out of fear that it will be taken literally-biologically or literally-sexually. But this caution does not mean that the fact is any less clearly expressed. All these expressions are indications of God's being with men, figures of speech, if you will, but still true in such a way that they are not "merely" figures or suggestions, but that they point to the reality of God who is *for* us.

What has been said above includes the point than in any case we cannot speak about God in less-than-personal terms. He is not Destiny, not the deterministic Fate, and neither is he the First Cause or the Unmoved Mover. These are all expressions which are in conflict with our faith-experience in which we have experienced the personal approach of God. But neither do I know what to do with it when someone says that he is more-than-personal, supra-personal, and that we drag him down if we speak of him thus anthropomorphically. Perhaps it is not utterly impermissible to call him Absolute Being, or the Origin, or the Mystery of Existence, but I am convinced that these allegedly more-than-personal words say less than does the abhorred anthropomorphism; they fail to express precisely what is the most important thing about God, namely that he is our God, God-with-us. And we definitely must reject the attempt to equate God or, as then people often say, the Divine, with Love, Truth, or similar abstract ideas or principles. That God is love cannot be turned around to read the other way; these biblical words do not mean to say that he is the embodied essence of love, but that he is such that he loves us, that he comes to us and bears us as the one who loves. All these abstractions appear ultimately to turn out to be speculations about a God-by-himself and not really to take seriously the fact that he is in essence just as he discloses himself to us.

The name

Central in what has been said in the fact that God is the great Ally who has granted to us to know him, not by means of general propositions or announcements, but by his having been revealed to us in his actions in Israel and in Jesus Christ, and involving us in these actions. Of course this does not mean to say that he now has become something wholly disclosed. When he reveals himself, the mystery of his God-ness still is preserved therein. Indeed, we also see a pale reflection of this on the plane of relationships between people. If two people love each other and even really know each other because they have shared a part of their history and have bestowed their confidence upon each other, still one can never fully describe the other. Not only are words incapable of describing the beloved, but even in knowing him, the mystery of the other person continues to exist. There is always more of him to discover; it is always possible to get to know him better. This holds true even more where it has to do with our knowledge of the great Other who is God. We can, may, and must speak about him, though this speaking will always have more of the character of confessing and addressing him than of a description. Our words can actually mean him, but we must be well aware that they are inadequate and that we can never capture him in them. But more important than the consciousness of this inadequacy of all human talk about God (which is something entirely different from being mistaken!) is that even when he reveals himself in his character as Ally, God still never becomes the "available" one, one who is simply "at hand." In his turning to us he is that one who does not surrender himself to our power; we may know him as he really is, but in this knowing, the mystery of his being God still is respected.

As we have said, the Bible speaks about God in an anthropomorphic fashion without reserve or embarrassment. Perhaps this is possible only because in the same Bible stands also the second commandment which forbids us to make any image of him. This commandment does not mean only that God is more and greater than our images—even the most spiritual and exalted ones—but also that man cannot capture him in any conception and never can seize him in any image. The most pregnant expression of this insight in the Bible is perhaps the Old Testament name of God Yahweh. In it actually all that we have attempted to say in this chapter comes together. We must not dismiss as a sign of primitivism the fact that the God of Israel had a name, as though it was necessary to distinguish this God from the many other gods—although this is an aspect of the matter when viewed in terms of the history of religions. But in the whole of the Bible's testimony the name is the confession that God is not "a" god, but this very specific, this personal God, who has made himself known. For what is more personal than one's own name? In it God has communicated himself, so that we can speak to him and call upon him.

But there is still more. The writer of Exodus 3 was convinced that the name of God also expressed his innermost nature. We no longer know for sure precisely what he meant by the explanation of the name which he gave. In any case, it is evident to us that while God makes himself known in his name, at the same time he conceals himself, and does not surrender himself into men's hands. Man may know that God is present for him: "I am there." But in his being present he maintains his sovereign freedom. "I am who I am," "I am there just as I am." No further description, only the possibility of knowing of his helping and saving presence, his being-there for his people.

Thus the second commandment, like his name, is for us an expression of God's hiddenness, not in spite of, but precisely *in* his revelation as the God of the covenant, as God-with-man.

III. THE "ATTRIBUTES" OF GOD

About describing God

The most important thing that we can say about God is, as was shown in the preceding chapter, that he is not a God-to-himself, but the Covenant-God who wills to be with man. At the same time this says about man that in essence he is not man-in-himself, but man with God. God's willing to have man as his covenant-ally includes God's making a place for man beside himself, and his giving to this man a certain uniqueness and freedom. Given with the concept of the covenant is a certain mutuality, or reciprocity, without the abolition of the qualitative distinction between God and man.

In this context now we must speak about the so-called "attributes" of God or, as they are also called, his "virtues" or "perfections." The theological term is not important here—and it seems to me that none of those mentioned is very satisfactory—but what matters is what is indicated by it. In his "attributes" we intend more precisely to describe God. They do not indicate what people conceive of under the abstract concept of deity, but they all are words which say how God has disclosed himself in his coming to man.

When we try more precisely to define and describe God, this is not an impermissible attempt to objectify him and in this way to render him manageable. It is rather an expression of gratitude of the man who wishes to put into words the experiences which he has had with his Ally. Again we can compare it to a loving relationship between people, where one wishes to talk about the other, not in order thereby to make the other person into an object, but because he is constrained to this by his love. In so doing he knows that no description can evoke a complete and perfect picture of the beloved one, and that he also could portray the beloved one in other words. Hence it also is not surprising that people cannot give a complete list of God's "attributes." A certain subjectivity, a certain personal choice is unavoidable here. One needs only to think of the Bible in order to perceive the truth in this. Israel, knowing of its own repeated apostasy, confesses God as faithful and patient and makes an appeal to these "attributes" of God when it asks him for forgiveness; the psalmist who was downtrodden and hardpressed by his enemies calls on God in his righteousness to help, the righteousness in which God champions the rights of the weak; and the man, who is grateful and happy, praises the goodness of God. All these words say something about God, about the way in which he has disclosed himself and thus is, and at the same time they say something about the man who utters them, about his situation before God.

And it is not only that we can never make a complete list of God's "attributes." We also must refrain from trying to fit them into a particular scheme. The more systematically they are arranged, the more we get the oppressive feeling, not only that it perhaps could also have been done otherwise, but also and especially that we are involved once again in making a kind of blueprint of the character of God. As if we ever could make a blueprint of our human beloved, to say nothing of the Great Beloved!

> In the treatment of the "doctrine of the attributes of God," it is often pointed out with great verbosity that God is not the sum of his attributes; these attributes are not something that he "has," but he himself "is" each of these attributes; therefore the multiplicity of the attributes does not detract from the unity of his person. I must say that I do not comprehend the difficulty which is noted here. All this also holds true for the "attributes" with which we describe another person whom we love. There too with each of our words we mean the beloved himself, not "something" of him.

It does belong to the very nature of the case that those predicates which speak of God most personally, most anthropomorphically, clearly must have priority. We can more directly call him loving or faithful than almighty or all-knowing, because the former words much more explicitly express God's turning toward man. The more abstract the concepts become, the more easily they can be misunderstood, as though they referred to a God-in-himself, apart from the man who believes in him. Even more strongly put, without the anthropomorphic "attributes" the apparently loftier descriptions, which often are regarded as much more essential, actually are not usable, because they do not speak of the personal God who wills to be with man, but of what man understands as the Absolute.

> In earlier times, in dogmatics a distinction was generally made between the communicable and non-communicable attributes of God. Often, however, no precise definition was given of what was formally meant by these terms. In general the communicable attributes were understood to mean those attributes which one can ascribe to God and to man (goodness, justice), while the so-called non-communicable attributes, which were assigned a much higher value, apply only to Goid (eternity, omnipotence). But the distinction between the two categories was also defined in such a way that the communicable attributes describe what God is for man, and that the non-communicable attributes express what he is in himself, in his diety. It is evident that I reject the notion of non-communicable attributes in the second sense described here, because I refuse to speak of God-in-himself, apart from man. But even in the first sense the term seems to me not to make sense, for various traditionally "non-communicable" attributes have an anthropological and ethical side, as will appear below, so that even they too are "communicable."

The words which are also applied to men

If we treat now of the "attributes" of God as to their contents, we think in the first place of those words which frequently appear in the Bible to refer to God in his dedication to man: gracious and merciful, longsuffering, full of lovingkindness, and faithful. As to contents, they are hardly to be differentiated; all of them are uttered in praise of God's incomprehensible goodness that he wills to be the God of Israel, the God of man. It is not our intention here to analyze these words in their biblical meaning; besides, words like longsuffering and lovingkindness, which have disappeared from our everyday speech, could better be replaced by other words. They do refer to "attributes" of God but also of men. Indeed the two sides are closely related; because God is loving, longsuffering, merciful, man as God's partner is summoned to follow him in this regard. We are so used to speaking of an "imitatio Christi," an imitation of Christ, that we have almost forgotten that what is involved in this is an imitation of God himself. There is a close connection between the doctrine of God and Christian ethics.

> The above-mentioned words obviously formed a more or less fixed series which was used in Israel (in the cultus?) in calling upon God. The fact that the Septuagint, the Greek translation of the Bible from the last centuries before the Christian era, can translate the Hebrew words for grace and mercy with the same Greek word, and that the same holds true for the words "mercy" and "lovingkindness," indicates how closely related in meaning these words were.

God is *merciful* in his love. We must not connect this immediately with the so-called forgiveness of sins. It is pure grace that God wills to be there for man, that man may be there as man-of-God, and that God allows him space and freedom to live as man. To be human involves having God as Ally, and being covenant-man and covenant-woman; this makes human life a life truly touched by grace. Only after this is postulated would I want to speak of God's grace in connection with sin. In God's willingness to forgive sin it becomes evident how infinitely more, how much higher he is than man. He maintains his being as man's Ally even when the latter does not acknowledge this. God cannot deny himself and cannot make himself dependent upon whether man does or does not acknowledge him. He holds his own honor high, and his honor is that he is God with and for man. Perhaps we may even say this: his honor is the man of the covenant.

When we speak in this fashion of God's gracious holding to man as an expression of his divine essence, we come into an entirely different climate from that out of which Voltaire spoke his derisive words: "pardonner, c'est son métier" ("it is his business to forgive"). Voltaire is speaking in a bantering way, as an onlooker who makes the whole matter a joke. Yet his words are true; they can only be spoken, however, out of an incredulous amazement and gratitude. For the statement that God "must" forgive because he cannot be untrue to himself is the most tremendous thing a man who has experienced this forgiving grace can say about the holy God of the covenant. God remains *faithful* to himself and thus he also remains faithful to us. This is the only proper way in which the traditional word of the "immutability" of God can be understood. For in and of itself it is just as correct to say that God changes; he is angry, repents, relents, and so forth. In keeping with the preceding chapter, we should no longer say that this is "nothing but" a figurative, anthropomorphic way of speaking. It is a facet of God's being a Ally that he is "changeable" in this way; as we have already said, he takes his human partner so seriously that he re-acts to him. But in his "changeableness" he is not arbitrary, but trustworthy and faithful. Therefore man can rely on him, and knows where he stands with him; and therefore, in spite of all the precariousness and uncertainty of existence, he still can also take his stand in life with confidence.

Because God desires the covenant relationship with man, he desires, as we have said, to respect him in his freedom, even if this freedom brings with it man's denial of his covenant-ally. God has an indescribable *patience* with us and with the world. He is Covenant-God; therefore he allows us room and gives us time. When the Bible speaks of God's patience (longsuffering), it does not mean an inactive looking-on or a certain indifference. God's patience means that he is willing to wait for us, and for the world.

These adjectives, all of which try to describe the way in which God is our Ally, contradict the notion of an unmoved deity. This occurs most explicitly where the Bible speaks of God's *suffering with* his people. In the past theology has often been afraid to speak of a God who suffers. Without intending to do so, however, therewith, in my opinion it unavoidably detracted from God's love, and consequently from his being-God. For love makes a person vulnerable, and if it is not willing to suffer for and together with the beloved it is no love. If God could not suffer in his love, his love would be less than that of men, or at least so fundamentally different from what we understand by love that it would be meaningless to continue to use this word of God. The image that is employed in the Old Testament perhaps is the most impressive one of all: the lover who suffers under the unfaithfulness of the beloved. But there it also speaks of God's sharing suffering when his people suffer. It must be stated even more broadly. God has compassion, he suffers with all who endure injustice, with all who suffer lack and who are not able to stand up for their own rights. Here it becomes clear how much God's love and his righteousness are intertwined and in part even coincide. God challenges injustice and upholds the rights of those who are not able to defend their own rights, because he suffers with the weak and the oppressed. This is not all there is to say about God's righteousness, but in any case it is one side of it.

Has not our speaking about God as we have done tended too much to pull him down to the human level? All the preceding is true and valid only if it is uttered out of the awareness that God is the *holy one.* It is the holy God who is our covenant-ally, who is patient with us and remains true to us—and to himself. The import of all the words with which we speak of him comes out only against the background of his holiness. God goes far above and beyond all that we know of love, faithfulness, patience, and compassion. It must immediately be added to this that even though he surpasses what we know, yet in these words we are actually describing God himself. With the term "holy" we attempt to go in some way beyond all this, to express something of the perfection of God, and something of the sense of awe that seizes man when he realizes the inconceivable fact that he may exist together with this ineffable God. The image used in Exodus 3 of God's holiness as a consuming fire that yet does not consume seeks to represent precisely this idea. Holiness must not be equated with the merely numinous, awe-inspiring, unapproachable. The holy God does consort with man, and is his Ally and his redeemer.

Moreover, the concept "holiness" also contains a moral aspect, as is true with the word in our ordinary usage. In the recent past, theology has often been so fearful of a flat, humdrum ethicising of this idea that it has been in danger of forgetting that the word "holiness" also describes God in the moral perfection of his "attributes." The association of God and man is set in bold relief by the demand that man imitate God precisely in his holiness. This word, which more than any other portrays God in his being-God, his God-ness, in his being different from man, refers to an attribute in which man also must share. Man is called to be holy because God, his Lord and Ally, is holy.

> In the Bible the word "holy" has an (originally cultic) aspect whereby God's qualitative otherness is indicated, but it definitely has a moral aspect as well. God in his holiness loves justice and cares for the oppressed. The two sides must not be separated. In the vision of God's holiness in Isaiah 6 the awe-inspiring majesty of God is portrayed, but also his (moral) purity as over against human unrighteousness.

The "un-" words

More than by means of his anthropomorphic "attributes," in the past the attempt has been made to describe God's nature in a negative way, by denying all limitations which are native to man. Thus he was called invisible, unchangeable, infinite. But in my opinion these words are unusable, because a pure denial does not indicate anything positive. To speak in negations points, I think, to an unknowable deity, a transcendent power, an X, about which ultimately there is nothing to say. The anthropomorphic "attributes" are actually adjectives which characterize God as Ally. Is it only a game with words to say that the "un-" words can only have meaning when used as adverbs? God is unchangeably gracious, invisibly present, infinitely loving.

The "all-" words

There remain the so-called "all-" or "omni-" words to describe God. Insofar as these are involved in the objectifying and abstract realm, they too are to be rejected. An almighty, all-knowing, and omnipresent being either is a supersuperman or is coterminous with the universe, in short is everything. Yet these words, if they are differently interpreted, can be very meaningful. They can then express actual experiences of faith which man has had with his covenant-God. The description of God as almighty, omnipotent, does not mean that God "can simply do anything in the world," but is a confession that he is mightier than all the forces and powers with which man has to contend in his life. Or, better, one actually may not even start from such a general confession. For all the "omni-" attributes it is true that in the first place they say something about God in a particular human situation. In a definite life-situation God has again and again proved himself to be mightier than that which works against or denies man's relationship with him. Out of these special experiences, then, man comes to the confession of God's omnipotence, as an expression of his absolute confidence in the might of his Ally. The person who confesses God as the almighty is expressing therewith the certainty of faith that in spite of everything, existence is good, and that his life is shielded and secure.

> In the Old Testament the word "almighty" perhaps does not appear at all, and in the New Testament only a few times. Only the Septuagint uses it repeatedly to translate two terms, the actual meaning of which we can no longer determine with certainty. This is no reason for our dropping the word, because it does soundly express a biblical idea; it is however a warning against regarding omnipotence as the most important characteristic of God.

In connection with God's omnipotence the question always arises as to why there is so much evil in the world, if God actually is a loving God. So long as one believes in a God who wills and brings about all that happens, and who intervenes in nature and in history at will, this question is in fact insoluble. Then one is driven to the alternative that either he is almighty, but then does not really love mankind, or if he loves us then he actually is not almighty. And the consideration that man cannot calculate and comprehend God does not put the question to rest, and threatens once again to make God the Unknown.

However, if one understands God's omnipotence as the invincible power of his love, the question of evil is not solved, but it does appear in a different light. God's love, we have said, is the love of the Ally who also leaves room alongside himself for man, and likewise leaves room for the world of nature in which man lives. Man and nature have their own existence. Hence we can say of so-called natural evil, that is, evil not caused by men, that it is not willed or caused by God, but that it lies in the course of natural events with their own development and laws. God does not interfere there with his power. Instead, it is man who, called to govern nature, is in a position more and more to do away with natural evil. The most burning question, however, concerns the misery that people cause for each other, human evil and human guilt. Here again we do not arrive at an actual explanation, and since human freedom is at issue here, we must not even attempt that here. Freedom always has an aspect of the non-causal, the incalculable. But that man has this freedom is a sign that God as covenant-God respects him as his partner, that he does not wish to force man, but leaves him free, so that he can even do things that God does not will. It sounds paradoxical, but one could almost say that the fact that man can sin, that he can do so much that God does not will, is a sign of God's love.

Thus when one continues to maintain, in spite of evil, that God is all-powerful, this is an expression of the experience of faith—whether of the individual man or of the community—that God has shown himself to be more powerful than calamity, sorrow, and guilt. And it is by God's grace that man also does not succumb to the evil that he suffers. As God's ally he too is stronger and more powerful, and the evil and the suffering and all that is against him do not overcome him. Thinking of this, one could almost say that man also shares in God's omnipotence.

From what has been said it appears that the confession of God as omnipotent includes the conviction that what God does not will ultimately has no future and that one may hope for a new reality in which that will become fully evident. More concisely stated: God himself in his omnipotence stands surety that in full human freedom the covenantal relationship of God and man, in which God is God for man, and man is man for God, will prevail.

> Thus the confession of God as omnipotent has an eschatological orientation: only "at the end" will he actually be revealed in his love which overcomes all things.

God's omniscience and omnipresence also must not be understood abstractly as a knowing everything or a being-present everywhere. Here also one must begin with the specific, the particular, that God knows something, is present somewhere, in order then to come to the general. God as the *omniscient* is an expression of the experience of faith—once again individually or in community— that he knows what from time to time befalls me, or us, and it also says that he knows me, he knows us. Apart from this confessional character the concept "omniscience" also is distorted and entangles one in endless philosophical problems about a deity-in-himself who knows all that there is to know, who knows what is going to happen and what can happen in every event.

And precisely the same holds true also for God as the *omnipresent.* This too is, in the first place, an expression of the experience of his specific presence. Here in such and such a situation he has shown himself as present. And on this rests the conviction that I am, that we are, that the world is in his hand, even when I do not sense his presence, even when he conceals himself. The Old Testament notion of God's traveling with his people seems somewhat primitive; but precisely therein it is being said that he is not tied to a particular place, that he is omnipresent. This omnipresence must never be understood as availability, as a being-present always and everywhere. The figure of God in heaven takes care of that. The idea of heaven is meaningful only as a symbolic expression. Heaven is not a concrete place up yonder where God is, but is an indication that he is not with us as things are, and not even as our fellow men are with us, but as only he himself, the great Other, is with us.

> The concepts of the omnipresent God and God-in-heaven belong together; the latter idea prevents our understanding the divine omnipresence pantheistically, and the former prevents our making God-in-heaven into a deistic deity.

In conclusion, God as the *eternal* likewise is not a philosophical expression, but once again a confession about the covenant-God. Perhaps the word "eternal" could best be understood if it were replaced by "all-temporal". Then it would be clear that it expresses the same with respect to the time in which man lives as does omnipresence with respect to the space in which he lives. God's eternity does not refer to an endlessly long duration of time forward and backward, nor to timelessness, just as his omnipresence does not mean to say that he is "everywhere," nor that he is "nowhere." Here too one must begin with the specific: God has now and again, repeatedly, shown himself to be a covenant-ally. And out of this then arises the certainty of faith that he has time for man; just as he had time for him yesterday and has time for him today, so will he also have time for him tomorrow. And just as heaven is the symbol that God as the Other wills to be present with man wherever he is, so his eternity says that he wills always to be with man, that the totality of man's temporal existence, in the past and in the future, is encircled, attended and guarded by him.

IV. PREDESTINATION AND ELECTION

Predestination

In the two preceding chapters we have done nothing but illustrate from various angles the point that God is essentially a covenant-God. He wills to be the God-of-us-men and he wills us to be men-who-belong-to-him. By postulating in this way God's will for a covenant relationship, we are speaking in fact about predestination.

It is not a self-evident thing that we should choose to use this term here. In the Old Testament the word probably does not appear at all, and in the New Testament it is used only rarely. Besides, it is so heavily loaded and has given occasion to so much misunderstanding and enmity in the church that one can ask whether it would not be better to drop it altogether. But precisely because it has played such a major role in the church's history, at least in some countries, it must not be silenced. Otherwise it could continue to hang like a frightening specter in the background of our thinking about faith, and all the more dangerous because of being suppressed.

Here again we must strictly maintain that our speaking about God, and thus our speaking about his predestination, may not be done abstractly and speculatively. Thus in predestination once again we are not talking about God-in-himself, but it is the confession of men who have come to know God as their Ally. And the content of their confession is that God in his incomprehensible goodness wills to be with and for man, to be his partner and covenant-God, and that man from his side may be with and for God, his partner and covenant-man. By casting this confession in the form of predestination, that is, of a divine decision that precedes everything, certain truths of faith are once again underscored. (1) In the covenant, this partnership of God and man, we are not talking about two equal parties. God is infinitely greater and more powerful; he possesses an infinite "pre." (2) The same thing can be expressed with a slightly different emphasis: it is God who bestows this covenant relationship; the initiative issues solely and entirely from him. In this respect also he possesses an infinite "pre." (3) God is not dependent on man. He wills—or, in terms of predestination, he has determined—to join himself to man. That is to say, he has destined himself to be a God of men. These words may not be taken to refer to a God *before* the covenant; they are intended only to place special emphasis once again on the gracious character of the covenant. This then is the obverse side of the fact that man experiences it as a gift that he, insignificant man, may be the covenant-partner of the great God. (4) Predestination perhaps is the clearest form in which man can testify to his certainty that God is faithful and that, come what will, he may be God's man. God has, after all, destined him to be such "from before all things," that is, without his being able to do anything for or against this decision. Therefore we can better understand "predestination" as a prior decision rather than as predetermination. It has reference to God's destiny for man.

If predestination is thus understood as a confession, in which man exalts the freedom and power of God's love, it becomes the summation of the gospel itself: the proclamation that God is for us, and therein anticipates us.

> In the history of the church, predestination has often been misunderstood as an absolute decree issued by God-in-solitude before creation, to which moreover he now is bound for all eternity by his own immutability. However, he is immutable only in his love, in his will to be our Ally.

Election

To speak about predestination is possible only for the person who knows that God is his Ally and that he is destined and called to be God's man. That is to say that only the believer, i.e., the elected person, can talk about predestination. As I see it, predestination is not altogether the same as election. I do not mean this in the sense that the former has a positive and a negative side; this idea is clearly rejected in what is said above. But in predestination we confess the eternal covenant-will of God; and in election we confess the means—or, better said, the route—by which God puts into effect and actualizes in history his covenant-will, which applies to all.

> The Bible often speaks of election, while the word and the idea of predestination appear there only relatively seldom, and then only in connection with election. The idea of predestination appears to be a radicalizing of that of election. It is noteworthy also that the verbal forms of "electing" are much more frequently used than the noun "election." This latter word does not even appear in the Old Testament at all. Thus in the Bible the idea of the action is primary.

1. We must make still more specific *the connection and the difference between predestination and election.* In both of them the initiative lies with God, and in both of them we are concerned with the covenant. But while in predestination we are thinking of God's eternal purpose to be together with man, in election we are thinking of his action in history. In the former, the primary accent is placed on God's covenant-intention which applies for all time and to all persons, while in the latter, it lies more on the dynamic and vital. God wills—so we confess in speaking of predestination—to be the covenant God of all men; in order to actualize that will, he chooses—so we confess when we speak of election—a particular people and makes his covenant with this people. This chosen nation knows and recognizes that God is its Ally; it knows that it is privileged to be his nation and that it stands in his service. Election pertains to the community as well as to the individual. In the Old Testament perhaps the election of the nation of Israel is somewhat more central, but within this nation again and

again individuals are chosen, kings, priests, and prophets, in order preeminently to give form to this covenant or to call the people back to it. And perhaps in the New Testament the individual men are somewhat more prominent, but these individuals still are representatives of the new Christian community, and they are wholly incorporated within it.

> In dogmatics, the "doctrine of election" has indeed developed as an explanation of the fact that some men believe and others do not. Starting from the point that apart from faith no salvation for man is possible and that faith itself is a gift of grace, people reasoned that some believe and others do not because apparently God has arranged that it should be thus. Election, however, is not a rationalistic, causal explanation of faith, but is, on the basis of faith, a praising of God's goodness.

2. In our days many prefer to use another word rather than election. They want to avoid any suggestion that out of the great mass God would arbitrarily pick out certain persons, to join himself to them alone and to bestow salvation on them alone. In the word "election" they sense something of undue preference. However, we are indeed talking about a specific and special, a "particularistic" action of God, and precisely the term "election" lets this be said clearly. According to the testimony of the Old Testament writers, God has revealed himself only to Israel as its covenant-God; he has chosen this nation out of all the nations of the world. And then again out of Israel he chose a David to be king, or an Amos or an Isaiah to hold the people to the covenant. The same thing is true with the New Testament: Jesus chooses the twelve apostles from among his own people, and the community is chosen from among Jews and Gentiles. And in this biblical testimony again our own experience is recognized; the community and the individual believers today know themselves specifically and particularly called and thereby in a certain sense set apart. This is all the more true since in our time the so-called universal Christian society no longer exists, and it is no longer the accepted thing for a person to be a Christian. Hence we cannot abandon the "particularistic" thrust of the idea of election. God's love is not a vague affection for everybody that is spread out over the whole world like a kind of mist, but a focused, personal love.

This so "particularistic" election, however, has a *universal import.* We are thinking here about what has been said about predestination: God has destined all men to be his covenant-men. He wants to be the God of all men. The elect are a reflection of that intention. In their relationship with God they represent the others; they are leading the way, as it were, for those who are not (yet) chosen. And not only this: they are also the way by which, or the instrument through which, God intends to work to draw these others also into his covenant. This also belongs to the very nature of the case. To be chosen after all means gratefully to accept God's love, which is not for us alone but for all men. The person who knows this love will therefore necessarily strive also to bring under its sway the others who do not (yet) know this love.

3. Therefore we cannot place in contrast to the elect the reprobate, or rejected ones; instead, they are those who *are not elected,* who have been passed over. For these, too,—thus we as believers must say—God's predestination is applicable. That is, God wills to be known to them also as their covenant-ally. Therefore also we shall not be inclined to speak of this passing-over as

arbitrariness. It is true that here we are touching upon the unfathomable freedom of God, behind which we cannot go, but it is the freedom of his love. He chooses men in order to come, through their instrumentality, to the other, the non-elect. Therefore the divine passing-over always contains something provisional; God can also make himself known to the non-elect, so that they too will become elect ones. To put it more concisely: those who are the elect are in a certain sense chosen for the sake of the non-elect.

4. From what has been said above, it follows that awareness of one's own election carries with it the *apostolate,* in the broadest sense of that word. The elect person knows that God has destined and purposed man to be his covenant-partner and to constitute a part of his people. Alongside the amazement that one is thus favored, there stands the amazement that not everyone can happily accept this divine destiny. And this holds true not only for the individual, but also for the community. Consequently, the community that gratefully confesses that it is chosen and called by God to his covenant can never, by its very nature, be exclusive. For it knows that God is a God of mankind.

5. When it once is clearly seen that all talk about election is a *confession of God's love,* one will not be led astray into talking objectively about whether others are or are not among the elect. Only one's own election can be gratefully confessed, whether as individual or as community. That has nothing to do with boastfulness. It is, on the contrary, the expression of an unutterable amazement that we too may belong to that company. To know of God's love, to know that he has destined us to be his covenant-ally, is never something self-evident; it always remains an incomprehensible marvel. The saying that it is not we who chose him, but he who chose us, expresses something of this amazement, and even something of the gratitude that his love has become so overwhelmingly evident that we could not but acknowledge ourselves won to that love, and on our own part love him. Hence, election can be experienced as an advantage, but never as a right; it is never a possession which we have at our disposal. Election must never be misunderstood as exclusivity.

If election is understood in this way, the traditional question whether human freedom is not abridged by it cannot actually arise. In essence it is the same as in a human relationship of love. When two people love each other, they can only be sincerely grateful that they are thus blessed; it is not something that they can "will" or determine, but it is rather something that conquers them. And yet it is they themselves in their own responsibility, who love each other. Thus it is I myself, wholly I, who may love God, not because I made a decision to do so, but because I simply cannot help it; his love has become too powerful for me. In this sense, then, the old-fashioned theological term of the "irresistibility" of God's grace may rightly be employed. Love—and this is true also of genuine human love—always comes upon us "irresistibly."

> One single time in the New Testament it is said that Jesus Christ was chosen before the foundation of the world, and in Eph. 1:4 the same thing is said of the believers. Here what is meant is not a kind of definition of time, in which the divine decision is placed before creation; instead, this is a radicalizing of the idea of the initiative of God's elective action. Just as the confession of God's predestination issues from the insight that God, who has disclosed himself as *our* God, wills to be the covenant-ally of all men, so the placing of our election before the

foundation of the world issues from the gratitude for the utterly unmerited love of God.

6. Knowledge of God's elective action, in which he has called us to live here on earth as his allies, is salvation; it is, in the words of the gospel of John, eternal life. For salvation is not a kind of reward for later on, but is the reality of the relationship with God now. This is the reason that the confession of election also directly impinges upon *ethics.* For if the relationship with God is salvation, it is inconceivable that a person would not want to live in this covenant relationship to which he is elected. From this perspective, Christian ethics always takes on the aspect of a considerable self-evidentness. It is unbelievable that we may be fellow-workers with God; and it is inconceivable that we should reject such a privilege or deal carelessly with it. Thus we are liberated also from the grim compulsion fearfully to do our best. The same thing holds true also, however, on the human plane. Where someone must put forth tremendous effort to please his beloved, this is an indication that there is something amiss in the relationship of love.

Reprobation

We have already pointed out that the correlative to election is not reprobation, but rather not (yet) being especially chosen. Still we must give some attention to the idea of reprobation or rejection. In this connection, almost even more consistently than in relation to election, we must maintain that this is not some eternal, inscrutable decree of God, but an action of his in history that is enacted between him and his ally. Where God has called a person or a nation and destined them for a particular work, it can happen that this nation or this person retreats from this calling and does not fulfill that destiny. We have already said that this should be inconceivable; for if life in relationship with God is salvation, how then can a person be so foolish as to reject his own happiness? But if he incomprehensibly does this, then God sets this person aside; then he can no longer use that person as his ally, and he rejects him. For just as God wants man as his ally, he does not want him as a non-ally. This not-wanting is his reprobation. But this does not mean that therewith now he also drops this person. For prior to and above his reprobation stands his covenant-intention, his love. We can talk about rejection or reprobation only against the background of the confession concerning predestination, that is to say, the awareness that God wills to have even the rejected person as his ally. In the words of Ezekiel: God does not will the death of the ungodly, that is, of the person who rejects his election, but rather wills that we will turn and live. We might almost be inclined to say that God hopes for this conversion. Therefore we may not speak of an irrevocable reprobation.

> It is needless here to point out again that election and reprobation thus may not be subsumed under the common rubric of predestination. ·God's predestinating will is only a will to salvation. It is significant that in the New Testament the words "election" and particularly "elect" are frequently used; however, the verb "reprobate" does not appear at all, "cast off" appears only in Rom. 11:1, and the corresponding noun in Rom. 11:15 only. And in this latter verse there is still a question whether God is the subject of this rejection. In any case, in the epistle to the Romans God's "rejection" is only provisional; this is to be followed by God's "acceptance."

In connection with this lexical comment one naturally must consider the fact that the idea of rejection in the Bible is not necessarily expressed by this word.

The idea of reprobation can function only in preaching, and there only as a warning, as a call to conversion, by pointing out how destructive and foolish it is for a person to place himself outside God's election and not to allow it to be true that he is God's ally. But there can be no talk of believing in reprobation. For if a person himself has experienced the overwhelming power of God's unmerited love, he cannot believe that this power would not be effective also in the life of another. And in the consciousness of his own guilt and sin to believe in one's own reprobation is self-contradictory. To believe, after all, means to be conscious of God who holds fast to man and wills to be his ally, simply out of his pure, unmerited goodness, in spite of sin and guilt. And as soon as a person is aware of this God, he is no longer one of the reprobate, but one of the elect.

V. THE CREATION

Creation and covenant

It was not an arbitrary decision that prompted us first to speak about God as ally before speaking of him as the Creator. For as long as we do not know who is this God who is the Creator, the affirmation that he has created the world is nothing more than the report or the hypothesis that the world owes its existence to "a higher power." For faith, at least, that is not very important. Only when we know that he who is the covenant-ally of man and who wills nothing but good for man also is the one who created man and the world does this affirmation assume its true dimensions. Thus the Bible, and particularly the Old Testament, upon which the testimony of the New Testament writers is based, speaks about the matter. The point of departure and the constant center of the faith of Israel is the conviction that God delivered Israel out of Egypt, made her his people, and bound her to himself. On the basis of the experiences that Israel had with her deliverer and ally in the course of her history, she arrived at the recognition that her God is also the God and Lord of all nations and of the whole earth, and that everything that is belongs to him, because he is the one who created all things.

In a certain sense it is misleading for the Bible to begin with the two creation narratives of Genesis 1 and 2. This has helped to promote the idea that one must begin with belief in a Supreme Being, who is not yet more specifically identified. Whatever then is subsequently related about this Being is something supplementary, found in another, a second, chapter of the story. But what we know of the way in which these creation narratives developed points in exactly the opposite direction. That is to say, these narratives are designed from the very outset as a kind of prologue to the history of the covenant, which, beginning with Abraham, relates God's dealings with Israel. It is true that every people has its own creation stories, which describe in mythological terms the origin of man and the world, and especially of the gods as well. Such narratives undoubtedly existed among the tribes of Israel also in very ancient times, and it is also true that the biblical writers appropriated much from these ancient creation motifs. But they have re-worked and re-shaped them into a testimony of the creative work of Yahweh, the God of Israel. To put it in another way: the Bible does not tell of a Creator who then subsequently becomes Covenant-God as well, but it tells of the Covenant-God who is the Creator of mankind and of the world.

Thus it is in harmony with the biblical thought-world when we do not regard the creation narratives as an objective declaration in which it is explained "where everything comes from." Everyone knows to how many difficulties and unnecessary tensions such an interpretation has led, once it became evident that this so-called explanation did not agree with the data, conclusions, and probable hypotheses of research in natural sciences. It must never be forgotten that "creation" is an expression of faith, which is given out of the situation in which man *now* stands. It is meant to be preaching or consolation, a confession about the covenant-ally and about the world in which the covenant-man lives, with its beauty and splendor, but also with its dark and negative aspects, its evil and harshness. Sometimes in the Bible, as for example in many of the psalms, there are hymnic utterances about the creation; then it is an exaltation of the covenant-ally who is so mighty that he has created "everything." But it can also be a comfort for a person in his misery or for a nation under assault. Then the confession of God as Creator is intended to say: if the covenant-God is so mighty that he has created the whole world, man need not doubt that his almighty covenant-ally can also help him. Thus belief in God as creator does not intend to give an explanation of this world, but to place it in a particular light.

> As a rule, people have oriented themselves, with reference to the doctrine of creation, to Genesis 1 and 2 so completely that non-theologians often are hardly aware that the Bible also tells of creation in an entirely different connection. In many places it is spoken of in hymnic terms, while the reflective theological way in which it is done in Genesis actually is an exception. In the psalms, God's mighty acts in creation are extolled together with his mighty acts in Israel's history (for example, Psalms 33, 136, and 148). In Deutero-Isaiah, creation and redemption are even interwoven (for example, Isaiah 44:21-28; 51:9-11).

It is sometimes said that in the doctrine of creation the main theme is not the creation but the creator; not the world and mankind, but God. I believe that this is a false alternative, produced in part by the mistaken idea of a God-in-solitude. When a person confesses God as creator, at the same time he is thereby expressing how he understands himself as God's creature in this world that belongs to God. The one is so closely connected to the other that one can only speak of the two together.

It is also a misunderstanding to think that in the doctrine of creation the main concern is with the past. Here the times are intertwined. The creation is confessed in the present. The confidence in the absolute power of the Ally *now* brings with it the insight that he also stands "at the beginning"; he has so fully disclosed himself to man in the world as Lord that he also must be confessed as Origin, or, better said, as Creator. And this same gracious power which is experienced now also prompts the recognition that God also will stand "at the end"; he is so absolutely the Lord of the world that he will also bring it to a good end, a perfect end. But as creator he not only stands "at the beginning" and "at the end." He is creatively present in the course of history, in every "today." Hence it is true that God was creator of the world, that he will be creator of the (new) world, and that he now is its creator.

> What is said here about the three dimensions of time is confirmed by the Bible. The Old Testament has various words for "create." The most common one

also signifies "make" or "do," and is used with God or with man as the subject; hence it is an indication that in this respect also, namely in his creative activity, man can imitate God. The theologically most specific word, however, is used only of God. Obviously the divine creation also has a dimension that is utterly unique and is different from any creation of man. I doubt whether this special quality lies, as is repeatedly asserted, in the fact that God can make something out of nothing, while man on the other hand can only make something out of already existing material. In any case it is a fact that this specific word for "create" in the Old Testament also is used where nothing is said about a *Creatio ex nihilo*, a creation out of nothing. Of more importance, however, is the fact that the word is used to speak of God's first creative activity "in the beginning" (Gen. 1:1, 21, 27; Ps. 89:48; etc.); to speak of the "creation" of Israel (Isaiah 43:1, 15) or of an individual man (Ezekiel 21:35); to speak of the new and marvelous saving acts which God "creates" in the course of history (Num. 16:30; Isaiah 48:6; Jer. 31:22); and to speak of God's final activity, when he will "create" a new heaven and a new earth (Isaiah 65:17). The New Testament points in the same direction. The word "create," which often appears in non-biblical Greek with the meaning of "found," is used here only of God; the more vague term "make" only rarely has the meaning of "create." Thus the specific word refers both to God's original creation and to his creating of the new man in Jesus Christ (Eph. 3:10, 15; Col. 3:10). In connection with God's actions in the end-time the word does not appear (is this only accidental?).

God's creation "in the beginning"

Theologically, it is not necessary in the doctrine of creation to place the divine creation "in the beginning" in the first place. Our following the traditional order here is done because it is logically obvious and because in the Bible also the original creative action of God is described as the beginning of his entire history with man. Moreover, it is precisely the idea that the world owes its existence to a creative act of God that causes the greatest difficulty for man today, with his evolutionist image of the world that is based on the natural sciences. That too is a reason for beginning with this idea.

We saw above that the words of the Bible that God created "the heavens and the earth" give expression to the belief that he, who is the covenant-ally of man, is Lord of the world in which man lives. This thought is further underscored by the idea that he has created *ex nihilo*, out of nothing. If "at the beginning" there was something else besides God, a material out of which he could create, then that "something" could form a menace for man; this "other" then would exist independent of God and consequently could, in a certain sense, compete with him. "Creation out of nothing" is intended to say that the Ally is master of all that is, and that however far back man may go in his thinking, there never was anything that was not subject to God's lordship. Therefore man ultimately has nothing to fear in this world.

It is not permissible simply to state that "the Bible" teaches the *creatio ex nihilo*. I am not thinking in this connection of the texts in which it speaks of a primeval struggle between God and various forces of chaos (for example, Ps. 89:11; Isaiah 51:9). Where this ancient mythological conception of creation appears in the Bible, it has become nothing more than a fairy-tale motif. But nowhere in the Old Testament is the doctrine of a creation out of nothing clearly found. It is true that Genesis 1 appears to point in this direction; however, in any case the primary accent does not lie on this point, but on the divine order, whereby the chaotic and threatening is conquered. Later theological reflection on the power of God however has led to the idea of a creation out of nothing. We find this idea first expressed explicitly in the first century B.C., in the apocryphal book II Maccabees 7:28, while it is presupposed in the New Testament in Rom. 4:17 and Heb. 11:13.

No one knows the way in which God created the world "in the beginning"; no one was there, and it actually has not been made known in some supernatural way or another. God has become manifest as mighty Ally in the events of history; that he then must also be the creator is an extrapolation of this knowledge of God that is compelling for thought that is grounded in faith. In order to describe this creation, various conceptions were used by the biblical writers. Thus for the description of Gen. 1, presumably use was made of narratives that stem from Egypt and Mesopotamia, which were plagued by floods. There, setting the bounds for the menacing flood, whereby God makes an earth habitable for man, could become a figure for his gracious creative act. In Palestine, bordering on the dry desert area, where we may look for the source of the second creation narrative (Gen. 2:4b-25), the idea that God makes the land moist and fertile serves to portray his salutary creation. And, to give one final example, in Col. 1:15, 17, the young Christian community speaks, on the basis of its faith in Christ, about the creation in him. All these are forms and conceptions in which the biblical writers have portrayed in their times the idea of creation. The fact that the Bible allows different models of creation to stand alongside each other shows that it does not intend to bind us to one particular conception. We are not required simply to adopt one. Instead, we must speak about the creative work of God in words that are acceptable to contemporary man, or, said more concretely, in words that do not run counter to our scientific knowledge. Just as the biblical writers bore witness to God's creation with the help of knowledge that was current in their times, so must we do the same with the help of our knowledge. Thus no effort need be made to show that, for example, the modern evolutionary view of the world "actually" is in harmony with the biblical conceptions. That would amount to the dismal position that "the Bible is right after all" (Translator's note: The author here uses the Dutch title of the book by Werner Keller which appeared in English under the title *The Bible as History*.). The only thing we can say is that if a certain affinity exists between present-day scientific thinking and the conceptions of the Bible, this can make it easier for us to represent the belief in creation in our own time.

For example, it can be pointed out that according to Genesis 1, God's creative activity extends over six days, and thus is not an instantaneous event. Moreover, it is conceived of as the first chapter of history; there is no break between creation and what then follows. Here lies a certain affinity with contemporary evolutionary theory. Further, in the Bible man is described as the climax of creation, and this also is an idea that at the moment is supported by science. There undoubtedly are still other points of affinity that could be named. But once again, we are not bound to the conceptions with which the creation is described in the Bible, and we need not go through various contortions in order to interpret or re-interpret the biblical data.

If a person sees the world as God's creation, this implies a certain way in which that person deals with the world. He will never be able to hold it in contempt, for it is the place that God has given him in which to live as God's ally. On the other hand, however, he will never be able in any respect to deify the world or to give it an absolute position; it is, after all, in no respect divine, but is wholly a creation. Perhaps these two sides could be expressed by speaking of the world as a place of blessed secularity. Here we may only state, without working out the implications, that this idea has implications that are far-reaching for culture and for science.

The good creation

The insight that man's Ally, who wills nothing but good for him, is the creator brings with it the certainty of faith that the creation is good. This observation, however, must be qualified. For whether the galaxies are "good," and whether the cat that plays with the mouse is "good," are questions that faith cannot answer. We call the creation good only because it is the place that God has given to man, to live there as his covenant-man and to practice partnership with him. It has to do, therefore, not with the creation in and of itself, but with the creation in relation to our human situation. Of this creation faith says that it is good.

But this expression also must be qualified. It may not be understood in such a way as to allow a cheap and easy optimism that closes its eyes to the harsh and dark aspects of the creation. Here we once again encounter the question of what we earlier called "natural" evil, such as natural disasters, sickness, death, and the birth of handicapped children (above, p. 17). We must not try here to know or to explain too much. Still I believe that the following can be said. Man, himself also a creature, is placed by God over the creation to administer it, to govern and even to improve it. The creation is not perfect; we may even say that it is not yet finished, and that man is called as God's partner to share in completing and perfecting it. When in spite of all that appears to argue against it, we confess the goodness of creation, by this we mean that it is good with respect to what the God of the covenant intends with and for man. The creation is good as the place and the workshop for God's ally.

When we speak in this way are we not speaking about creation exclusively from a human perspective, anthropocentrically? Indeed we are, and I think that this is proper. We do not know, and as men we cannot know, what is God's intention for the celestial bodies and what he has in mind for the animal world. But we do know that he is our good Ally in this world that belongs to him, because he created it, and that therefore this creation is "good" as the realm in which his covenant with us finds its place.

Now can it be seen by looking at this world that it is a creation of God, or, to say it in other words, does it point man to the Creator? Insofar as one is thinking here of an "objective" observer, I think that this question must be answered in the negative. There is too much in nature and in what happens there of meaning and non-meaning interwoven, purpose and aimlessness intertwined. But for the person who knows God, the heavens indeed proclaim the glory of God — but really his glory, not that of a First Cause or of a Higher Power. The believer will be able to recognize in the order and regularity of nature something of the faithfulness of his Ally, who through the laws of nature has granted to the life of man on earth a certain security and calculability. He will also recognize in the vastness of space and the mystery of the microcosm something of the unfathomability of God, who indeed is a God for men but whose nature is not exhausted by this affirmation, who is not different from this, but is more than this. The same truth is found in the words "heaven and earth" with which the Bible refers to the creation. Biblically seen, heaven is the realm over which man has no control. While we spoke above about creation wholly from man's perspective, the "heavens" break through our anthropocentric and geocentric way of thinking. The universe is more and greater than "the good creation," and God is the Creator of the totality of the universe as well; he has power over it as well, so that man ultimately has nothing to dread from it.

God's continuing creation

There is a question whether there is an essential difference between God's original creative act and his creative work in history. For earlier believers, for whom the creation was in principle finished, once God had made it, the situation was different. But in our time we are convinced that the world has come to be through a gradual process of evolution and that this process has not yet come to an end, even though at the moment when thinking man appeared on the stage a fundamentally new factor entered the picture. Therefore we can speak sensibly about creation without doing violence to our understanding only if we do not think of an instantaneous event, but of a continuing creative activity of God. But it is not modern natural science alone that compels us to adopt this view. The problem of evil that (still) exists in the world also points in the direction of a creation that is not yet completed, but is still continuing. A little earlier we said that through thinking man a fundamentally new factor has entered into the evolutionary process. In the language of faith this can be expressed thus: that God's creative activity is altered since he made the creature, man; since then he has been working, "creating," together with or even through the instrumentality of his ally.

But when we confess God as Creator even in the present, we are not thinking solely of the continuing development of the existing world. We have in mind also the repeatedly new and special creative deeds that he has done and is doing in history: he has "created" Israel, he has "created" the church, and every believer confesses that he himself is "created" by God. It is obvious that here faith alone will speak of a creation of God; this is not subject to empirical demonstration or proof. But the same is true also of any of God's activities.

Now when we speak of God thus as creator, this not only says something about his continuing to be creatively active in the world, but also something about our world, namely that it is open to God. The world and existence are not irrevocably determined, and they are not firmly fixed in the range of what can be determined and measured; history and nature are not processes that operate exclusively in the realm of causality and can be calculated perfectly by science.

> Along with the term *creatio ex nihilo*, dogmatics also uses the terms *creatio continua* and *creatio continuata*. These ideas cannot be appropriated if one understands them in the same way as did earlier theology. For if *creatio continua*, continuing creation, is understood to mean creation ever anew, so that every moment the world is being made in a new creative act of God, then all continuity

is lacking. And *creatio continuata*, continuing creation, suggests the idea that the world, once created, now continues of and by itself, so that God need no longer have anything to do with it. It is true that both of these ideas bring out certain elements of truth. The former can point out that the creation is not yet finished, but is still continuing and that the ever-living and ever-active God still is engaged with it; and the latter can point out that the creation has a certain identity and independence in which it persists. Together the two can express the conviction of faith that God attends and accompanies the world in its blessed secularity, that is, in its being, for men, relatively calculable and subject to their manipulation.

The declaration of faith that God still is constantly active as creator, both in that the creation is still being completed and in that ever new and different things are happening, can also be expressed in these terms: that he is not present with his creation as an inactive observer, but that he accompanies it and goes with it through history. This includes the conviction that he is active as creator not only in the "accidental," in the new and contingent that happens in nature and in history, but also in the "ordinary," in the constant and causal. And here again the idea must be expressed that it is the gracious Ally of man who is the one accompanying us. Therefore this accompanying of the world and of man — or perhaps we must rather say, of man in the world — is a beneficent and gracious accompanying, a protection and a preserving.

This accompanying by God can be called providence. There is no compelling reason to use this word; in any case, it does not appear in the Bible. But because it has often played a significant role in the thinking of the church and moreover has given occasion for much misunderstanding, it is better not merely to pass by it in silence. Providence does not mean that God sees things in advance, that he sees them before they happen. Furthermore, it does not mean that everything that happens is determined by God, in such a way that providence becomes a kind of synonym for an all-encompassing causality. We have already rejected such mistaken associations when we spoke about God as the almighty one (above, pp. 16-17). Here again all speculative views must be avoided. The providence of God is one special aspect of the covenant relationship. Man may know himself to be protected and guided in this world because the Ally accompanies his creation, his creature, and "provides" in whatever is necessary for the covenant relationship. Therefore providence also is rightly confessed with regard to all that threatens life; in spite of the fact that so unutterably much happens that God does not will, he does not abandon man and the world; he remains the gracious companion.

> The word "providence" (derived from the Latin verb "providere," which can also signify "to provide with" and "to care for") does not appear in the Bible, though the idea which it expresses of course does appear.

> If providence is understood to mean that everything happens just as God wills it, then one must, following logical reasoning, arrive at the conclusion that it is God's will that some men believe and are saved, and others do not believe and therefore do not share in salvation. A mistaken doctrine of predestination then is derived from a mistaken doctrine of providence. But in this way everything is turned upside-down. The first thing is God's predestination; he wills to be God-for-men. From this, then issues the confession of his providence; as God-for-men he has created men and he "provides" them with what is needed.

God's creative work "at the end"

From the present, in which God has disclosed himself as mighty Ally, the line was drawn by faith back into the past, and the insight that he is the creator became a necessary conclusion. From the same present the line also is drawn forward, to the future. God stands at the beginning, and he also stands at the end. And just as we can talk about this "beginning" only in faith's imagination, so also is it possible to talk about this "end." I do not propose to say much about this subject now, because a separate chapter is to be devoted to it. But in any case, even there we cannot claim to offer an actual description of this "end."

The kingdom that God will establish, and the new heavens and the new earth that he will create are images that give expression to the assurance that the world is moving toward a goal and that it has a future. These images have reference first of all to history; they say that God will reach his aim for humanity. But they also have reference to the creation; the creation too will someday reach its goal; it too will be finished "at the end." We do not know what all this implies. We can only believe, in trust and confidence in our Ally, that it will be a blessed goal and that God as the companion of his creation stands as the guarantor of this goal.

VI. MAN: CREATURE AND SINNER

What is man?

The subject of man is practically limitless. The question as to what is distinctive about man, what it is that actually marks him as man, can be answered, for example, in the area of biology, psychology, sociology, or philosophy. The question can assume the form: "who am I?" Then the answer will have to be sought by means of self-contemplation. In this way, however, man never escapes from himself and thus never really comes to the other person. The phenomenon "man" can also be investigated in a scientific and objective way. Then, however, one never comes to himself.

Theological reflection will, for its image of man, start out from God and his confrontation of man. This does not mean that thereby the other ways of approaching the subject are disqualified, or that these can only offer us insight into how we think about man, while theology teaches us how God thinks about us. It is not all that simple. Even a theological, biblically formed image of man is based upon human reflection. The difference is that this reflection is grounded in the knowledge that God is the Ally.

In the preceding chapters we have repeatedly said that God is not a God-by-himself, but a God who is with man, who loves him and sustains him. This insight is summed up in the idea that God is essentially the Covenant God. However, this at the same time says something about man. If God is the covenant-ally of man, man is the ally of God. If God is with man, man is with God. Stated negatively: as surely as God is not a God-by-himself, just so surely is man not a man-by-himself. And this holds true of every man, whether he knows it or not, whether he wants it to be true or not. It is obvious that here there is a direct connection with the doctrine of predestination, according to which God, in his all-powerful determination that preceded all things, determined to be man's Ally and destined man to be his ally. Of course a man can also live as a non-ally, but he cannot nullify God's intention; the fact that God also wants him as ally remains a fact. There is no such thing as an objective godlessness; as long as man lives, he is with God.

But God is not only the Ally of man; he is also man's creator. But again, this expression not only says something about God, but also something about man, namely, that he is created by God, that he is a creature. Man cannot discern this about himself from his own existence; he is brought to this insight by reflecting upon the supreme power of God which he has experienced in his life. Only the creator can lay such sovereign claim upon something of his own making.

Thus we arrive at the following definition of what makes man man: he is that creature that may be God's ally. The truth of this definition is recognized only by the believer, as can also be said about all theological utterances. As a "subjective" expression of faith, however, it dares to say something that "objectively" holds true for every man.

Man as creature

According to the definition we have just given, man is a creature. As such he belongs wholly and entirely to the creation. In his creatureliness he is involved with nature; he is himself a part of nature and is subject to its laws. Thus he is not in any aspect of his being divine, not even in those aspects in which he surpasses the rest of nature. Not only with respect to his body, but also with respect to his soul or spirit he is non-divine.

Everything that was said in the preceding chapter with respect to the creation in general must now be repeated with respect to man as a part of this creation. He is utterly dependent upon God, but he also has a relative independence and selfhood. Moreover, he is, in his createdness, "very good." It is true that here again it must immediately be added that this goodness of man is not a judgment that is based on what is evident, though the opposite likewise does not apply, that it must *per se* be branded by experience as false. It is an utterance of faith, which knows that man is made by the God who loves him and who therefore wills nothing but good for him. This being-man in his creatureliness, then, may also be accepted with thanksgiving, because it is good in all its aspects, even its transitoriness and frailty, even in its finitude and limitations. Man is, after all, in every respect a limited, finite being. In his relatively short life he does not have time to do all that he would like to do. His being limited to one place also signifies a restriction for him; when he is here, he cannot at the same time be elsewhere. He can never realize all his possibilities; he will have to choose, and if he chooses one thing, he will not be able to do the other. In every direction he comes up against his limitations. It is true that in the course of the centuries he has expanded the room that he has, and he will do this still more in the future. But he will never be able to do and to know everything; he will always remain limited. However, there is no reason for him to rebel against this in a futile struggle. Being man within these limits that are imposed upon him is, after all, good. For God has allied himself precisely with this weak, finite, and limited man; this is the creature that may be God's partner, the creature that is good for the covenant relationship.

> The relationship of body and soul will not be discussed here. In my opinion, theology has nothing specific to say on this point. Of course it is possible, and in my opinion interesting as well, to explore what the various biblical writers understood by the diverse anthropological terms such as body, flesh, heart, soul, and spirit. However, their views cannot be normative for us, not even if these happen to coincide with our contemporary views. For on what basis should the writers have possessed any special knowledge in these matters? When we in our time are convinced of the indissoluble connection of body and soul, this is based on psychosomatic observations and not on biblical anthropology, which in

this respect exhibits the same features. One can, however, ask whether the intuition of the biblical writers does not perhaps issue in part from their faith-conviction that the whole man, in all his aspects, is created by God and is dependent upon him.

Man as God's ally

The possibility of man's being God's ally and partner is not something that is added to or over and above his being human. It is not correct that man is first of all a mere creature and that then, as further definition, he may also be an ally. It is part of the very essence of man that it is God's intention to have him as ally; he is, we might say, created for that purpose.

It is not possible to give a full description of this being an ally, for it is as broad as being human itself. In any case, it includes man's capacity for "experiencing" God, the ability to thank and praise him, to call upon him and even to contend with him.

But this still is only one aspect, the aspect that is directly related to God. Man lives in the creation together with his fellowmen, and we must speak of his being God's ally with this in mind as well.

As creature he is, as we have said, a part of the creation, and he stands on the side of the creation. As ally, however, he stands altogether on the side of God above the rest of the creation. This again must not be understood in a speculative sense. Whether man stands above the Milky Way and various solar systems, or whether he stands above hypothetical inhabitants of Mars, we do not know and cannot know. But we do know that he is called, as God's co-laborer, to preserve, to order, and to develop this earth where he lives, to cultivate it, in the broadest sense of that word. Both of the creation stories bear witness to this: the earlier one by telling that man, placed in God's garden, is given the commission to cultivate and to preserve it (Gen. 2:15), and that he gives the animals their names; the later one, which has a more thought-out and taut theological form, by speaking of subduing the earth and ruling over all the animals, fishes, fowls, and creeping things (Gen. 1:28).

> The splendid Psalm 8 in the translation of the Netherlands Bible Society has been given the superscription, "Man, the crown of God's creation." This heading only partially covers the contents of the psalm. In viewing God's heavens with their moon and stars man becomes aware of his littleness (veses 4,5); when the psalmist then speaks of the greatness of man, who is placed by God as ruler over the works of God's hands, he names the sheep and cattle, the animals of the field, the birds, and the fishes. The psalmist — and the same is true of the writers of Genesis 1 and 2 — sees man as ruler over the earth, that is, over that part of the creation in which he lives, his environment. For us, so many centuries later, our environment, over which we may in God's name exercise dominion, has become much more extensive. At the present we are at the point of extending it to what lies beyond the earth. Yet our environment still has its limits. Hence it is better not to speak of man as the crown of creation in absolute terms.

In this dominion which is given to him, man does God's work, and he himself shares in God's creative labor (above, p. 29); as God's co-laborer he is called to represent God to the creation. Thus as creature and as God's covenant-ally he stands between nature and God. And thus he may not, in a mistaken so-called modesty retreat from his task of cultivation in ruling over and improving nature. But on the other hand this dominion may not become something arbitrary and tyrannical. For the creation is not man's property. It is entrusted to him, and he is permitted to govern it for the Other, the good Creator of heaven and earth. This is how lofty man's thinking about man must be!

Man as a reflection of God

In this ruling over sub-human nature man reflects his great ally. We have already encountered this idea several times in the preceding chapters. *Imitatio Dei*, the imitation of God, is in the last analysis only another term for the same thing. This is the reason also that it has been possible to speak of God in such human terms; actually God does not resemble man, but man resembles God. It is no wonder that, as we have said, man then can also share in the "attributes" of God. This resemblance to God, this reflection of him, comes out most clearly in the connection between man and man. Just as God is with man, so also may man be with his fellowman; and just as God has time for man, comes to his aid, and has patience with him, so also men may have time for each other, come to each other's aid, and have patience with each other. For man is not only created as God's partner; he is also created as partner of his fellowman. The one is just as essential as the other.

In the creation narratives, especially in the second, the incomparable power of *eros* and the primeval bond that connects man and woman are given expression. The Old Testament commandments are aimed primarily at giving form to the connection of men in the life together. Central concepts such as peace and righteousness also point to the fact that men are put in each other's society by God and are bound to each other. And finally, the New Testament exhortations to mutual service and love intend to define men in relation to each other. God has placed a bond between man and man, as surely as he also has placed a bond between himself and man.

Being and destiny

In the preceding we have spoken about man in a curiously dual fashion. On the one hand he was described in "is"-terms: he is covenant-man, is ruler over nature, is bearer of culture, is together with his fellowman. On the other hand, these same aspects were seen as destiny and calling: he is destined to be God's ally and co-laborer, destined as God's representative to exercise dominion over the non-human creation, destined, in reflection of God's nature, to be man in relationship with his fellowman. It is obvious that man's actual being and his destiny do not coincide. This insight, however, is not specifically Christian, but it arises out of universal human self-consideration. A man is not just man in the same way a stone is a stone, or an animal is an animal. He must first be actualized in his humanness.

In our context this means that he must be actualized, or fulfilled, in his being an ally. God has created him for this purpose, and this is what constitutes the nature of man. But at the same time it is also his destiny, which as it were still lies before him. For the covenant relationship between God and man and between man and man is based upon reciprocity. Therefore man must will, in freedom, to be the covenant-ally of God and of his fellowman; this very freedom points to the independence which God gives to man. Hence being human is both gift and obligation, and the obligation is already itself a gift. For the possibility for man to love God and the fact that man has the destiny to be God's co-laborer and his deputy in the world is the most marvelous thing that God has given him; this is how important man is to God. Similarly, it is a gift that God has destined him to be bound to his fellowman.

Because it is a matter of his intended destiny, however, there is also the possibility that man will not fulfill this destiny. Here we are not dealing with necessary causality, but with the freedom which God gives to his ally. Man cannot nullify the fact that God is his Ally, nor the fact that he was created as God's ally. But he can refuse to live as such, and can, as far as he is concerned, break the covenant. Thus he can live in conflict with his destiny, as though he were not man-of-God. This non-fulfillment of his creaturely destiny to be ally is called, in the believer's language, "sin."

Man as sinner

The word "sin" in its real meaning belongs to the language to faith. Only when God has been revealed to us as the Ally of man and when we, as a correlate to this, know that man is called to be ally of God and of our fellowman can we speak of sin. For sin is a failure to realize our humanness before God, an acting in conflict with the good destiny given to us by God. Therefore we shall confess it first of all with respect to ourselves, whether individually or as a community. It is not our business to judge how another man stands before God. This does not mean that the consciousness of sin arises within us spontaneously. It is as with our knowledge of God; in the testimonies of the Bible we recognize him with whom we are confronted in our own lives. Thus also we recognize ourselves in Israel, who again and again broke the covenant with God, in the disciples who at the critical moment left Jesus all alone, in David who wrongfully took Bathsheba as his wife, and in Pilate who washed his hands in purported innocence. In this connection it is incorrect to start out from the point that man is a sinner a priori and that the individual sins then issue from that state. The point of departure is on the contrary our concrete deeds and omissions in the real historical situation; it is in these that we fail to respond to the destiny which God has given us. Only when the inconceivable and appalling nature of our deeds has penetrated our very being do we realize that even earlier we have not shown ourselves to be God's covenant-partners and that, no matter how far back in our thoughts we go, there was never a time when we did so. Thus we are driven to confess to our Ally: we have sinned, we are sinners.

Must we now extend this insight and say that all men are sinners, that "man" is sinner? Yes; but this may not be a judgment that is pronounced from the stance of a spectator, or one of which the truth in its universality may be empirically determined. We are, ourselves, in the first place this sinful man, and if we speak in generalizing terms here, we can do so only on the basis of our being bound up together with our fellowmen.

We may hear repeatedly that one must not speak first of all about the sinful actions or the sinful omissions of a person, but of his sinful attitude. This tendency is often carried so far that some are willing to let the word "sin" be used only in the singular and reject its usage in the plural. But I consider this placing the sinful attitude foremost a dangerous thing, because thereby it is easy to get bogged down on a static sinful attitude of man. The next step then is for one to say that all that he does is, without distinction, sinful, and that he is incapable of doing good. Such an utterance becomes empty of meaning because it tries to say too much; often it is more of a dogmatic conceptual construction than an actual confession of guilt. The only correct significance of the words that we are utterly sinful is that in our totality we are sinful, that we do not sin with one part of our being while another part does not sin, but that we ourselves, just as we are, with our body and our soul, our mind and our conscience, sin. Indeed, the Bible also points in the direction indicated here. It speaks more . *i* sinful deeds and thoughts than of a so-called sinful attitude of man.

The inexplicable nature of sin

God has given man the freedom to live as his ally and to respond to his love with love in return. Therewith the possibility also is given for man not to make use of this freedom that is given to him. This does not mean that thereby the fact of sin is in any respect explained. It remains utterly incomprehensible that man, who is made to be God's partner, is not that; it is inconceivable that he does not actualize the destiny for which he is designed entirely. Moreover, it is not permissible for theological reflection to try to eliminate this inexplicable character. For sin is, by definition, that which God does not will, what he in no way has created, and what therefore cannot be placed within his good creation. It does not lie in human nature as such, and thus not in man's physical being, his finiteness, or his limitedness. Man may, after all, be God's ally and follow him just as he, man, is; that is to say, just as he is, his being man is good. Furthermore, we cannot explain our sinning by the situation in which we find ourselves. It is true that this situation always is already partially determined by the sins of others, and that we are thereby invited to sin, so to speak. When we have to justify ourselves to men, we can almost always rightly appeal to the "circumstances." But when we are aware of standing before God, we are conscious that this excuse will not serve. Then it becomes utterly inconceivable that we do not (are not willing to) respond to our destiny.

Moreover, sinning may not be explained by our saying that it is impossible to avoid getting "dirty hands." Otherwise one would miss the point that sin is not tragedy but guilt. We must actualize our covenant relationship with God ever anew, and in ever new ways. In so doing it is indeed often impossible to keep our hands clean, because acting in this world — and even refusing to act is a kind of action — is in fact coupled with getting our hands soiled. But if a man does in a particular situation what he knows himself to be called to do as covenant-man, we may not speak of sinning. The doing of God's will, even though this frequently consists of choosing something a bit better as over against the worse, is not sin, not even when in the process our hands are soiled. Could we not even say that the God of the Bible also, in his history with his people, has gotten "dirty hands"?

Man himself often experiences his sinning as something inexplicable and irrational, almost as something he is compelled to do, which however still does not nullify his consciousness of his own responsibility. Here the figure of the devil has its place. As symbol of personalized evil he is deeply rooted in human experience. For evil, the satanic, can become a real power which captures man, so that he does things that he does not "really" will. Man has received from God the freedom to be his ally. It can happen that he does not make use of this freedom, but squanders it, so that he becomes unfree.

The nature of sin

The concept "sin" can be described, as to its content, in all sorts of different ways. In any case it does not have primary reference to the transgression of (divine) commandments, but to the failure to fulfill the covenant-destiny. This can be expounded further with reference to one's relationship with God, to the connection with one's fellowman, and to the dominion over creation as God's deputy. We can also take as our point of departure the definition given above, that man, who is creature, is God's ally, and that consequently as creature he stands on the side of the creation and as ally on the side of God. He sins if he neglects one of these two poles. If he forgets that he is a creature, he makes himself like God and rebels against his creaturely limitations. If he forgets that he stands on God's side, he does not deal with nature as God's representative and sooner or later he will become either a tyrant over nature or a slave to nature. And if one considers that man as covenant-man is essentially bound to him who is more than man himself, one can define sin as man's being wrapped up in himself, as resting in what is given. Thereby it becomes evident that sinning is not only a wrong decision or action, but also the refusal to decide, simply letting things happen.

But regardless of the content with which one describes sin, one will never be able to grasp it in all its facets, and any systematizing of it will always retain a certain amount of arbitrariness.

Summary

It is only from the perspective of faith that one can speak of man as creature and of man as sinner. Only when God has become manifest to us as our gracious Covenant-ally do we ourselves become manifest as men whom he calls to his covenantal relationship and who again and again refuse to heed this call. In the light of God's covenantal relationship we recognize ourselves as sinners. However, we cannot of our own accord recognize that we are made by God very good; this is for us simply a conclusion to which we are necessarily driven by faith in the supreme Ally.

So both must be said together: we are, as God's good creation, sinful, and as sinners we are God's good creation; while we are people of the covenant, we live as though we were not God's allies, and while we live as not being allies, we remain God's covenant people. For — to come back again to our starting point — there is no such thing as an objectively God-less man. But we only come to know that when we have come to know God in his all-powerful love that never lets us go.

VII. MAN: EXPLICATION OF SOME DOGMATIC IDEAS

In the preceding chapter we spoke about essential aspects by which the human condition is defined in the light of faith. Now we shall treat some dogmatic concepts which have played a major role in theological anthropology. The material could also have been divided another way. We could have treated, in a first chapter, the creation of man and the primeval paradisiac goodness, and in a second chapter, the fall, the nature of sin, and original sin. But I have not used this obvious division; in my opinion, one must, insofar as it is possible, speak of man as creature and as sinner in the same breath, because either apart from the other is an abstraction. Besides, I did not want to devote a separate chapter to sin; that would place too much weight on the subject and it could appear that man's breaking of the covenant is of greater weight than the faithfulness of God which maintains the covenant. In a certain sense the present chapter could have been omitted altogether; we have already said everything that is essential. What follows here only serves to make the preceding more precise; in the process then we also can repudiate certain mistaken associations.

Biblical data

At present there is general recognition that the first three chapters of Genesis, which tell about the creation and the fall of the first man and woman, do not intend to give a description of something that happened long ago, but rather to say something about "man" as he is. This undoubtedly contains a truth; the very fact that "Adam" is, strictly speaking, not a proper name, but means "man," indicates that Adam and Eve are supra-personal figures, representing all men and women. Yet these narratives of the beginning do not exhaust their meaning for the biblical writers by the existential content alone. They also simply meant, with the means at their disposal, to describe the beginning of man and to tell about the history of the primeval era. In this connection the modern tension between faith and science must not be projected back into the Bible. What is said there about the creation of man is based upon profound reflection which arose out of Israel's covenant-experience with its God. This reflection of faith functioned in that time also as properly recognized "scientific" views. It is obvious that these can no longer have any authority for us; the biblical writers after all had more limited scientific knowledge at their disposal than we in our time possess. Therefore we may not appeal to the Bible for any sort of scientific hypothesis. The view that all men are descended from one set of parents is not proved by the Bible, nor is the opposing view of a descent from multiple beginnings refuted by it. Moreover, we may not triumphantly point out that according to the Bible man owes his existence to God's final act of creation, in order to confirm our evolutionary world-view, in which man is the last and highest stage of a long development. The writers knew nothing of evolution. It is another matter for us, who do have such knowledge, and we shall have to take account of it in our utterances of faith. This means that we shall have to surrender the idea of a perfect paradisiac condition. Indeed, the same also holds true for the idea of the fall. Neither as a historical description nor as an explanation of how man came to be as he is can the story of Genesis 3 be considered.

In comparison with traditional dogmatics, the biblical material is conspicuously more sober. Thus, for example, we do not find in the Bible any description of the perfection of Paradise.

> Only Ezek. 28:11-15 appears to give such. But this description, which presumably is borrowed from a pagan myth, does not refer here to primitive man, but to the king of Tyre!

There is also a question whether the Bible knows anything of the concepts of inherited sin and inherited guilt. The classical prooftexts for these ideas are Rom. 5:12-20 and Ps. 51:7. The exegesis, particularly of the New Testament passage, presents difficulties and is disputed. In any case, the intention of the passage is to place the grace that is in Christ in the spotlight by setting it against the background of the universality of sin. Paul is convinced of a certain connection of all men in sin and death, but he does not give a more precise explanation of this connection, and he does not explain how sin has passed from the one Adam to all men. The whole passage is more of a hymn of praise than a theological exposition. And as for Psalm 51, this is a personal, existential lamentation in which a psalmist who is unknown to us confesses his own sin and guilt in the most radical fashion. Indeed only seldom is anything said in the Bible theoretically and abstractly about "sin"; usually it speaks of specific sins that have been committed. Genesis 3 gives the most fundamental consideration of the matter. Here it speaks, from the perspective of the human situation in the world, about the anomalies in human life, the ambivalent relationship of man and woman, the peril of having children, painstaking labor, death, and all these are related to the greatest anomaly of all, sin. In the following chapters, Genesis 4-11, then, in repeatedly new fashion sin is described as the most basic disruption of existence in more and yet more different aspects.

References to the story of man's creation in the rest of the Bible are scarce. Only seldom is there any reference to the sin in Paradise: neither the prophets nor the gospels speak of it. Obviously the question of the origin of sin played no crucial role.

Paradise and the fall

Paradise is for us the symbol that man was created good, in harmony with God, with his fellowman, and with the world in which he lives; and the fall is the symbol of the fundamental disturbance of this harmony. Together they illumine the human condition, as the latter is made manifest to us in the light of God's covenantal relationship. In "Adam" and "Eve" we recognize ourselves, or, better said, we *are* Adam and Eve.

"Paradise" and "fall" as indication of the two sides of human existence may not be detached from each other. We know nothing of a pure being-human in a perfect state, one that lies prior to our current being-sinful or separate from it. It is not necessary here to go into that topic; that was done in the preceding chapter. But it is also forbidden to let the two aspects of "paradise" and "fall" coincide; they are not to be separated, but they must be distinguished. If we were to identify man's being a creature with his being sinful, then sinning would necessarily be given with man's being man, and thus it would lose the character of guilt. This distinction is assured by the way in which we experience ourselves. This does not mean that we can read from ourselves what man actually is like; we ourselves are too ambiguous and too opaque for that. But if the picture of man that we sketch on the basis of our belief in the Covenant-God is in agreement with reality, then we must be able to recognize ourselves in this picture. And indeed we know of ourselves that we are "really" different from and better than what we exhibit in our actions, and we do not experience this failure as fate alone (though that too!), but above all as guilt.

> The dogmatic idea of a "status integritatis" to indicate an original primeval integrity must be rejected; man has never been in such a condition, either individually or collectively. Even in the Bible, in fact, nothing is told us of a non-sinful condition of the first men; the first thing they do is eat the apple! Yet the idea of a human paradisiac state is a meaningful symbol that being a creature is in itself not a defect. And because, logically considered, the creaturely status precedes the sinful condition and the latter is experienced as an action in conflict with our "real" nature, the condition of integrity "precedes" — to translate it into theological language — all human activity.

Inherited sin

Along with the rejection of an original sinless ideal state, the idea of an original fall which dragged down with it the whole of humanity also has become untenable. There is a question whether thereby the whole idea of original sin, or inherited sin, also disappears. We have already said that this idea does not offer any explanation of sin. Man's sinning is in principle inexplicable. Even if it could be placed in some causal connection or other with an original, primeval sin, that still would provide no explanation; for then the original sin would have to be explained, and thus the incomprehensibility would only be shifted to an inaccessible past. The many questions that are evoked by the concept of inherited sin are indeed well known. What is the connection between our sinning and that of our forefathers? Must we think here of a kind of infection that is handed down from generation to generation? Does not the term "*inherited* sin" imply a negative assessment of the biological process of procreation, and thus wrongly regard sexuality especially as the locus of sin? And does not the unavoidability of inherited sin detract from man's moral responsibility? How can one then realistically speak of guilt?

Along with these questions and negative aspects, however, there are in the concept of inherited sin also some very definite elements of truth. It points to a fundamental perversity, which defies further explanation but nonetheless is very real, in which we refuse to respond to God's love and do not realize the humanness for which we are designed and to which we are destined. It reminds us that in our wrong actions we do not stand alone and that in them we are neither special nor original. We cannot even boast that we have invented our own sins; in them we only do what an infinite number of men have already done before us. Here we may even think of a handicap received from our parents. It is an undeniable fact that we can influence the lives and fortunes of our children for evil and that we can transmit our faults to our children. This perhaps holds true even more strongly for the society in which we grow up; our actions and thoughts are to a significant extent determined by that society. As members of society we share in the responsibility for the evil and the injustice that are committed by society. And with this we arrive at the last and perhaps the most important element of truth in the concept of inherited sin, namely, it points to the non-voluntary aspect of sin. Our sinning is based only in part on an actual decision of the will. This insight is again confirmed by our own experience. We are driven to it by the situation of human existence, with all its ambiguities which make it impossible for us unequivocally to do the good. Thus in a certain sense our sinning is also always fate. Sin can be experienced as a real power that has captured us, or, better said, to which we have given ourselves up as captives. Where this aspect of sin as fate is not recognized, as a rule sin is rationalized and put on an exclusively moral level. In practice this almost always means that it is rendered trivial.

If one wishes to maintain the term "inherited sin," it must in any case be purged of all mistaken associations. But because the truth for which it stands can just as well be expressed in another way, it seems to me better, in order to avoid all misunderstanding, to abandon this heavily freighted and ambiguous term.

> Dogmatics speaks of the *status corruptionis*, the condition or state of corruption in which man finds himself. Indeed, we know ourselves as people who sin again and again. Yet the theological term is too static and too abstract; sinfulness is not a characteristic of man apart from and prior to his (sinful) actions. For the same reason I have reservations about saying that man is sinful "by nature." Here again a sinful nature is posited a priori. Moreover, the expression "by nature" is ambiguous. The "nature" with which God created man is, after all, good, equipped for the covenant relationship with him. Therefore one could say, with just as much or even more right, that man is "by nature" good.

Man as God's image

The essence of the Christian view of man is often summarized in the words that man is the image of God. It is not absolutely necessary to use precisely this term for this purpose. It is not a central term in the Bible, and it appears only a few times; besides, it is not everywhere clear exactly what is meant by the term. But even if we could precisely determine the meaning of the term in the Bible, that still would not be sufficient. As an indication of the essence of man, the idea "image of God" has acquired in theology a broader significance and a definite value.

Attempts have been made to define this image in many different ways. In the past it was sought for in man's reason or in his freedom of will, or otherwise in his personhood or his moral consciousness. These aspects of humanness, however, are of no special weight for faith's view of man. In my opinion, "God's image" must be understood as a reflection of God, as was discussed in the preceding chapter. Man resembles God in that he is not man-by-himself, just as God also is not God-by-himself. Thus man is the image of the Covenant-God in the fact that he is essentially related to God above himself, to his fellowman alongside him, and to the creation beneath him. Only in this way is justice done to the plain meaning of the word "image" in the sense of "representation."

> The expression "image of God" is borrowed primarily from Gen. 1:26, 27. It does indeed contain the idea of a likeness, a reflection. Thus the special connection between God and man is given, from the very beginning, with the word "image." Yet this probably is not the point with which the writer was primarily concerned. It is also generally assumed that the addition, that man is created as male and female, does not offer an exposition of this being in God's image, although the connection between male and female undoubtedly was important to the writer. He appears however to be impressed primarily by the position of dominion which man occupies on earth. In this he saw an analogy with God's having dominion. This is also the idea that is expressed in Psalm 8, where the words "almost like God" say the same thing as "image of God."

There has been much concern in theology over the question whether the image of God has been lost because of sin. Generally speaking, this image has been equated with an original righteousness which the first men possessed in their state of primeval integrity. Then it was necessary to posit, with sin, the loss of the image. But because this image was also used to identify what is specifically human about man, a difficulty was encountered; for the sinner too still remains recognizably human. But if the distinctive thing about man is seen in the fact that God is his covenant-ally, then the humanness of man must be defined primarily not in terms of man, but in terms of God, who in his faithfulness remains the Ally even of the man who sins. With respect to man, this says that he is created to be God's ally and collaborator; he is designed for that end, and that is his "design." But when he sins, he fails to actualize this design; instead, he lives and acts in conflict with it. And, as is the case with any talent or capacity, it also holds true for the capacity for the covenant relationship, that if it is not used, it grows weaker and weaker and in the long run it atrophies.

Thus when man is identified as the image of God, this image-being points, on the one hand, to the capacity of man which he must actualize; it is in the way he lives and acts that it first becomes evident that he resembles God and reflects him. In this respect the idea of "the image of God" has a normative and critical function. It serves to indicate the destiny that God has given man, and man is under condemnation insofar as he does not respond to this destiny. By failing to use his capacity, or by misusing it, man then can also obscure the image of God that he is, and can even lose it, and instead of reflecting God he can become a reflection of the "devil." On the other hand, as we have already said, man must not be defined primarily in terms of himself, but in relation to God. Without taking anything away from what has just been said, it is true that man is and remains God's image, because out of pure grace God remains his Ally.

> The duality that resides for us in the concept "image of God" is also characteristic of the way the Bible speaks of it. On the one hand man *is* God's image; regardless of whether he fulfills the destiny that is implied in his being that image (for example, Gen. 1:26, 27; I Cor. 11:7); but on the other hand it is only the man who is made new in Jesus Christ, that is, the man who in Christ fulfills his destiny, who becomes God's image (for example Col. 3:10; cf. II Cor. 3:18).

Thus in its meaning of "reflection" of God the term "image" indeed offers an excellent denominator under which we can include everything that must be said about man from the perspective of faith. For it points to a view of man in which the relationship to God is central from the very outset, so that it cannot be confused with any natural scientific or philosophical view of man.

VIII. ISRAEL IN THE OLD TESTAMENT

All that has been said up to this point about God, about his being man's Ally, his predestining and electing, and everything that has been said about man, about his being called to be God's ally and his failing to fulfill his destiny, could be said only on the basis of God's dealing with Israel. Therefore we must now speak about that matter. Indeed, all that we shall say hereafter about Jesus would be without any foundation without the preceding history of God's dealing with his people.

Covenant and law

God is the God of all nations, and in one way or another, beyond our ability to perceive, he deals with them all. But his dealing with Israel, his relationship with this people is specific and unique. The Old Testament is evidence of this. It is the testimony of the experiences of the people of Israel — or of individuals or groups of that people — with God in the course of their history. Compared with the testimonies of any other peoples, these experiences appear to be qualitatively different. In Israel God has made himself known, in an incomparable way, as Covenant-God. Of course all sorts of factors of common history and origin have formed this nation, but in all these historical factors the nation itself traced its existence back to God's own action. God himself set the nation apart from all other nations and chose it for the purpose of relating himself to this nation in a special way. It is the apple of his eye, his special jewel, his "Sonderschatz," to use one of Buber's terms. And the nation may know him and may live as the people to whom he has bound himself, as his covenant-people. For the covenant between God and Israel is summed up, and indeed can best be summed up, thus: "I will be your God, and you shall be my people," words which appear, with variations, again and again in the Old Testament. The covenant comes altogether from God, it is his declaration of love for Israel, and to this extent one can say that it is a one-sided arrangement. But again, on the other hand that is not true; the word "covenant" includes the idea that two parties are involved; it has to do with God's love that seeks a response of love in return, and of trust, on Israel's part.

Israel's fundamental covenant-experience as the abiding center of its faith is indissolubly bound up with the deliverance from Egypt and the giving of the law at Sinai. It is impossible to reconstruct precisely what happened there historically. The description that the Bible gives in the book of Exodus, in the form in which we now have it, dates from a much later time. For faith this is ultimately of no importance. In any case it is clear that an act of deliverance preceded the establishment of the covenant. This is the first thing: God becomes manifest as the redeemer, as the one who helps his people and brings salvation to them. And this becoming manifest takes place through an event in history that is in principle historically datable (approximately 1290 B.C.?). God is a God of history, a God who makes history with his people and who is Lord of history. And closely connected with the leading of the people out of Egypt is the giving of the law. Actually the word "law" is not a happy translation of the biblical concept of "torah." The latter is not a collection of legal prescriptions which Israel must follow as an obligation, so that God will be gracious. It is rather the beneficent revelation of God's will for his covenant-people, an exposition of what it means, as to content, to live here on earth as the people of God. Therefore the torah cannot be fixed in content once and for all. When Israel still was not much more than a few loosely related groups of nomads in the desert, different directions for living as covenant-people were necessary from those required when, after the entrance into Canaan, an agrarian federation of twelve tribes had developed. Living as God willed in the time of the independent monarchy had a form different from that in the time of the Babylonian exile, or when the nation was a province of the Persian or the Hellenistic world-empire. Many of the stipulations of the torah that appear in the Old Testament seem unimportant to us now, and often we are unable any longer even to recover the meaning of them. But they declare that God accompanies his people as a whole, as well as the individual among this community, even to the various aspects of everyday life. It is unwise for us to make a strict distinction between the so-called moral laws and the cultic laws, ascribing then to the moral laws, which regulate the relationships between men, an abiding significance, and to the cultic laws only a temporary and transient value. It is precisely in the cultic laws that the character of the torah as grace comes out most clearly. After all, they give directions as to how the nation or the individual may approach God as covenant-partner, and how God has provided in the sacrificial ritual a way of restoring the covenant relationship that has been broken by transgression. Because the cultic and the moral belong together, even the cultus loses its meaning if in social life the justice for which God stands is trodden under foot; then the cultus becomes an external thing which is in conflict with God's intention.

It is improper to ask whether the torah is from God or is a collection of regulations made by men. Of course they are human regulations; this holds true not only of all sorts of relatively secondary prescriptions, but also of the "ten commandments," the abiding core of the entire torah. But as human regulations they are an expression of God's covenant will for his people in particular times and in certain situations. God's self-revealing will is known only in the form in which men actualize it and bear witness to it.

Israel's election

God chose Israel to be his people in particular; they are privileged to know him as do none of the other nations. This is an unbelievable privilege which the nation can only accept in wondering gratitude. This brings with it, as a self-evident consequence, that Israel then also is to live as is becoming for the people of God

— which Israel after all is. They are called to be a holy nation, chosen by God to do his will. And thereby they will then become the way by which God's revelation will also reach the other nations. It is the task and calling of this nation to reflect God's will in their manner of life. They are chosen to be God's test-plot, his experimental garden, so that the Gentiles, seeing Israel, will recognize what God evidently wants of men, and on the basis of this recognition will be converted to the God of Israel, who is also the God of all peoples. When it is said in the prophetic writings that someday all the nations shall come to Jerusalem, this does not arise out of a nationalistic or imperialistic feeling of superiority, but it is the expression of the expectation of faith that someday the whole earth shall be full of the knowledge of the Lord. For it is through Israel that God's revelation is intended to reach the Gentiles. Israel must be transparent to God, or, to say the same thing in different words, it must represent God to the nations. But the other holds true also, that Israel represents the nations before God. It stands, so to speak, for the other nations, so that in his love for Israel God likewise has these other nations in view. This idea in fact is included in the figure of the test-garden. In Israel there must be actualized what God will someday actualize for the whole earth. The words of Ex. 19:6, that Israel shall be a kingdom of priests, perhaps have this dual representation in mind: that of God to the nations, and that of the nations before God.

> One of the most impressive testimonies of this universalistic dimension of Israel's election is the story of Abraham's call, which presumably assumed its basic form in the tenth century B. C. This dimension lies not only in the words of Gen. 12:3, "In you shall all the races of the earth be blessed," the translation of which is not certain, but primarily in the way in which the covenant with Abraham as pre-history of the covenant of Sinai is placed against the background of the primeval history. When God's dealing with humanity came to a dead end, his dealing with Israel begins in Abraham, in order once again to reach humanity through this detour.

Israel is God's people and is destined to live as God's people. We can express this in various ways: that its election and its calling are two sides of one and the same thing, or that its existence and its destiny belong irrevocably together. In view of the fact that Israel in its election is representative of all peoples and of the whole of humanity, we could also speak in these same terms about "man" in general in chapter VI.

Israel's unfaithfulness

But from the very beginning there was a discrepancy between Israel's destiny and its actual existence. The entire history of the covenant between God and his people can be described in terms of Israel's unfaithfulness to its calling and God's repeatedly renewed attempts to identify Israel in terms of its commission. One may think here of the story of the golden calf, or of the framework in which the ancient legends of the judges were set: the nation's apostasy — punishment by God — repentance — deliverance; and then the cycle begins again with a new apostasy. Even the monarchy in Israel can be seen as an expression of the nation's unfaithfulness to God: it was not satisfied with God's invisible kingship, but wanted to have a human, visible king, like the other surrounding nations. But God did not abandon his people. The king himself now becomes the instrument par excellence through which he will make his people obedient. In the Old Testament the covenant of Sinai and the royal covenant, that is, God's covenant with David and his descendants, originally stood side-by-side without connection. It is good to keep this in view, for it is an indication that we may not see the covenantal history as an unbroken line. Again and again it is interrupted and God begins anew and in a different way. Yet we may also say that the covenant with David is an extension of the Sinai covenant; in fact, after the exile this connection was made in Israel itself. The king becomes the way by which the Sinai covenant must be fulfilled. On the one hand the king has become the representative of the whole nation; with him it stands or falls. But on the other hand he is also God's representative. He is his anointed, his messiah, through whom God's lordship must take shape. But one king after another defaulted; not one of them actually responded to his calling. And with and in the kings' failure the nation as a whole also failed. And again God does not give up. Now it is a man like the writer of the book of Deuteronomy who strives to keep Israel to the Sinai covenant, or it is the prophets who with their sharp denunciations try to call Israel back. It is almost as if God wants to give his people one last chance. But it is of no avail. And then these same prophets must proclaim with stern relentlessness the judgment upon the nation, and this is fulfilled in the fall of the state and in the Babylonian exile. And again God does not abandon his people. With the return from exile he makes a new beginning, he gives a new possibility, a possibility however which again appears to come to naught.

Thus the history of the covenant provides, with increasing clarity, the evidence that if the covenant is actually to fulfill its intention, God himself, in his love and faithfulness, will have to overcome the unfaithfulness of his partner. Perhaps by giving his people a new heart and a new mind, perhaps by putting his torah in their hearts so that they will no longer break it, perhaps by bringing a small remnant of the nation to sincere repentance, perhaps also by giving a new Davidic king who in the name of the people will do God's will perfectly, or perhaps through one through whose innocent death the people will be brought to a confession of their guilt and to conversion. But the way by which God's covenantal love will prevail is for the devout in Israel less important than the certainty that, however it must be done, this love will someday overcome the resistance of the people.

Although there were always some individuals in Israel who did God's work — It must never be forgotten, for example, that the testimonies of the Old Testament arose within Israel itself — as a whole it appears here too as representative of all nations and of the whole of humanity in the fact that it does not fulfill its calling from God. On the basis of this fact we spoke about human sin as we did in the preceding chapter.

The promise

The history of God's dealings with Israel however can also be described in another way. We have already seen that the covenant points beyond itself, because it has in view the salvation of the whole world. It is oriented to the future and contains a promise for the future: for the future of Israel itself, when it shall live as a people among whom God's lordship shall take form with utter clarity; and for the future of the nations, when they shall be incorporated into this kingdom of God which Israel is destined to become. This openness to the future, this element of promise and expectation, is a characteristic mark of all the relationship between God and Israel, as the Old Testament writers bear witness to that relationship. The history of the covenant can also be described in these terms.

There is the promise of the land of milk and honey that drives Israel forward, toward the future, in its journey through the wilderness. And this divine promise is fulfilled, and yet not fulfilled, when the nation is once established in the land. It appears to be a precarious possession, constantly threatened by the nations round about, only a dim foreshadowing of the anticipated paradisiac land that means rest and salvation. There is the promise to David that God will perpetuate his house and kingdom. When Solomon, belated son of a marriage that was founded on injustice, by all sorts of detours and intrigues at last ascended the throne, this promise appears to be fulfilled. But again the promise is shown to be greater than the original fulfillment. After all neither Solomon nor any of his successors is actually a king entirely after God's own heart. And then when with the exile everything seems actually to be finished, there is the new promise that gives impetus toward the future, that God will lead the exiles back home and will provide a new deliverance and saving deed just as he once did in Egypt. And then when the return has taken place, again the promise is fulfilled, and yet not fulfilled. The return is seen not to have brought the expected salvation.

The prophets have given clearest expression to this structure of the divine promises which surpass the historical fulfillment. The promises which they proclaim in God's name have reference on the one hand to the immediate historical situation. In the debacle of the judgment they point to the remnant who, as representative of all Israel and as a guarantee of its restoration, shall be spared; in the exile they point to the return, and in the time after the return, when life has become drab, they speak of a rebuilding of the land and a rich and blessed life. All this was real comfort and it gave Israel assurance that in spite of everything it was the people of God, whom he would not abandon. But all these promises have still another dimension. They are clothed in words that point to a distant vision of ultimate and perfect salvation. They speak of a Kingdom of peace and righteousness here on earth that at the same time surpasses any earthly possibility.

When we now, in conclusion, bring together the two lines that have been drawn, that of the covenant and that of Israel's expectation, we see on the one hand a growing consciousness of the breakdown of the covenant and on the other hand the assurance of faith that God still will cause this covenant to prevail. But the great problem obviously is man!

IX. THE "HISTORICAL JESUS"

Historical-critical study of the Bible

The name "Jesus Christ" itself contains a confession of the Christian faith, namely that Jesus, a man who lived approximately two thousand years ago, is the Christ in whom God has acted in a decisive way. "Jesus is the Christ" means that in this man God's saving intention has been made manifest and implemented. "Jesus is the Christ" means that a man who died at a certain time back then now is our Lord and Savior today. All these are big words. In the chapters that follow we shall try to give more content to them. At this point we wish to direct our attention to only one side of the matter, namely, to the fact that the person whom we confess to be the Christ for us is the historical man Jesus. Whatever we shall say further about Christ, we shall be speaking in any case about this man. This includes the acknowledgment that if historical investigation could ever prove he actually never existed or that his words and deeds were contrary to what we now proclaim as Christian faith, this faith would no longer be tenable; it then would clearly be built upon a fiction. We may not dodge this issue by saying that historical scholarship will never be able to prove our faith. It is true that it is not historically demonstrable that Jesus is the Christ and that in him we are dealing with God. But this utterance of faith proposes to say something about an historical person, and whether this alleged historical person actually lived or is nothing but a fabrication cannot be determined by faith, but only by scholarship. And the same holds true for all that this historical person said and did and experienced. These are historical facts from the past which can only be determined on the basis of historical research.

Now the data which we have concerning these facts are of such a nature that we must ask whether it is not impossible for us to form a picture of this historical man, Jesus of Nazareth. For these we are exclusively dependent upon the writings of the New Testament, and these are writings of men who were anything but "objective" or "unbiased." The few scant reports about him that we find in Jewish or other writers are unimportant and provide no firm grasp for us. This is not surprising, for except for those who acknowledged that he was the Christ, Jesus was not a figure who deserved historical notice: a Jewish teacher who traveled about with a little group of disciples, who through his conduct brought down upon his neck the enmity of the leaders of his people and evidently because of his political aspirations was put to death by the Roman authorities. This sort of thing happened frequently in that time.

Of the New Testament writings, only the gospels provide us with historical data about the life of Jesus. In the letters of Paul, the earliest writings that we have from primitive Christianity, only the fact of his birth and his crucifixion are spoken of, and a few of his words are handed down, which, apart from the words of institution of the Lord's Supper, are of no startling significance. It is clearly a different matter with the four gospels, the earliest of which, Mark, was written about thirty-five years after Jesus' death, and John, the latest, about sixty to seventy years. Moreover, all of them contain material that is earlier and that was passed along orally in part, and in part also was already written down. At first glance the gospels appear to offer us a biography of Jesus. But that is true only in a very relative sense. None of the four intends to give an historically exact description of the life of Jesus, but they are "*Tendenz*-writings," which have only one aim: to show that this man is the Christ. The historical data are placed entirely at the service of this testimony. This involved a major process of sifting. Only those deeds, events, and words of Jesus that were relevant for this testimony are told. Thus for example we know nothing of his youth, of his characteristics, of his outward life, of his private life, or of his personal friendships. And the material that is included is described in such a way that it is obvious that here we have to do with the words and deeds of the Christ in whom the community believed. They did not intend primarily to pass along something that had happened earlier and was now in the past, but it was their intention to confront the reader with the risen and presently living Lord. Historical event is interwoven with what the evangelists or their sources wanted to say with that event. Thus not only a reduction but also an expansion of the historical material has taken place. For there are also descriptions of happenings that never occurred, and there are words put in Jesus' mouth that he never uttered. An example of the former is the futile attempt of Herod to kill Jesus by the murder of the babies in Bethlehem. This story, which appears only in Matthew (2:13-19), is, as is generally recognized, formed as a parallel to the Old Testament story of the rescue of the child Moses; Jesus is described from the very first as a second Moses — only he is much more powerful than Moses, as will later appear. The flight into Egypt, moreover, gave Matthew the opportunity to have Jesus called back from there later by God, just as God had done in the past with Israel. In this way the evangelist expressed an idea which is fundamental for the Christian faith, namely that Jesus stands for all Israel, that he represents his entire nation. If one says that these things that are related did not "really happen," but that they are "only" legends, one does not thereby contribute anything to an actual understanding of them. They want to be read as an expression and an illustration of the belief that Jesus is the Christ.

And in order to gain an impression as to how a simple parable, which presumably came from Jesus himself, is re-shaped into an expanded allegory, one may compare the invitation to a banquet as told by Luke (14:15-24) and Matthew (22:1-14). In Matthew's version there are all sorts of features of the earlier form, which is better preserved in Luke, expanded in the light of later experiences. Now it has to do with a marriage feast which a king gives for his son, established figures of the messianic end-time, of God and the Son of God. Moreover, in the fate of the servants there is reflected the martyrdom of the Christian missionaries, and the setting fire to the city has reference to the devastation of Jerusalem in A. D. 70. Such a re-working must not be regarded as a falsification of the original words of Jesus; the evangelists did not work with the modern concept of historical reliability. Behind this re-shaping lies the belief that the words of Jesus have an external value and that they therefore were spoken for every age. Jesus' words for "then" are transposed in the gospels into words for "now."

> In 1835 David Friedrich Strauss published his first and most famous work, *Das Leben Jesu* ("The Life of Jesus"), which provided the impetus for the entire so-called Leben-Jesu-Forschung ("Life of Jesus Research," usually equated in English with the "search for the historical Jesus"). He wanted to discover, behind the Christ of orthodox doctrine, the life and character of Jesus as he actually was. This investigation, however, was a great deal less undogmatic and objective than it purported to be. Instead of starting from the conviction that Jesus is the Christ, the Son of God, Strauss and his disciples took as their unexpressed starting-point the position that he was nothing more than an ordinary man, an "impressive personality" or a "religious genius." This form of research has come to a dead end. It has become evident that there are not enough data to provide a complete biographical or psychological picture of Jesus. The gaps have been filled in by the pious imagination of scholars, so that one ultimately had a great variety of pictures of Jesus, in which every picture strongly resembled the investigator's picture of the ideal man. Moreover, it also gradually became evident that there were certain aspects of Jesus' teaching that were utterly alien to the religious ideas of the man of the 19th and early 20th centuries. The man Jesus appeared significantly less understandable than had originally been thought.

The refinement of the so-called historical-critical study of the Bible in our time has given a new impetus to the search for the "historical Jesus." This research must not be taken as an undermining of faith. It is nothing more than a tool which can be used for good or for ill. It makes it possible for us to penetrate behind the biblical text and to discern which material presumably comes from the writer and where he has made use of earlier material, why he took over precisely this material, from what circles it comes, how he has changed it, and in what context he has placed it. Alongside the critical analysis of the text that has been handed down, historical criticism also has a constructive function, which is at least just as important, namely to reconstruct, as well as is possible, the historical event and the traditions which are used by the biblical writers. No reconstruction is absolutely certain; any such reconstruction can only lay claim to greater or lesser probability. This awareness must bring with it a large measure of modesty, but must not lead to neglect of the effort at reconstruction. To return once more to the parable of the feast: even the form in which Luke offers this very probably does not come in its entirety from Jesus but, to use a technical term of historical criticism, is partially "inauthentic." The sending out of the servants three times, first to the prominent persons, then to the needy in the city, and finally to the people outside the city, points to the spread of the mission from Israel to the Gentiles. Thus this motif presumably stems from a time when the Gentile mission was already in process, and did not belong to the original parable of Jesus.

What is said above makes it clear that the distinction in "authentic" and "inauthentic" does not involve a value judgment. In the so-called "inauthentic" words of Jesus there is frequently contained the preaching and the application of the "authentic." Just so, the non-historical narratives also on the one hand obscure our view of the "historical Jesus," but on the other hand interpret him for us. The historical Jesus must have been such an uncommon man that these extraordinary stories could be told about him. If this unusual dimension in the picture of Jesus is lacking, this must be an indication for us that the reconstruction offered does not fit somewhere.

> The more conservative scholars are convinced that a great many of the words which the Bible presents to us as coming from Jesus are "authentic," or that at least his genuine words can be discovered from then. The so-called radical-critical scholars on the other hand take a very skeptical stance with respect to the genuineness, regard by far the most of these words as having been formed by the community, and think that only a few utterances can be attributed with any certainty to Jesus himself. All, however, without distinction make use in one way or another of the method of historical criticism.

Jesus, proclaimer of the kingdom of God

Although there is wide divergence of opinion on many aspects and components, most scholars agree on the main content of what Jesus taught, on some important characteristics of his conduct, and on a few biographical data.

In proclamation of the kingdom of God, Jesus stands altogether in the line of the great prophets of Israel. They too spoke of the lordship of God which will be realized. In Jesus' preaching this proclamation is only greatly intensified, and it more strongly permeates all that he says and does than we find it in any of the prophets. The Kingdom is already dawning; it is already beginning to become reality and to prevail. The important thing is to commit oneself to it and to prepare oneself for it. With this message Jesus appeared before his fellow countrymen and to this he summoned them. In this summons, exultation occupies a large place. The Kingdom is open to all who give heed to his preaching, and it signifies salvation and joy. And even God rejoices over every single person who is willing to enter.

> There is a question as to how fully Jesus' preaching of the kingdom of God must be set in the apocalyptic thought-pattern of his time. In apocalyptic, the coming of the kingdom is preceded by a great cosmic catastrophe which would bring an end to the world and its history. In any case, Jesus did share with apocalyptic the conviction that the kingdom would be the decisive turn in history, and that it would be completely new.

The miracles which Jesus did must also be seen in the context of the coming of the kingdom. Although precisely here the legendary additions are particularly numerous, it is hardly to be doubted that Jesus' activity is reminiscent of that of the exorcists. Exorcism is a phenomenon that is difficult for modern man to comprehend, though it appears in all ancient cultures: the adjuring, overcoming, and expelling of evil spirits by means of special rites and formulas. Jesus shared with his contemporaries the conviction that sicknesses, and especially mental illnesses, were caused by demonic forces. However, he did not attack these devils and demons with adjurations and magic formulas, but with his word of power. This was altogether in harmony with the in-breaking lordship of God: he was pointing out that in principle the strength of the antigodly powers was already broken. We no longer believe in demon possession in a literal sense, or in evil spirits which cause illnesses. Therefore we shall have to express what happened in Jesus' healings in different fashion from that of the evangelists. These healings are for us indications that misfortune and sickness are in conflict with God's will and that in the healing of people, whether in mental or in physical respect, something of the salvation of the kingdom of God is becoming visible. Indeed even the biblical writers do not place their emphasis upon the miraculous element in Jesus' miracles. As was noted, there were many exorcists in that time. They saw the healings rather as signs of the power of God which was at work in Jesus and as manifestations of the kingdom which was breaking through in him.

In his teaching and exposition of the Scripture Jesus appeared as a scribe. We do not propose to offer a detailed treatment of his ethic; this would take us too far afield and would call for a judgment about "authentic" and "inauthentic" words of Jesus which I am not able to give. For much in this area is under dispute. Yet the essence of what he taught is clear. Jesus did not set himself in opposition to the torah, although he appears to have ascribed rather slight weight to the cultic regulations. Alongside this, however, we find in him such an unprecedented radicalizing of the law that thereby he called the entire traditional religious system in question. In the preceding chapter we saw that in Israel the torah was an expression of God's gracious will and that the many prescriptions show how even in the minor matters of everyday life God shows man the right way. Israel and its biblical scholars, particularly the Pharisees, knew that the torah was not something from the past, but that in each new age and circumstance, it must be interpreted and applied ever anew in a new way. The many prescriptions which existed in Jesus' time were the result of this actualizing interpretation. But these many prescriptions almost inevitably brought with them the danger of formalism. Moreover, the law, actually the revelation of God's saving will, threatened thereby to become an independent entity which was placed between God and man.

> These prescriptions are labeled by Jesus in the gospels as "traditions of men." There is a question as to whether this expression had such a denigrating sound as we hear in it. The standard term in Judaism was "traditions of the elders."

> The highly negative light in which the Pharisees are placed in the New Testament is, historically seen, unjust. They were the Jews who most of all wanted to take seriously God's Torah, down to the most minute details of everyday life. It is questionable whether the picture of the relationship between them and Jesus as drawn in the Bible agrees with the historical actuality. Historical criticism makes it probable that much here in dark colors has been inserted in a time when the Jewish religious leaders were vigorously opposing the still infant Christian community.

Jesus pushed aside this entire legal system. God's will cannot be captured in a series of regulations. In utter dependence on God, and at the same time with a strong self-consciousness he appealed to God himself and confronted his hearers with the keenest immediacy with God's holy will. Again, this too must be seen in the light of the dawning kingdom: man may live in God's very presence. This same immediacy indeed is noticeable in Jesus himself: it actually is his most distinctive characteristic. This is attested, among other ways, by the way he addressed God: Abba, dear Father. His relationship with God appears to be of an unprecedented intimacy and confidence. In Jesus' announcement of the kingdom is incorporated also his association with "tax collectors and sinners." It is difficult for us fully to sense the unprecedented and revolutionary character of all this. "Tax-collectors and sinners" were people who did not trouble themselves with God's commandments and who thereby violated the holiness of the people of God. No wonder, then, that the God-fearing Jews avoided them. And with such people Jesus even sat at a table. That was not only a proof of an almost inconceivable solidarity with people, but it also had a symbolic worth which went far beyond that. A meal was, after all, the fixed symbol of the kingdom of God. In Jesus' table-fellowship with the outcasts, the kingdom as it were is set forth as present. God's rule obviously signifies, in particular, salvation for those who need him most: those who are estranged from God, those who are outcasts from society, the despised, the lost, and the poor.

The crucifixion

The story of the crucifixion in Jerusalem belongs to the most detailed and earliest material in the gospels. This does not mean that we have here a larger number of historically reliable data. The crucifixion, originally the great stumbling-block for faith, is described altogether as the proclamation of the first community; the account is given in terms of a testimony. Thus for example the many references to the Old Testament in the passion narrative are striking. With these the evangelists wanted to show that in his suffering Jesus stood altogether in line with the suffering righteous ones from the Psalms.

The fact of the crucifixion cannot reasonably be doubted. It can also be assumed as historically established that it was a Roman sentence which was based on an accusation by Jewish leaders. Further, the inscription above the cross makes it appear probable that the accusation was of a political nature in the first place. But as to precisely what the course of events was and precisely why Jesus was put to death, about this we can express only conjectures. From the gospels it can be inferred that at the outset Jesus found a hearing for his preaching with more than a few, but that he also evoked, in increasing measure, the resistance of his countrymen. His preaching of the "righteousness that exceeds that of the scribes and Pharisees," his thrusting aside the entire system of rules and prescriptions, and his association with "sinners" brought down on his neck the enmity of the religious leaders of Israel. His conduct disappointed the Zealots, the revolutionary underground resistance fighters, who presumably at first cherished high expectations of him, and alienated them from him. The strong self-consciousness in which he proclaimed God's Lordship which had already dawned in his own person, his preaching, and his deeds, rendered him suspect to the aristocratic priestly class which, open to the culture of the Roman world empire, had great interest in maintaining the status quo. On the basis of historical-critical study it is generally assumed that this class played the most prominent role in the accusation before the Roman authorities. And finally, Pilate condemned him as a politically dangerous pretender to the kingship over an independent Israel.

The titles

This last point brings us to the frequently propounded question about the so-called messianic consciousness of Jesus. To me personally the question appears to be wrongly stated. Self-consciousness is a psychological category, and the sources which we have do not allow us psychologically to penetrate Jesus' inner life. The matter takes a different cast if we ask whether there are "genuine" utterances in which Jesus said or confirmed that he was the Messiah. But even when stated in this way the question appears unanswerable. To begin with, we do not even know how the label of "Messiah" was employed in Jesus' time. According to some it was a designation used for very diverse figures, who had in common only the fact that in some way or another they were related to God's final time of salvation. According to others Jesus' contemporaries (except for some sectarian groups) used this title exclusively as a reference to a king or someone like a king, in any case a specifically political figure who would liberate Israel from foreign domination. It is very likely that certain groups among his people saw Jesus as messiah in this latter sense. But we do not know whether Jesus himself assumed and perhaps reshaped this title. It also is not very important, for the title "Messiah," particularly in its Greek translation as "Christos," acquired a new content of its own. It expresses the idea that in his saving activity Jesus is the salvation of the world. And this faith does not rest upon certain utterances which Jesus perhaps made about himself. What is said here about the title of Messiah applies equally to the other titles which are put in Jesus' mouth in the New Testament, such as, for example, that of the Son of Man or the Son of God. Much has been written about all the titles, and a unanimous conclusion has not been reached about any of them. It continues to be a disputed question whether Jesus ever applied one of these titles to himself; and even if he did so, there still remains the uncertainty about the sense in which he did so. But again it must be said that this entire set of questions is not important for faith. For what is unique about the "historical" Jesus, which is not to be fitted into our ordinary human categories, does not rest upon certain utterances which he made or did not make about himself, but is contained in his words and his deeds and the totality of his conduct. And the young church was pointing to all this when it gave him all these messianic titles and called him Christ the Lord and Son of God.

X. JESUS AS THE CHRIST

In the preceding chapter we attempted to describe the historical man Jesus of Nazareth insofar as this is possible from the available sources. There we arrived at the picture of an exceptional man whom it is difficult to fit entirely into our usual categories. However, this route could not bring us to the certainty that this man is the Christ. And yet that is, put in its most concise formula, the quintessence of the Christian faith. For the name Christ has become for us the symbol in which we summarize the totality of the saving significance of Jesus.

> Perhaps it will be good here briefly to say something more about the title "Christ." It is the Greek translation of the Hebrew "messiah," and means, literally, "anointed one." In the Old Testament the term is used one time to refer to the high priest (Lev. 4:3), but ordinarily it is used of the kings of Israel, of Saul, David, and David's successors, and as an exception also of the king of the Persians, Cyrus, to indicate thereby that he is the instrument of God (Is. 45:1). It is noteworthy that in the Old Testament writings the anticipated king who is to bring the promised time of salvation is never called Messiah.

> We do not know precisely in what sense the Jewish primitive church in Palestine gave Jesus the title of Messiah in addition to other titles; moreover, the development of the steadily richer conception of the Messiah can be described only in approximate terms. In any case the Hellenistic community took over this Jewish title in the Greek form "Christos." There it relatively quickly gained a dominant position. This appears from the fact that very soon the believers were called "Christians" (Acts 11:26). Finally, the title Christ is crystallized and becomes a kind of proper name. (Cf. also the comment in the preceding chapter about the messianic self-consciousness of Jesus.)

We do not propose in this chapter to speak about what we mean when we say that Jesus is the Christ, the salvation of the world. Here we shall deal only with the question of how people arrived at this confession.

The crucifixion

With great authority Jesus had proclaimed the coming of the kingdom of God, which was already dawning in his words and deeds. His entire manner of life had been a summons to men to let themselves be included in the movement of this coming kingdom and to travel the way which he had pointed out to them. He had given offense to most of his countrymen because in consequence of his extraordinary sense of a relationship with God, he did not refrain from going beyond the precincts sanctified by tradition. But some had cherished a faith in him and his words and had hoped that he would play a decisive role in the establishment of God's rule. Then the crucifixion followed, and thereby the ground was cut from under every possible expectation. Jesus' entire activity had come to naught. He obviously was not the one in whom salvation was announced, and the divine authority of which his conduct had borne witness evidently had been nothing but appearance. Thus the cross signified a great disappointment for all who had expected something of him. The words of the travelers to Emmaus (Luke 24:19-21) surely give a faithful picture of the disappointment of Jesus' disciples after the crucifixion — regardless of whether the episode described there is historical or not: "We lived in the hope that he would be the one to redeem Israel, but our chief priests and rulers handed him over to be condemned to death." If the crucifixion had been the last thing to be said about Jesus, a Christian community never would have arisen, a New Testament would never have been written, and if we knew anything of Jesus — which is unlikely — we perhaps would have regarded him as an outstanding man, who had great sympathy for the poor and the despised, and perhaps as a prophet with an impressive message who was unjustly condemned to death, but not as the Christ, not as the one in whom God himself has definitively come to the world. Something must have happened, of such an extraordinary nature that it can account for the belief in Christ after the profound disappointment which the crucifixion had brought.

The appearances

One can say that it is Jesus' resurrection from the dead that offers this explanation, but that is not enough. The resurrection is exclusively God's action, a pure miracle, about which no one can know anything; even Jesus' disciples were wholly outside the secret. If then on the basis of the biblical testimony we accept the resurrection in grateful faith, we shall have to ask on what experiences of people that testimony is based. Posing this question is not a sign of unbelief or of an impermissible rationalism; what is involved here is the grounding of our faith. The testimony about the resurrection after all did not simply appear out of thin air. Then in our inquiring we are confronted with the appearances of Jesus. He was seen, the Bible says, after his death by certain persons, and as a result these persons gained the assurance that he was not dead, but had arisen and was alive. The testimony about the resurrection rests upon the appearances.

But this still seems not to bring us much further along; the appearances seem hardly less enigmatic and mysterious than the resurrection itself. The stories of the appearances which are handed down to us in the gospels and by Paul are sharply divergent; it appears impossible to fit them together in a single harmonious whole. They also exhibit certain legendary features, a point to which we shall later return. Moreover, Jesus' appearing after his death is for us something utterly preposterous and totally contrary to our ordinary experience. All this appears not to argue in favor of the reliability of the narratives; we are inclined to explain them in psychological terms or to write them off as mythological items. But we would be letting ourselves off too easily. In the first place, as we have already said, "something" must have happened; otherwise the emergence of the Christian community all at once with its message that Jesus was alive after the original defeat and dismay of the disciples is inexplicable. Moreover, all the biblical narratives, regardless of how much they differ among themselves, agree on this one crucial point: that Jesus in truth is seen after his death as something that people had experienced is more strongly attested than almost anything else that is handed down to us about his life. For only about this do we still have the words of an eyewitness, who moreover stoutly reinforces his testimony by appealing to other witnesses who had had the same experience that he had had. When Paul wishes to prove to the Corinthians his authority as an apostle, he refers them to the fact that Christ has appeared to him, just as he had earlier appeared to Peter, to the twelve, and afterwards "to more than five hundred brethren at one time, most of whom are still alive." The aim of this last addition is evident. Paul wishes to defend himself against a possible countering charge that this so-called appearance of Jesus was only his own imagination or fabrication. Therefore he points out that many others have experienced the same thing as he himself — and if the Corinthians are not willing to believe this, they can question these others personally. People of our time would confirm their trustworthiness in precisely the same way. Hence I think that we can hardly avoid the fact that Jesus appeared after his death, although we can have our doubts about the historicity of the individual descriptions.

If we ask how we are to conceive of these appearances as to their content, the only point from which we can start with some measure of certainty is the personal testimony of Paul. On the basis of his words already cited above, we may assume that his experience on the road to Damascus was of the same kind as the experiences of the others whom he names. Insofar as we wish not to speak here only in negative terms — that is, not merely to say what did *not* happen — perhaps we best can think of a vision and an auditory perception that had such convincing power that it gave to those to whom it happened the absolute certainty that they had encountered him whom they knew to have died and to have been buried.

> In the last century and the beginning of this century these appearances were explained in psychological terms as mass hallucination. It is impossible to give absolute proof that they were not this, but hallucination on such as massive scale would be hardly less a "miracle" than the miracle to which the Bible testifies. In current literature one hardly ever encounters this so-called rationalistic explanation. On the contrary, the appearances are sometimes called objective visions; this term is meant to say that they did not arise out of the subjective, psychological frame of mind of the eyewitness, but that an objective reality corresponded to them. Although there actually is not a great deal against this — I myself have spoken of beholding in visions — I am somewhat dubious about any and all categorizing. But that does not apply here alone. Every believer perceives that it is impossible to describe precisely how Moses' meeting with God on Sinai took place.

The resurrection

What lies between Jesus' crucifixion and his appearances to the disciples? We do not know. No one was present, and even the gospels do not give a description of this. Jesus was dead and buried, his life and history were utterly closed, finis. If then there is to be, in one way or another, a continuation — or, in fact, we rather must say a new beginning — this can only rest upon a mighty act of God, which cannot be precisely conceived; after all, a dead person can do nothing more, nothing more is to be expected of him. We have no word of our own that can describe this unknown act of God. Here, following the New Testament, we use terms borrowed from the figure of sleep, "awakening," or "arising," symbolic designations for something that transcends our knowledge and our understanding.

> The Dutch word "opwekken" is less clear than the Greek in showing that we are dealing here with figurative language; the Greek uses the ordinary word for "awaken." The same is true of the Dutch word "opstanding"; the Greek word also appears in non-biblical usage and denotes "standing up," or "becoming awake." In the New Testament the predominant pattern speaks of awakening or being awakened from the dead; only in the later strata of the New Testament tradition does the term "arising" appear alongside this one. Perhaps this indicates a tendency to make Jesus equal to God insofar as possible: he himself has the power to lay down his life and to take it up again (John 10:17,18). This brings with it the danger that his death becomes only a kind of sham. But if one considers that the noun "awakening" does not appear in the New Testament at all, one can ask whether there is not too much weight being placed on the varied usage of words. We should think of the so-called Apostles' Creed; when the resurrection of the flesh (of man) is confessed there, everyone obviously thinks only of an act of God.

We also hear elsewhere, both in Judaism and in other religions, of dead persons being awakened to life. In these accounts the accent is placed on the power that issues from the wonderworker. Cases of raising the dead are even related about Jesus, not as mere miracles, but as signs of the dawning kingdom of God. In all these cases the story has to do with bringing back to life one who has died. There is no doubt that even in the minds of the evangelists (if they ever even raised the question) the daughter of Jairus (Mark 5:21-43), the young man of Nain (Luke 7:11-17), and Lazarus (John 11:1-44) later died again just like any other man. But the resurrection of Jesus is something entirely different from the case of a dead person who comes back to life; he no longer has death before him but behind him. God has called him through death and out of death to a new, different, richer order of existence. Something radically new has happened, something unique, that has no analogy in history. The gospels of Luke and John express this by relating that in his appearances Jesus at first was not recognized by his own people — although it becomes evident that it is he. There is also a similar tension in the matter of his corporeality or non-corporeality. The same Luke who tells how the disciples are allowed to touch him to be convinced of his bodily presence tells also how in an utterly unexplainable and sudden fashion Jesus is present and then disappears again.

We said above that we do not know what resurrection is, that what God does in it eludes our knowledge. The same is true of the manner of existence of the one raised; a man cannot know what lies beyond death. When Paul begins to speak about it, he can only stammer. Then he speaks about a changed spiritual body and about glorification, but these are only indications of the ineffable state of being, not descriptions of it. Only one thing is clear: this new order of being does not nullify the preceding life. It is the historical man Jesus, as he walked about in

Palestine and died at the beginning of our era, who is glorified. It is the crucified one who is raised and lives; the cross remains in effect; it was not merely a brief interlude.

> Although I am convinced that the *fact* of the appearances cannot rightly be doubted, I hold many features of the appearance *narratives* to be relatively late legendary formations. This applies, for example, to the narratives in which the resurrected one has a meal with his friends, and to his encounter with Thomas. Perhaps they were intended from the very outset as figurative. But in any case the description is too much in conflict with the account of Paul, our only eyewitness, and is too concrete and material for me to be able to credit it. However, the narratives do not thereby lose their value. Precisely in their realistic portrayal they testify that the whole man Jesus, Jesus as he was in body and soul, is raised and lives. And the story that Thomas is allowed to touch with his finger the wounds of the crucifixion (only in John 20:24-29; but see also Luke 24:39) shows, among other things, that the cross is not blotted out.

The empty tomb

Up to this point we have not spoken of the empty tomb. According to all four evangelists the disciples knew, before they encountered the resurrected one, that the tomb was empty. Is this only legend, developed as rationalistic proof for belief in the resurrection, or is it a historical fact that is described with legendary features (the earthquake, the angels, the grave linens left behind)? Nothing can be said here with certainty, but there are some arguments favoring the view that the tomb indeed was empty. But even if we assume this, it does not mean that we "believe in the empty tomb." We believe in the resurrection, and that Jesus lives, and whether the tomb was empty or not is in this context a relatively unimportant circumstance. It should be remembered that even according to the gospels, it is not the finding of the empty tomb but the appearances that first brought the disciples to faith. Matthew, who speaks most fully about the empty tomb — he alone tells of the guard at the tomb and of the angel that rolls away the stone —, even explicitly recognizes that the resurrection is not the only explanation for it that can be given.

> The consideration that Matthew obviously found it necessary to report and refute the rumor that the disciples had stolen the body is, in my opinion, one of the arguments indicating that the tradition of the empty tomb goes back to a historical reality.

I myself am of the opinion that the connection of the empty tomb with the resurrection is a hindrance rather than a support for faith. As a presupposition of the resurrection it appears to imply a realistic conception of the resurrection as the coming back to life of a corpse (think of the medieval paintings), which is not in harmony with the way the Bible speaks about it. Besides, it can lead to our dismissing of the anticipation of our own glorification (on this see p. 109) as a mythological conception; our graves certainly will not appear to be empty.

The mission

The resurrection is the basis and pivot of the Christian faith. In the words of Paul: "if Christ is not risen, then our faith is vain" (I Cor. 15:14). We should actually say it even more strongly: if Christ had not risen, there would be no faith at all. It was the conviction that he had arisen that made the first disciples Christians. Only the encounter with the resurrected one impelled them to believe and to testify that Jesus was the Christ. And this encounter made them missionaries. Hence it is extremely significant that the gospel of Matthew and the "inauthentic" ending of the gospel of Mark put the missionary commandment in the mouth of the resurrected one. And on the basis of the testimony of these first eyewitnesses all later ones — we ourselves included — have come to faith and have become, in turn, new witnesses to the resurrection.

Significance of the resurrection

In the foregoing it has been stated *that* the resurrection made it possible to believe that Jesus is the Christ. Now we must answer the question *why* it has had this result. We propose to try to do this somewhat schematically, in four points.

1. The resurrection is the legitimation of Jesus. By raising him from the dead God has shown that he says "yes" to him. This divine "yes" applies to Jesus' entire life: his total dedication to God, his complete submission to God's will, his willingness to surrender his life. It extends also to the divine authority with which Jesus acted: this was not arrogance on his part, but it was rightly his because God himself stood behind it. From this awareness, then, the church also confessed that Jesus is Lord, something that in the strictest sense can be said only of God himself. But the authority with which Jesus acted was the authority of God himself.

> Even the title "Lord" like that of "Christ," went through a development. During his lifetime Jesus was addressed, in keeping with the common, secular usage, with the title "kyrios" (cf. our "sir"). The primitive community made a special connection between this title of address and the return of Christ. We may think of the Aramaic formula "Maranatha,"."Our Lord, come!" (I Cor. 16:22; cf. also Rev. 22:20). It was first in the Gentile-Christian community then that it became an actual title of honor, to denote Jesus' divine authority and dignity — one could even say his deity. In the writings of the so-called Apostolic Fathers (first half of the second century) it often is impossible to distinguish whether God or Christ is intended by the title of Lord.

This "yes" of God is also extended to include Jesus' extreme radicalizing of the law and his association with "sinners," this offence to his devout fellow-Jews and to the pious of all ages. God evidently wills that precisely the unworthy, the wayward, the irreligious should be sought and accepted without any prior condition, just as they are.

2. The resurrection is further the exposition, the interpretation of Jesus. It is through God's "yes" that Jesus' person and conduct first become transparent. Now it first really becomes clear that his healings were not manipulative exorcism and that his forgiveness of sinners was not moral laxity, but that therein the salvation of God's kingdom had broken through. And now it becomes evident that even the crucifixion had not nullified all this, that the cross by no means is proof of Jesus' failure, but rather is the way leading to salvation. Only from the perspective of the resurrection — nay, even more — only together with the resurrection does the cross signify salvation. Hence it is only now that those who believe in him can actually confess him as deliverer, savior.

It is a noteworthy fact that in the New Testament and early Christian literature the words "deliver" and "deliverance" (=salvation) appear frequently, while, with the exception of the Pastoral Epistles, the title "Savior" is only rarely used. We cannot fully explain why this is so.

3. The resurrection, however, is not only legitimation and exposition; it does not only have reference to the past, to the history which is concluded with the crucifixion. It also has significance for the present. It speaks to us of the presently living Lord and of the continuation of his history and his work. Thus the resurrection also has to do with the Holy Spirit; we shall deal with this subject later.

4. And finally, the resurrection also points toward the future. Something totally new has happened here. With Jesus' resurrection from the dead, God breaks into the world as we know it in an unprecedented fashion; here in the midst of our ordinary world he is making a beginning with a new world. Said in another way: in the resurrected Jesus the new world, which is the end and the fulfillment of the old one, is present in the midst of this old world. We must be careful here not to speak too emphatically; Jesus appeared only to a few, his resurrection remains an event that can be ignored or denied, and we do not yet know what the new world or glorification is. But we believe that the glory that has become Jesus' lot through his resurrection is the ultimate destiny of our own lives and of the entire world. In the resurrection Jesus has become the beginning and the guarantee of the future. And for this reason also the church calls him the Christ.

XI. GOD IN CHRIST

We spoke first about the earthly man Jesus, and after this we said that through his resurrection the believers came to confess that God stood behind him totally. The resurrection is like a spotlight that places the entire past life of Jesus in a new light; in that light it becomes evident that from the first God was acting in him. It is not only as the resurrected one that Christ is both Lord and Savior, but he was that also during his lifetime, although at that time this was not yet clearly to be seen, not even by his closest followers. When we say now that Jesus' life must be seen in a new light, we take back nothing of what was said earlier about the "historical Jesus." From the perspective of the resurrection, faith sees more, but nothing in that new vision changes the fact that he was a particular man, with a human consciousness and a human will, a man who could be cherished and could feel distress and suffer pain; in short, a man who was subject to all the limitations and potentialities that are given with being human. But in the light of the resurrection we believe that in this man God himself has come to us, that God himself is present in him and is acting through him.

God in man

Here we stand at the center of the Christian faith, and it is therefore difficult to find words that are adequate. To approach the mystery of the person of Jesus Christ, in the past the words "Jesus Christ, true God and true man" have ordinarily been used. They have served to guard the church against slipping into views whereby the salvation that is given in Christ might be prevented from sounding through clearly. Yet there are grave objections also that attach to this confessional formula. For example, it suggests that Jesus had on the one hand a human side and on the other hand a divine side, that he was man and, in addition, was God as well. Building on this, then, people came to say that he did certain things in his capacity as man and other things alongside these in his capacity as God. However, in this way Jesus becomes for us a curious dual being. And if one tries to avoid that danger, it becomes almost unavoidable that one lets his humanity be swallowed up by his divinity. Both alternatives render it impossible for us to see Jesus as a real and authentic man. Hence I wish to drop the old formula "God *and* man" and instead of this to speak of God's presence *in* this man. Only at the end of this chapter will it become evident whether in this way justice can be done to the truth which the earlier confessional formula intended to express and to safeguard. However, the advantage of this change is obvious. If we speak of God in the man Jesus, this central creedal utterance does not appear as a foreign element in our faith. We do believe in a God who acts in and through human history. Thus he has made himself known in and through Israel's history, without its ceasing to be ordinary human history. It is an extension of this when we now say that God has acted in and through the man Jesus and through him has made himself known, without Jesus' thereby ceasing to be actual and full man. But it still is no more than a similarity. For it is true that God has acted in the history of Israel, but in this history many things happened that were in conflict with his will. And it is true that he was present and that he has become manifest in the actions and the words of the great individuals in Israel, of Moses, David, and the prophets, but we cannot say of them that their entire lives and their entire persons were filled with God's presence. And that is what we mean with the confession "God was in Christ." God's presence in Israel found in Jesus a unique and perfect concentration. In him God is as totally present as he can be in a man. Therefore the first community called Jesus the Son of God; this title is, after all, extremely well suited to point to the exceptional bond between God and this very man.

> Like all titles of honor, "Son of God" has undergone a development in the various traditions in the Bible. In keeping with this fact, one cannot simply appeal to the Bible for Christology in the narrower sense, i.e., the doctrine of the person (as distinguished from that of the so-called "work") of Christ. The believers consciously began to reflect on the person and the function of Jesus on the basis of the resurrection. The resurrection set in motion a process whose beginning we see in the biblical writings but was far from being completed with the last book of the Bible. This process was not a straight line in which one idea was the logical further development of the preceding one. Instead, many different efforts were made to gain a clear insight into who Jesus Christ is. Reflecting still further on the biblical data, the church developed a Christology which in the fifth century found a certain conclusion in the formula: Jesus Christ, one person in two natures, the divine and the human. This formula continued to be the unassailable basis, although in later times it was still further worked out and refined. The church borrowed the terms "person" and "nature" from the thought categories of that time. In our times they have acquired a meaning different from what they had then. Therefore we cannot adopt these concepts unless we are willing to enter into profound philosophical and historical expositions. We shall have to find another way to express the fundamental truths of the belief in Jesus Christ.

True man

Replacing the expression "God and man" with "God in this man" has still another advantage: in this way justice can better be done to the true humanness of Jesus Christ. When we speak of his true humanness, this means in the first place that he was a real, genuine man. God's presence in him is not to be understood in such a way as to suggest that Jesus has broken through the boundaries and limitations that are set for a man. He did not know more and he could not do more than it is possible for a man to know and to do. This includes the fact that he was a man of his time; he thought in the concepts and with the ideas of a Jew in Palestine of that time. Even in the miracles that he performed and in his so-called sinlessness he was not more than a man. What needs to be said about his miracles has already been said in Chapter IX. There it was pointed out that in the miracles Jesus did nothing that was not done by other men of his time also. If we compare his miraculous deeds with those told by writers of antiquity about other men, only one thing actually is striking: the fact that there was so little of the spectacular about them and that they were so little intended to call attention to Jesus himself. The characteristic feature is rather that they were so totally directed to the service of the kingdom of God.

Even in what people usually call his sinlessness Jesus does not go beyond the possibilities of his humanness. Actually the term "sinlessness" is not a very fortunate one; it is too static and too negative, and it creates the impression of referring to a fixed attribute which as it were attached to Jesus. We may speak of Jesus'sinlessness only in the sense that in the concrete situations of his life in which he found himself confronted with decisions, he demonstrated perfect loyalty to God and to his fellowman. His sinlessness is not a self-contained quality, but its meaning is that in his life he did not commit any sin; that he did not yield to any temptation to which he, like every man, was subjected; that he always did God's will. When we give an active interpretation in this way to his sinlessness, we are in fact saying the same thing as the epistle of Hebrews, where it is stated that Jesus "learned" obedience through the difficult course of his life which led to the crucifixion. But this complete obedience was not superhuman. In Chapter VI we said that it actually is inconceivable that man, who is made to be God's partner, constantly acts in conflict with this intention. Jesus did not act in conflict with his destiny; he did not do the essentially inconceivable things that we all do. In fact we always are turning things around: it is not Jesus' not sinning that must be explained, but our sinning. Jesus acted in harmony with being man, as this is created by God, and we act in conflict with it.

> In the church's teaching Jesus' sinlessness is related to his being free from original sin. Thus it would have been physically impossible for him to sin. However, this puts Jesus in an exceptional position as compared to that of all other men and obscures the insight that his obedience to God is maintained in the face of actual temptations. In Chapter VII I have already raised objections to the doctrine of original sin. Reflecting on the humanity of Jesus, who was like us in all respects but did not sin, further strengthens those objections.

The fact that Jesus did not sin is not something that can be objectively perceived or determined. All we can say is that we do not know of any sin that he committed and that from the gospel narratives we gain the impression that he was remarkably free from any consciousness of guilt. But that is not enough to justify the conclusion that indeed he never sinned. This conviction issues from the belief that he was true man.

And this brings us to the second and even more fundamental significance of Jesus' true humanity. He was not only fully man, but also man as God intended him. He was concerned, not with acting in his own interest, but in God's interest. He traveled an extremely difficult road, to the end that God's will alone should be done through him and God should be magnified in his life. In fact this total submission to God is the positive side of what was called above Jesus' refraining from sin. Therefore this true humanity also cannot be proved, although it is in harmony with the picture of him that we gain from the gospel narratives. These do give us the impression of a man who so totally placed himself at God's disposal in all that he did that his life became, as it were, transparent to God. Thus everything that is to be said about the man Jesus can be summed up by saying that he was fully and completely God's partner in covenant, who lived in unbroken unity with God. And this means that in this man, who lived in perfect communion with him, God's covenant-love now at last can appear to its full advantage. Therefore also two things can be said about Jesus Christ: in him we are confronted by a man who has realized the God-given destiny of his humanness — and in him we see fully what God's will for man is; that is, we can look into God's heart and thus we are also confronted by him.

> With this I have come very close to the old confessional formula to which I earlier objected: Jesus Christ, true God and true man. But my objection was directed only against the fact that in these words the *being* of Jesus Christ was described and thereby one became entangled in all kinds of insoluble intellectual difficulties about the relationship of Christ's human "nature" and his divine "nature." Then people came to some remarkable questions: whether Jesus could ever have made a mistake, whether he knew in advance what would happen to him, whether he could have avoided the cross if he had wished to do so, and so forth. By presupposing that Jesus was really and fully man, such apparent problems are avoided, while the truth with which Christology deals is preserved: that this man was so much at one with God that in him God and man and the unity of God and man have been revealed.

God's initiative

Does what was said above mean now that Jesus was an ordinary man? As soon as we pose this question, there arises at once the counter-question: what actually is an "ordinary" man? Is it man such as we are, or is it man as God intended him to be?

Perhaps we can clarify what was distinctive about Jesus if we refer back to what was said earlier about Israel. There we saw that this nation fell far short of being the true covenant-partner of God, and that therein it is the mirror of the failing of us all. The "ordinary" man is obviously the man who does not fulfill his destiny. Therefore we also said that if the covenant is ever actually to correspond to its intention, God himself will have to see to it (page 49). And now that is just what he has done when he gave this totally obedient man Jesus. He is the one sent, the chosen one, filled and equipped by God with his Spirit. It is true that all this in a sense was also said of the prophets. They too were specially called by God and equipped with his Spirit for the task for which he had destined them; in that respect they were anything but what we call "ordinary" man. But what applies to them all applies to Jesus in fulness and completeness such as we can attribute to no one else. Thus Jesus' appearing is based upon God's free trust and initiative.

But once that is said, the other also must be said: that Jesus in his free obedience surrendered himself wholly to God and did God's will, and that he thus, in freedom, was the true man. In Jesus' case too, and particularly in his case, God's gracious presence leaves room for his human covenant-ally.

The chosen man

Yet we have spoken of Jesus too much as of a detached and isolated individual. That is not enough. According to the unanimous biblical witness he is related in a unique way to all men and women. After all he is not *a* true man, but *the* true man, in whom the covenant is fulfilled. Thus in him it is not only a matter of God's being with *man*, with *all* men. To put it in another way: in his covenant relationship with God Jesus is not just an isolated individual, but therein he represents us all. If that were not so, he would not signify salvation for all men. All men are embraced in him.

That can become clear only if we do not forget that as a Jew Jesus stands in the covenantal history of God with Israel. Israel is after all the people that God formed and chose to be his very special people. In doing this, however, God is not concerned for this people alone, but for all peoples. It is, as we said earlier, an essential aspect of the election that in it there is always a concern also for the others, those not chosen. In connection with Israel we developed this idea in two directions. Israel is called to be the covenant people in such a way that in and through this people God becomes manifest to other peoples also. And Israel is God's experimental plot, in which he has the entire world in view; it represents all peoples in his sight. But the last thing that we had to say on the basis of Israel's own testimonies in the Old Testament was that Israel did not respond to this twofold call that was implied in her election.

But we saw that God did not abandon Israel. He made a new beginning, and the calling that Israel neglected he transferred to this one Jew, Jesus, whom he specially chose and sent for this purpose. And to this one he gave his Spirit, so that he received power to take up and to fulfill Israel's calling. In Jesus all Israel is summed up; he *is* Israel, as it were. Hence all that applies to Israel applies also to him, with the crucial difference that what was destiny intended for Israel became actuality in Jesus. Just as with Israel so also with him we must think of God's election. And for him too this election has the same two sides. He is chosen to be wholly and entirely God's covenant-partner, who in his being one with God is transparent to him. We have already spoken of this in what was said earlier. But there is another side also: God has all mankind in view; Jesus represents Israel before God, and as representative of Israel he represents the whole of humanity as well.

The saving significance of Jesus Christ

In all that is said about the person of Jesus Christ in his unity with God, the main point, in the last analysis, is not who he is in himself, but who he is for us. The question is not his essential nature but his function. But this function cannot be divorced from his essential nature. He has this particular function only because he is who he is, the true man who is uniquely at one with God. I wish further to speak briefly about this function under three aspects. In so doing, I shall deliberately speak of his one function that has these different aspects, because here everything is interwoven. In the last analysis Jesus Christ has only one function, namely, to be salvation for the world. It is not necessary to make separate mention of the fact that in that salvation God is likewise glorified. God has, after all, staked his honor on the salvation of mankind.

1. In Jesus Christ it becomes manifest who God is and who man is as God has

meant him to be.It is not accidental that in this chapter about the person of Christ we have had to refer back again and again to earlier chapters. It had already been made manifest in Israel's history that God is a God who wills to be together with his people, but it only acquires its full confirmation in God's being united with Jesus Christ. Man's having been created and "destined" to be united with God in full freedom also finds its confirmation in Christ. And that election signifies being set apart by God for the sake of the others who are not specially chosen. Fulfillment of God's covenantal intention — it is true that we can discern this in Israel and in the individuals who are further singled out and chosen from among the people of Israel, but it first becomes unequivocally clear in Jesus Christ. In him it is unmistakably clear how the particular is directed to universality; this individual man is chosen and called for the sake of the world.

2. This indicates our transition to the second aspect. In Christ the God of Israel has become the God of the whole world. Or, rather, it is wrongly stated thus. From the very beginning the God of Israel was the God of the whole world, but only Israel knew him as such. There is a "before Christ" and an "after Christ." Before him God's saving activity was concentrated upon Israel, so that through obedient Israel his salvation might be poured out over the entire world. Jesus Christ is that Israel that has become obedient and thus the universalizing has become a reality. Now all men are called to God's covenant. In this respect the distinction between Israel and the Gentiles is nullified.

3. And then the atonement. It is often the case that only this topic is considered when the saving significance of Jesus Christ is discussed. Therefore here I have deliberately placed the atonement in a broader context, as one aspect among several, without at all intending thereby to diminish its importance. In and through Jesus Christ we are reconciled with God and God with us. But the next chapter will deal with this subject.

The incarnation

Jesus then can have for us a unique and definitive saving significance only if God has come to us in him and has acted in him as fully as this is possible in a man. The church has expressed and sought to safeguard this truth by means of the doctrine of the incarnation, God's becoming man. I have no difficulty with the idea that God embodied himself in the man Jesus. God is a God of men. He actually enters into human history, he becomes discernible for us only in history. And just as he enters into human history and expresses himself in it, so he has expressed himself in particular and in a unique fulness in the history of Jesus. In this sense I can speak of an embodiment of God in Jesus. However, I am aware that in saying this I am not saying the same thing as does the church's tradition in her doctrine of the incarnation. She connects this with the idea of the pre-existent (i.e., before his becoming man) Son of God, who at a specific moment became man, or, as it is expresed in dogmatics, assumed human nature.

The idea of the incarnation of the pre-existent Christ is found particularly in Paul's writings and in the gospel of John. In this way is expressed the belief that in Jesus Christ God himself has come to men. The doctrine of the incarnation (though we still can hardly speak of actual doctrine in the Bible) thus is a form in which the saving mystery of Jesus Christ is put in words. Among scholars in the field it is a disputed question whether the three synoptic gospels also are acquainted with the ideas of pre-existence and incarnation.

I think that nowadays the "God-in-Christ" can be expressed better in another way than with the aid of the doctrine of incarnation. The conception that God becomes man, if it is taken realistically, is strongly reminiscent of all sorts of mythological stories. Still more important is the fact that it really does not make anything clearer. In the history of the church it has created as many difficulties as it has resolved. We may say that in any case this doctrine indicates that Jesus Christ did not first become Son of God at a particular moment in his life, but that he was one with God from the very first. Indeed one cannot speak of a particular moment at which this perfect and unique alliance of Jesus with God and of God with Jesus came into being. But I also fail to see why it should be necessary to posit the view that this relationship was already present from or even before the first moment of Jesus' life. This association, as we have stressed in the foregoing, is the correlate of Jesus' obedience. Whether even the infant or the child Jesus was already obedient is a question with which only later legends about Christ have concerned themselves. It appears to me that for faith it is a bit of useless speculation.

The truth-content of the doctrine of incarnation, as I see it, lies in its declaration that in the history of Jesus Christ God has the initiative. But the belief that Jesus is chosen by God, that he is called, equipped, and sent by God to do God's work — this too presupposes God's initiative. And from Jesus' side, his perfect obedience to God's will was his response to this election by God. God's election, the gift of the Spirit, and Jesus' obedience are the pillars on which is based the Christology developed here. Our salvation depends on what Christ has done for us, and in another thought-world the doctrine of the incarnation was a help. When this help can no longer function, we may replace it with another.

The virgin birth

The biblical data about the so-called virgin birth are ambiguous. Only Matthew and Luke speak of it, but even with them this idea remains curiously unconnected with the rest of the gospel narrative. Further, the Bible speaks naturally of Jesus' father and of his parents, and there is not a single indication that Mary later knew that there was anything special about her son (see, for example, Mark 3:21; Luke 2:50). As I see it, on the basis of the Bible only one thing can be said with certainty: that the belief in a miraculous birth of Jesus is not an indispensable element with which the Christian faith stands or falls. For example, Paul, who is our earliest witness of Jesus, appears to have known nothing of a virgin birth.

Yet it is not immediately clear that here we are dealing with the forming of a legend by the early church. It is frequently assumed that the account of this birth arose or was formed in order to indicate that Jesus was the son of God, or to make it clear that he was sinless, or was free of inherited sin. Both explanations appear to be obvious; however, though they do appear in later church history, they are not found in the Bible. The remarkable thing is precisely the fact that in the Bible the story of the miraculous birth remains an unattached element without any continuing theological relevance being attached to it and without any further reference to it ever being made. One can ask with some puzzlement why it actually is related.

Thus I arrive at the conviction that belief in the biological factuality of the virgin birth is utterly unimportant for salvation. It does not explain anything, nor is anything based upon it. And as interpretation and symbol of the belief in God's initiative and the uniqueness of Jesus I consider it dangerous, because thereby we threaten easily to forget Jesus' ordinary humanness.

XII. PEACE BETWEEN GOD AND MAN

Reconciliation and the doctrine of reconciliation

Actually there is hardly any need for a separate chapter on reconciliation, after the preceding chapter. Everything in fact is already said. For if Jesus Christ is the man who is perfectly at one with God and if this one man represents all men, then in God's being with this one man it is given that God is with all and that his covenant with mankind continues. And this continuation of the covenant, in spite of the fact that men have broken it, is reconciliation. Yet believing thought inquires further here. It wants to know what precisely it means to say that God has reconciled men to himself specifically through the cross. In this connection it must be kept in mind that the cross may not be isolated. Jesus' death was the consequence of his life. It was, after all, the unprecedented radicality with which he had proclaimed God's judgment and grace that ultimately had led to his crucifixion. And just as the cross may not be detached from Jesus' life that preceded it, so also it may not be detached from the resurrection that followed. For only in the light of the resurrection can we say that the cross brought salvation and reconciliation. Thus in the reconciliation the entire life, the death, and the resurrection of Jesus Christ are involved, and reconciliation can rightly be called the center of the Christian faith. But that holds true for reconciliation, not for the doctrine of reconciliation. Of course we may and must attempt also to think through reconciliation systematically, but in doing so we must be conscious of the fact that the richness of this event is too great for faith to be able to rest in some doctrine about the event.

Even in the Bible we do not find a complete and pre-packaged doctrine. The various writers speak about the saving significance of Jesus Christ, and then in particular about the significance of his cross, in many different words and figures of speech, all of which illumine particular aspects of the event of the atonement, but which do not lend themselves well to being fitted together into a comprehensive whole. Thus for example terms are used that are borrowed from judicial language (condemnation, acquittal, accusation), or that call to mind the purchasing of freedom for slaves or captives (paying a ransom), or that speak in the figurative language of the sacrificial cultus (the blood of Jesus, the lamb of God, Jesus as high priest, the expiation of sin). But the figures remain side-by-side, not connected, and they are more alluded to than worked out.

Now it is a fact that in the Bible only rarely is a systematic doctrine of other aspects of the faith offered. It is rather the task of the church to formulate this on the basis of the biblical data. But there has never been one particular, universally acknowledged ecclesiastical doctrine of the atonement. It is true that there have been particular thought-patterns that have been employed for thinking about the atonement, and there have even been specific outlines proposed, but none of these proposals has ever possessed universal validity. In every case the biblical data also clearly are susceptible to a different interpretation.

But not only does it appear difficult to explain to ourselves and others how the atonement came about, even though the event itself occupies a central position in the faith. It is difficult even to find words with which we can speak about it. More than elsewhere the biblical or tradition-hallowed words here have acquired a particular special value. For many believers the heart of their faith beats in expressions like "We are redeemed by the blood of Christ," "He is the lamb that takes away the sin of the world," or "He has borne the wrath of God for us." They have the feeling that if an effort is made to transpose these and similar expressions into another language-field that is closer to our contemporary way of thinking, the mystery of Christ's saving work is thereby betrayed. And this feeling can hardly be refuted with logic; it is too emotionally charged for that. Yet we cannot leave the matter with the old words. For alongside those who use these words to give passionate expression to their faith, there are others in whom the same words evoke resistance. And their antipathy often is equally emotionally laden, so that they too are no longer in a position to penetrate to the intention of the terms. Moreover, there are then the great many who do not merely stumble over the words and expressions but who in a more basic sense are at a loss with the whole traditional doctrine of the atonement. Hence the matter of the atonement itself compels us to try to speak in terms that can strike a responsive chord in people of our time.

Ordinary language

If we are to talk about reconciliation in and through Jesus Christ, it is reasonable to begin with the ordinary meaning of the term. In general usage it points to a two-sided event. It says that two persons or parties who were at odds or in enmity with each other have reestablished peaceful relations. The same applies with reference to God and man. Something has happened whereby their relationship with each other is altered. God has once again achieved peace with man, and man with God. Therefore the question whether in the atonement something has happened with God or only with man is basically misconceived. Because what is involved is a vital relationship between God and man, a change in this relationship also affects both of them. Now they both confront each other in a new and different way. To this extent both God and man are changed in the reconciliation.

Further, the general usage of the word "reconciliation" includes the idea that the two persons or parties who now are reconciled earlier had a good relationship with each other. Two strangers who had never had any dealings with each other do not need to be reconciled. Reconciliation thus also signifies a restoration. Hence we can talk about the reconciliation of God and man only against the background of their earlier relationship. Actually, to speak of association of God and man in general terms is too vague. When we are dealing with Jesus Christ, we may never for a moment forget that his place is in Israel. That is not merely a bit of historical fact, but it is relevant for the entire event of atonement and reconciliation. Instead of speaking of a general association, therefore, we prefer to start from God's covenant with Israel. Therein the reconciliation takes place, and it is the restoration of that covenant. However, we must immediately add that we cannot speak here of restoration in the strict sense of the word. For in its actual reciprocal character the covenant was never fully realized before the coming of Jesus Christ.

And this brings us to the third implication that is contained in the idea of reconciliation. This idea presupposes not only an originally good relationship, but also a break in this relationship. That is, the reconciliation that is accomplished in Christ must be seen not only against the background of the covenant, but of the broken covenant. Therefore we cannot speak of reconciliation without also bringing human sin and guilt into the discussion. Thus usage in everyday language already provides some suggestions as to content for our thinking about the reconciliation of God and man. This same language usage, however, points to the fact that here something out-of-the-ordinary is involved. That is, one can say that two persons are reconciled with each other, or that one is reconciled with the other, but it is very unusual to say that one reconciles the other with himself. And it is precisely this remarkable turn of meaning that we are using when, adopting Paul's use of the term, we say that God has reconciled us with himself. This points up the fact that although reconciliation is a two-sided event, there is no thought of two equal parties: God has the initiative, and it is he who is active here. The siruation here is the same as with the covenant. Just as there what is involved is a relationship, and thus both God and man, but it is God who unilaterally gives the covenant, so also it is God alone who in the reconciliation causes the covenant to continue. Like the covenant, the reconciliation rests entirely and solely on God's covenant-love. And man is invited to respond affirmatively to this love and to let himself be reconciled to God. That is the "action," so to speak, which is asked of man. Of course this "action" then is also to be worked out in his later life, but that is nothing more than the consdquence be worked out in his later life, but that is nothing more than the consequence arising out of that love and man's response to it.

The cross as guilt

It is our sins that brought Jesus Christ to the cross, and it is the guilt of all of us that is made manifest there. This often repeated confession is true, but only because the cross stands in Israel. The universal human sin, as a matter of fact, did not first come to light in the crucifixion, but already in Israel's failures in all its earlicr covenantal history. Israel after all is not just another people, but the chosen people, and as such the reflection and representative of all peoples. Hence also it is only in Israel that the cross is the revelation of the universal guilt of humanity. This cannot be grounded in a general belonging-together of mankind. Socrates' cup of hemlock points to the guilt of the Athenian judges and the Athenian people that they represented, but not to a guilt of humanity as a whole. If we disregard the special place that Israel occupies on the basis of its election, even the cross of Jesus is only a sign of the guilt of those who were personally involved there. We then could properly say, with Moses Mendelssohn, "What do we have to do with a deed that was done so many centuries ago?" But it is the representatives of Israel and in them all Israel that became guilty in regard to

Jesus. And just as Israel, in God's turning to this people, represents all of us, so also has it, as representative of us all, become guilty in our place.

> Hence we do not do well when, in a well-intentioned combatting of anti-Semitism in Christendom, we pose the idea that the responsibility for the crucifixion lay with the Roman authorities, in this case Pilate, and that only a small minority of all the Jews then living played a role in it. If that were all that can be said about it, then we could perhaps see in Pilate a type of opportunistic authority, and in the Jews who were involved a type of the establishment, but we ourselves would remain uninvolved, out of range. Scholarly biblical study can try to determine the historical share of Pilate and the others involved in the crucifixion, but for faith the guilt of the Romans has a different significance from that of the Jewish leaders. For only because it is true that the cross reveals the guilt of the Jews can we rightly say "mea culpa," here *our* guilt appears.

The human guilt that has acquired its full disclosure in the crucifixion has a dual shape: it is guilt in relation to our fellowman and guilt in relation to God. This was already the case with Old Testament Israel. It became guilty in relation to God and it became guilty through injustice in its society. To a great extent these two aspects are interwoven. The nation became guilty in relation to God by failing to actualize the society that he intended. In the cross the two aspects wholly coincide. Jesus Christ is the man who, in a fashion that far surpassed the prophets before him, in his entire life was devoted to the salvation of his people. The crucifixion shows that men will not accept it that another, in an absoluteness that will admit no compromise, gives himself for them in order to call them to their true destiny. They do not tolerate the true fellowman next to them. But behind Jesus stands God. Therefore the cross is also guilt in relation to him. The repudiation and rejection of Jesus is in fact — even though unwittingly and not consciously intended — a rejection of God. Where God so fully reveals himself and is so fully present as in Jesus Christ, men, represented by the chosen Israel, say "no" to him.

We said above that reconciliation, as the term functions in everyday language, implies a preceding break in a relationship. The word "break" appears utterly inadequate when speaking about the cross. Only words like opposition, rejection, and enmity can indicate the seriousness of what became manifest there. All these terms, which indicate a fundamental disruption of the relationship between God and man, again point to a two-sided event. It is true that the enmity, this negation of the covenant, issued from man. And it is also true that God nevertheless continues to maintain this covenant and wants to bring it to its fulfillment, to the achievement of his just purpose. But if we were serious in what we said earlier about God, that in spite of all the difference there is a genuine mutuality between him and man, an interaction in which he lets himself be influenced by what man does, then that implies that human enmity does not leave him unaffected. To man, who first has said "no" to him, he also, from his side, says "no". To put it in another way: because God wants the man who is a participant in covenant, he does not want the man who refuses to be a participant in covenant; this man he rejects (see p. 23). Here the Bible speaks of the wrath of God, and we likewise cannot avoid this concept. God is wrathful toward the man who is of such a kind that he rejects Jesus Christ and, in so doing, rejects God himself — yet in his wrath God does not abandon this man.

The cross as sacrifice

We have spoken about the men who were the active agents in the crucifixion. We must also speak about this same crucifixion with respect to him who suffered it. Actually we only need here to take up what we have already said earlier. Jesus Christ was wholly obedient to God, and his death is nothing but the confirmation of this obedience. Even when his life was at stake he did not shrink back, but remained faithful to God. He placed himself wholly and entirely at God's disposal, and this meant his death.

Was this death unavoidable? Yes and no. No, in the sense that Jesus had the possibility of acting more cautiously, of conforming more to the prevailing views. But that would have signified that he was not exclusively obedient to God, but let himself by guided by what was opportune. Then, however, he would not have been Jesus Christ, the one who in total obedience was one with God. And hence for him, considering who he was, his condemnation was in fact unavoidable. This consideration also sheds light on the often-asked question whether Jesus knew in advance that he would be put to death. Certainly not in the sense that he lived in order to die. His struggle in Gethsemane, in which his submission to God is put to the ultimate and final test, emphasizes the opposite. And even less in the sense that in some supernatural way or another he had foreknowledge of his death. But knowing of the fate of the prophets before him, conscious also of the opposition that his conduct evoked, it is only natural that he must increasingly have foreseen his death and taken it into consideration. Just so in our own time a person who in a totalitarian state openly opposes injustice knows that he cannot do this without penalty and that things will have to go badly for him. Thus it is his total service to God, the unbroken unity with God in which Jesus lived his entire life, that brought him to the cross. That is to say, Jesus gave his life for God.

But Jesus' service to God was at the same time service to his fellowmen. That was, after all, precisely what God willed for him, that he should place his life wholly at the service of his people. In this respect also his death once again was a confirmation of his life. When his fellowmen turned against him, he did not withdraw from them and thus save his own life, but he bore their enmity and remained loyal to them to the very end. By giving his life for God, Jesus also gave it for his people.

Hence it is fitting and proper when the church's teaching in the main sees Jesus' self-giving as especially concentrated in the cross. Before his death, which was the direct consequence of his submission and commitment to God and to men, it still was not a foregone conclusion that Jesus would not shrink back from the ultimate consequence. Only his crucifixion confirms and shows that in fact he has fully sacrificed himself.

> We no longer have cultic sacrifices. Therefore the New Testament images that are borrowed from that practice no longer have a function in our time, unless we first prefix to them a lengthy exposition. But such an exposition would have a fatal effect on the figurative language. Hence it is better to drop the biblical sacrificial terminology. In my opinion, it still makes sense to speak of Jesus' sacrifice only in the sense that Jesus sacrificed his life in his service to God and men.
>
> In the above we have not spoken explicitly about the sufferings of Jesus. It is

best for us not to dwell long on this theme. Suffering in itself after all is not something good or something that God wills. It may be discussed only in the sense in which we spoke of Jesus' sacrifice. Suffering was the price that Jesus had to pay for his covenantal obedience. Hence the question that has been raised in the past about to whom this price is paid misinterprets the figurative language of the words.

God has peace with man

It is not in harmony with the usage of the New Testament to speak of God's becoming reconciled. But if one does not mean thereby that God had to be brought to a change of mind, it is not incorrect to say that not only is he the Reconciler of man, but he is also reconciled with man. We said above that a twofold movement is involved, a movement of God toward man and, as a response, man's turning toward God. It is that first movement of God toward man that we have in mind when we say that God is reconciled with man, or that he has peace with man.

That God is *one* with Jesus Christ was the central idea of the preceding chapter. Jesus now at last has fulfilled the covenant from the side of man also. He is the first and only one who actually has not fallen short; he was man as God intends man to be. Hence it is incorrect here also to speak of transgression or of enmity. With this man God can have peace.

But this still need not signify that God now also has peace with us. Here everything hinges on the belief that Jesus was not merely a man, the only exception in the midst of all other men, but that he is the man who is given and chosen by God and whom God in his choosing has made the representative of all men. In him all men are incorporated, as we expressed it in the preceding chapter. He stands for all men. As he stands for all men in his obedience, therein he represents all in God's eyes. In his obedience God sees the obedience of all of us. Therefore he has also made peace with us.

1. The idea that God has peace with us because we are incorporated in Jesus Christ says the same thing as the more typically dogmatic words that God imputes to us Christ's righteousness. These words themselves even have the advantage that they more plainly express the fact that the peace that God has with us indeed is Christ's work but yet has its ground wholly in God.

2. In what has been said up to this point the idea of representation has played an important role. It is impossible, I think, to make clear what reconciliation *in* Christ means without using this idea. I find the word clearer than "substitution," which is more commonly used in this connection, all the more since for me the latter term is too heavily loaded theologically; in fact I intend the same meaning by both terms. Representation is something that appears everywhere around us. If a Dutch football team wins the Europa cup, "we" have won. Or, actually that is not a good analogy, because "we" can "credit" this victory to ourselves, but it is too much external to ourselves. But if our government declares war or concludes a peace agreement, "we" are bound by that, and we have war or peace. Just so also a people become responsible in their leaders (Hitler's Germany, the so-called police action in Indonesia, Algeria). To express the realistic character of the substitution or representation, Anglo-Saxon theology has formed the term "corporate personality." The best known example of this corporate personality is

found in Isaiah 53, where it cannot be discerned whether the Servant of the Lord signifies an individual or the people of Israel.

3. In connection with the crucifixion I have not spoken of punishment. I regard as incorrect the idea that appears in certain forms of the doctrine of the atonement, that Jesus bore the punishment for our sins, if by this is meant that Jesus Christ is punished by God in our place. How could God will to punish the man after his own heart? God was after all well-pleased with him. As a matter of fact, in the New Testament the word "punishment" does not even appear in this connection. In any case, it was not God who put Jesus to death, but men in their blindness, and it was not God who punished Jesus, but the men who condemned him.

4. Moreover, in my opinion the idea of the transfer of guilt or the assuming of guilt clarifies nothing. We can speak of guilt only in the sense that Jesus allied himself with men in their guilt and that under this being-guilty of theirs he suffered. We can however say that Jesus cancelled and did away with the guilt. For like covenant and reconciliation, guilt is a relational concept; it is guilt in relation to another, in relation to God. Jesus Christ in his obedience stands before God just, and God sees us, as represented by him, also standing before him just. He has peace with men, so that he no longer sees their guilt. To use a Pauline term, he no longer imputes their guilt.

Man has Peace with God

We began this discussion by saying that atonement, reconciliation, is a two-sided event. It is not enough to speak of God's turning toward man. Man must also turn toward God and must himself come to stand before him in a new way. This is, after all, what God is concerned with.

Here we shall have to speak of the persuasive power of love. It is the experience of the ordinary life that the love of another who accepts us and who is even ready to endure our rejection finally can overcome our resistance. Love can be such a power that we must acknowledge ourselves to have been won over to it. And if that is true even of human love, how much more then is it true of God's love. He has sent Jesus Christ, just as he also sent the prophets, to bring us back to himself. Already therein we recognize his love. And we recognize this still more when we consider that this sending meant suffering and death for Jesus and therefore suffering for God also (p. 15). God suffered because people rejected Jesus and thereby also rejected God himself, but above all he shared in the suffering of Jesus. For what kind of love would it be that did not suffer too when the beloved one suffers! This idea also is altogether in line with the thought of Paul. He too speaks of the love of Christ that is so great that Christ was even ready to die "for the ungodly," and he too knows that in this love to the very death God has shown us his love (Rom. 5:6-8). And finally, God's love has also become manifest in his raising Jesus Christ from the dead. The resurrection is the demonstration that God did not let the matter rest with mankind's rejection of Jesus Christ and thus of himself. He did not accept men's cutting themselves off from him. Resurrection means that in spite of crucifixion God remains committed to man.

Thus in the cross and the resurrection of Jesus Christ God's love is made manifest, a love that is ready to suffer and to forgive. This love is stronger than our resistance, so that we acknowledge ourselves voluntarily to be won over by it; just as we indeed only can come to recognize our resistance for what it is in the light of this love.

To summarize the above in a few words: through Jesus Christ God has reconciled us to himself. He has peace with us in spite of our sin and our guilt. has done sinks in upon us, we can no longer persist in our self-chosen enmity toward him, but we gratefully accept the peace that he has made with us. Thus it is understandable that Paul considers "the ministry of reconcilliation" as part of the reconcilliation-event. It must be proclaimed to us that God has reconciled us to himself and has peace with us. And only through this proclamation does his love become manifest to us and do we confess ourselves won over, so that now from our side also we have peace with him. Since proclamation is an essential part of the reconcilliation, it also becomes evident that a person must constantly be reminded of his having been reconciled. Thinking about reconcilliation necessarily issues in ethics. It must be demonstrated in our lives that we have abandoned our enmity against God and live in peace with him. Hence also we may not say that the reconcilliation has happened once-and-for-all, but we must add that it must be expanded through time, that is, that it must always be happening again and again.

The Mediator

Of all the titles that the church gave Jesus, that of the Mediator most clearly expressed his place in the reconciliation-event. It is true that there are certain dangers connected with this name. It must not be used so as to create the impression that there is no direct connection between God and man. Any suggestion that God is so unapproachable in his holiness that an intermediary is necessary must be avoided. Further, the title of Mediator must not be understood to mean "go-between"; it must not carry the idea that in some way or another Christ had to persuade God to try again with man. One can regard these mistaken implications as so dangerous that one rather avoids this title particularly since it is only occasionally used in the New Testament. Yet it, like no other, indicated the two-sided character of reconciliation: that God has peace with us because Jesus Christ was the fully obedient man; and that our sinful resistance to God is overcome and we are brought to respond in love because God in his love has become manifest in Christ. God sees us in Jesus as his covenant-partners, and in him we see God's love. And thus God reconciles us to himself.

In the discussion of reconciliation the terms "objective" and "subjective" with reference to the doctrine have played a rather prominent role in the Netherlands. These terms are used with varying meanings. By "objective" is meant either that God is thought of as as the "object" of the reconciliation (he is reconciled) or that the reconciliation occurs "objectively" (i.e., outside of man). By a subjective doctrine of the atonement people understand either that God is "subject" only (he does the reconciling) or that the reconciliation has "subjectively" affected man, so that God does not change, but only man. Here we have strongly emphasized that in the reconciliation a double movement is involved, that of God toward man and that of man toward God. But we have also insisted that this twofold movement had its initial impetus solely from God, because he chose and prepared Jesus Christ, delivered him into the hands of men, and finally cancelled the guilt of men by raising him from the dead. Thus this entire distinction appears to be unsuited to express the truth of the reconciliation, and the sooner it is abandoned the better.

Other concepts for speaking about reconciliation

In the reflection which I have tried to offer here, the concepts of enmity and peace have played a prominent role. I am conscious, however, that thereby I have not allowed other important ideas to have a hearing, or at least not an adequate hearing.

1. Thus for example reconciliation also could have been thought through using the concept of *forgiveness*. In this word the gracious character of the reconciliation is especially expressed. Because God wills to forgive man, he sends Christ; that is sheer grace. And this forgiveness does something to man. A child that knows that it is accepted by its parents without reservation or condition — even when the parents have reason to be angry with the child — thereby feels safe and secure, and therefore can confront life in confidence. Thus man also is changed by the knowledge that he is forgiven and accepted by God; he comes to a new and trusting stance in life.

> After all that has been said to this point, it will be evident that I regard as untenable the idea that God cannot simply forgive and that Christ therefore had to provide satisfaction. It was Anselm of Canterbury who at the end of the eleventh century was the first to attempt consistently to think through the event of atonement and to this end, in true Christian freedom, utilized the conceptual material of his time. One of his central ideas was satisfaction, making compensation, a word that does not appear in the Bible. His suggestion had a particular resonance in the medieval situation, although even there it did not escape refutation. In any case, in our own different thought-world, in which the words that he used have a different sound, it is neither permissible nor possible to adopt his outline.

2. The concept of *redemption* lies very close to that of reconciliation and is often used as a synonym for it. It has a somewhat different accent. While in reconciliation the idea is removal of enmity, redemption implies liberation from a burden. This too is a figure in which the saving work of Jesus Christ can be expressed. Through God's seeing us in the obedient Christ, we are delivered from the burden of our guilt. It must be added that redemption is liberation from guilt, not from sin and suffering. For placing the idea of redemption in a central position brings with it the danger of forgetting the provisional and incomplete character of the reconciliation. The world is not yet set right; to use Paul's language, it is still groaning, and like the believers it is still looking toward full redemption.

3. Still other associations are evoked by the idea that Christ has gained the *victory* for us, that Christ has wrestled with the power of evil, and this power could not draw him away from God; in his life he overcame this power. But that is not all. When in the crucifixion it appeared as though evil had gained the upper hand, the resurrection revealed that God is mightier. Reconciliation, considered in terms of victory, means that in the final analysis the power of all the anti-godly forces that strive to separate us from God is a powerless power; it cannot separate us from God. The strength of this figure of speech is that it expresses, better than any other, the fact that the sin that brought Jesus to the cross is more than man's wilful hostility. As we said in an earlier chapter (p. 38), sin is experienced as a real, supra-personal power. Atonement as conquest signifies that we are no longer captives of this power.

> Even though the early church did not have a fully worked-out doctrine of the

atonement, an important role was played by the idea that through his death Jesus Christ had gained the victory over the devil. Hence the theory of the atonement in which Christ as victor is the central motif is often called the classical theory.

The various concepts and images that we have used — and there are still others also — are not mutually exclusive, but they also do not easily fit together to form a unified whole. But that is good too; for if we were to set out to create an actually complete doctrine, the event of reconciliation between God and man wrought by Jesus Christ would be rationalistically made trivial. In the final analysis it — like God himself and his dealings — escapes our thoughts and our grasp. Therefore we may not make our own doctrine of our own conceptual material absolute. As was said earlier, even in the Bible various figures and words are employed to describe the reconciliation. Following that example, our speaking about it also will always have to exhibit a great deal of openness, and we shall have to allow others the freedom to talk about it in other, different words.

XIII. THE HOLY SPIRIT

The Spirit as God's presence

The Christian faith has to do with past, present, and future. It is concerned with what God has done in the past, in the history of Israel and of Jesus Christ. Undoubtedly for most Christians not so long ago the focal point of their faith lay in the view that salvation had happened once-for-all, back there on Golgotha. Hence it is not surprising that Jewish theologians repeatedly charge Christianity with being so backward-oriented that it renders history meaningless; if the crucial event has already occurred, there is nothing more that is essentially new to expect. In earlier years this accusation had some justification, but it no longer is valid. In our time great emphasis is being placed on the fact that the consummation, which will bring the realization of the kingdom of God, still lies in the future. Believing has often become almost the same as hoping and trusting in that which — or in him who — will come, and living in the strength of that expectation. But even so the present remains empty. It lies bracketed in between the past to which it is oriented and the future toward which it reaches.

It is not true, however, that for the Christians the "now" is empty. In the "now" people are confronted with God, they come to faith, and their lives can be given a new direction; in the "now" a new fellowship is growing, of those who in faith in God's reconciliation are carrying his salvation to others; and in the "now" also here and there in the world something of lovelessness, injustice, or violence is set right, and something of humanity and righteousness is actualized. The "now" is the time in which the Spirit, that is, God in the power of his life-awakening love, is at work in the world.

In the first, introductory chapter, I said that God becomes "self-evident" to us when he shares himself with us as the Other, and so confronts us in our lives that we cannot escape from his reality. Only on the basis of the experience of being addressed and seized by him, as I said there, is it possible for us to speak meaningfully of God. That chapter dealt with the power of God's presence which we now "experience" in our lives, with religious experience, to use a somewhat old-fashioned term. It is this experienceable presence of God that is called the Holy Spirit. Our entire first chapter dealt with the Spirit, without the necessity at that point of actually using the term. This is significant. The Spirit is not "something," not an independent entity alongside God, but the evidence of God's active presence in the world. Perhaps an illustration from everyday life can clarify this. A child can experience the love of his parents and this love can be for him a source of strength in his life. But this love has not thereby become something that "exists" alongside or apart from the parents. So also the Spirit is only another word for God's love that flows to persons and works in them to awaken and renew life. The Holy Spirit — so one could define it — is God insofar as he can be experienced by us humans. We experience in our lives his renewing presence; we experience his giving us strength and supporting us. We encounter people of such great purity and such an evident unselfishness or of such a great wisdom in living that in and through them we perceive God at work. And we know a fellowship with others which for all its defects nevertheless is formed and held together by the power of God's love. These are all such lofty words that we hardly venture to utter them. We distrust our religious experiences and are fearful about speaking of them. Hence even much of what earlier Christians could say with a good conscience sounds to our ears unbelievable. But we shall have to take care that, in our so-called sobriety, we do not discard too much. The denial of experiences that we have in faith can also be nothing but a form of ingratitude toward God, by whom we are grasped so that we can believe in him. For faith-experience is not the same thing as subjectivity and emotionalism. But we have already discussed this in our first chapter, so it is not necessary here to enlarge upon that. Only this further point: if we believe in a God who is at work, who is involved with us humans — and these are simply other terms for the Holy Spirit —then there must be something of him to be observed, to be noted and experienced. Otherwise what basis would we have for believing?

> Thus we could drop the word "Spirit" (or the older English term, Holy "Ghost." Tr.). and if we consider how little many Christians are able to comprehend the term, and how much it is misunderstood, it would not seem unreasonable for the time being to avoid it. it is also helpful to realize that here we are dealing with a term that is borrowed from human existence. In modern languages as well as in Hebrew and Greek the word "spirit," which indicates above all the essence of the human person, is used for God's active presence. One may compare the expressions "filled with the Spirit of God" and "to act in the spirit of a certain person." If we keep this in view, we will not so easily be tempted to place the Holy Spirit alongside God as a separate entity.

> In Hebrew and Greek the basic meaning of the word that we translate as "spirit" is "blowing" or "wind." This meaning never entirely disappeared. Hence in the Old and New Testaments the word has retained overtones of the dynamic, free, unpredictable. Derived from this, then, the word further has the meaning of "breathe," "breath of life," and then even "life." In the Bible, more than in modern translations, the concept "spirit" suggests that it is God who through his presence gives life, who makes alive. All these nuances must be heard, for example, in John 3:8: "The wind blows where it will...; so is everyone that is born of the Spirit." "Wind" and "spirit" are the same word in Greek, and "blow" has the same stem. What is involved here is more than an etymological play on words.

If we "define" the Holy Spirit as the power of God's active presence, it is obvious that this involves a particular aspect of the doctrine of God. That is also the reason that it is impossible to describe the Spirit in and by himself; we can only say what he does, and we can point to his work that we experience and see. This is all put very broadly and provisionally, and in the following chapters it will be explicated and given content. But the basis of all that is said about the Spirit remains the experience that God shares himself with man and gives him power — to which it must be added even here that most people receive this experience in one way or another in or at least through the church.

The Spirit in Israel

If we pose the question as to where the work of the Spirit is to be seen most clearly, we shall have to point to Jesus Christ. But in this respect again Jesus may not be detached from his prehistory in Israel. Old Testament Israel recognized, saw, experienced (or whatever word one chooses to use here) that in her midst there were people who were so filled with God's presence that they were, so to speak, lifted out of themselves. God seized certain people who in and of themselves often were insignificant, inspired them, and made them leaders of his people, as is related for example of certain judges and even of David. When the biblical writers say of them that the Spirit of the Lord came upon them or seized them or that God sent his Spirit upon them, they are thereby giving expression to their belief that God himself equips and gives power for their task to these people, whom he intends to use at a certain moment in a special way. But the power of God's immediate presence appears most strongly in the Old Testament among the prophets: among the earlier ones, who experience him in dreams, visions, and conditions of ecstasy; and among the classical ones, the so-called writing prophets, in whom the ecstatic motif recedes into the background but of whom it is clearly evident that they are impelled, by virtue of having been laid hold upon by God directly, by virtue of the awareness that they can do no other, to address the people in his name. In this connection it is striking that many of them refrain from appealing to the Spirit for the message that they bring, undoubtedly because such an appeal was brought into disrepute by the so-called false prophets. But they do quite explicitly refer to the Spirit when they speak of the future: God will one day give his Spirit to his people and thus, through the judgment, will awaken them to a new life in obedience to him. Or, further: through his Spirit he will equip someone, a king or a prophet, who as leader will reclaim the people of God. Here the Spirit has altogether become the effectual power of the covenant-God who one day, when the time of salvation comes, through the inward renewal of his human partner will actualize his covenant intention.

The Spirit in Jesus Christ

This is the background against which we must speak about Jesus as the one in whom the Spirit has been made manifest in an incomparable fashion. We have already alluded to this when we spoke about Jesus as the true man (see p. 67). We said then that Jesus is so totally filled with God's presence that he is wholly and entirely God's covenant-man, who in his perfect and unique communion with God is one with him. Now, however, from the perspective offered by thought about the Spirit, certain aspects can be brought out which earlier were not yet so explicitly clear. (1) In Jesus, as the one who is perfectly filled with the Spirit, the future toward which the Old Testament prophets looked forward has dawned. In this respect it does not matter whether we think here more of Jesus as the summing-up of the entire nation or as the one who is equipped to reclaim God's people. The two ideas are intertwined, or, better said, they are essentially one and the same. In any case, the expectation is that one day God will pour out his Spirit in an unknown way and will cause the covenant that has been broken by his people once again to be in force, confirmed in Jesus. (2) Jesus, we have said, is in the whole of his humanness so fully one with God that in him we encounter God himself; he is, so to speak, transparent to God, the image of God, to use a biblical term. Therefore in him the covenant of God and man has become a reality in its full duality. Here, however, a misunderstanding could arise. It could appear as though Jesus was a kind of moral and religious superman and that therefore God wills to be with him so fully as a kind of reward. Then it would not be God in his love for men who has restored the covenant, but the man Jesus. In order to avoid this idea we have spoken explicitly of God's initiative. We have let this be evident specifically by setting the biblical idea of God's special choice of Jesus in the foreground. However, we then also pointed to the special equipping for his task that Jesus received. Now, from the perspective of thought about the Holy Spirit, all that can be made still more precise and we can even more clearly do justice to God's initiative. Jesus was indeed man, but a man who was totally grasped, totally filled, by the power of God's presence. And the power of God's presence is only another term for the Spirit. Hence we can also say that in Jesus the work of the Spirit has taken on visible form. (3) As bearer of the Spirit, Jesus stands in the line of those in the Old Testament whom God equipped and filled with his power, although this does not hold true of any of them so fully as of him. But here there is not merely a continuity, the extending of a line. For with Jesus something entirely new has entered into history. He is true man, as no one before him has been; he is the new man to whom the believers after him must be conformed. The words in the Apostles' Creed, that Jesus was conceived of the Holy Spirit are intended especially to express this. For it is never said of any prophet that he was conceived of the Spirit. These words indicate that with his life-giving Spirit God here has, as it were, performed a new act of creation. He has made a new beginning with a new man, after he has reached an impasse with his covenant-partner Israel.

> In the Bible there are two traditions in particular that express the belief that Jesus is filled with the Spirit. One, which is found in all the gospels, connects the gift of the Spirit with Jesus' baptism. Alongside this, Matthew and Luke have also preserved the other tradition, which originally stood separate from the one already cited, that Jesus was begotten by the Spirit. The latter then took its place in the Apostles' Creed, thus pushing the former and presumably earlier tradition more into the background. This is understandable, too, for that former tradition appeared too much to put Jesus on a par with the prophets. Besides, in the idea that Jesus was conceived of the Spirit it is better indicated that his unity with God did not begin at a specific identifiable moment in his life (cf. p. 71). He had the Spirit from and even before his birth from his mother's womb. And finally, the conception by the Spirit gives expression to the belief that Jesus Christ was given by God.

> But in the words that Christ was conceived by the Spirit, the point is a testimony of faith, not a biological statement. The idea that the Spirit should take the place of Jesus' human father is utterly absurd. Hence this testimony may not be placed on a par or closely connected with the so-called virgin birth. For quite apart from the question whether or not one feels obliged to accept this, in any case this birth does speak of a biological fact.

The Spirit after Christ

The Spirit, we have said, is the power of God's presence. Here, however, there is posed the question whether the working of the Spirit after Christ is changed or newly qualified. In order to answer this question we must start out from our own faith-experience. When we speak about the Spirit, that is, about God whom we experience in our lives, that is the only proper way. And then the matter becomes clear, so that for us as Christians the Spirit is related to, or perhaps we must rather say bound up with, faith in Christ. God, whose life-giving power we experience in our lives, is the God with whom we are confronted in Jesus Christ. He was always, before and after Christ, the same God. Yet in Christ he has let himself be known in a new and different way; in him he has explained himself in a new way. For we see in Christ what happens when a man lives totally out of the power of God's presence. In him the Spirit is fully and wholly embodied. This means that Christ is the definition and the criterion of the Spirit. Then it also is highly significant that Paul often speaks about the Spirit as the form in which the exalted Christ is present with the believers, and that he then has this coincide with the presence of God. In Rom. 8:9-11, for example, everything is interwoven, or, better said, it is all the same: the Spirit of God, the Spirit of Christ, and Christ who dwells in man. As soon as we speak in terms of content, it is also evident at once that Christ is the definition of the Spirit. for the Spirit is not only the overpowering might of God's presence, but above all and at the same time the sustaining power of his love; this actually has first become manifest in Jesus Christ and is first fully experienced in faith in him.

In another respect also the work of the Spirit is altered after and through Christ. Through Christ salvation has been spread abroad throughout the world. In the Old Testament, God was especially present only in Israel. It is true that even then it was not Israel alone that was concerned, and precisely in terms of the Spirit this truth is underscored. Outside Israel too there were, here and there, individuals who according to the Old Testament were motivated by God's presence; the story of the prophet Balaam is a clear example of this (Num. 22-24). But the dynamic power of God's love was first let loose for the world when men in belief in Christ went out into the world with the message of salvation. Only then did the Gentiles also, the "outsiders," experience God's love and its life-renewing power. In this respect also it is once again confirmed that the Spirit is, so to speak, the God who can be experienced. It is after all a historical, verifiable fact that only after Christ is the world confronted with the God of Israel. Thus through Christ the Spirit not only is defined in a new way; through him the Spirit also has become universal.

> It is obvious that in the foregoing we have not always spoken about the Spirit in one and the same manner. We have not held to one particular definition of the Spirit. I believe that this lies in the very nature of the case, 'for the Spirit can no more actually be defined or objectified than can God himself. As soon as we in our ideas and words think that we know precisely what we mean by the term, it appears once again to elude us. And if we start out from the point that the Spirit is the comprehensive indication of the power of God's presence that men experience in their lives, it also is obvious that this cannot be put into words once and for all. This presence can, after all, be experienced in many different ways. Hence the one thing we must maintain is that the Spirit is always the power of

God's saving love, which we have come to know in Christ. Christ remains the criterion.

We have already noted that *ruach* (the Hebrew word for "spirit") is also "breath of life" or "life-force." It is not a purely anthropological idea, for it is God who gives the *ruach* to a man and takes it away again. In this sense God's life-awakening Spirit of course in Old Testament times also was active outside Israel. There is, however, an inner connection between these two functions of the Spirit. For us, too, "life" is not an undifferentiated concept. It can be a kind of vegetating and it can have a powerful intensity. It is in keeping with this that according to the biblical writers all life is given by God and rests upon his presence, while this presence also can be experienced as a power which wholly seizes the man and inspires his actions in an unrecognized way.

Speaking about God with three terms

Now let us survey the route that we have taken. We cannot know God, cannot believe in him in the full sense of the word, before we have encountered him in our lives, before we have experienced him — or his power, but here that is the same — in our lives. Our experience of him is the first,the beginning point. But we cannot stop there. If God were to be equated with our experience of him, we would ultimately be experiencing only ourselves, or a divine center within ourselves. Hence we may not speak of him exclusively in this way. God is also the Other, the one who comes to the world "from without," the one who in full supremacy has the absolute initiative in relation to us. By speaking of God as Creator, we put into words this absolute initiative of him as the Other. But even this still is not enough, for the question as to who this Other is must still be answered. Thus we must go still further and say that this great Other is the one who has made a covenant with men and who so loves them that he does not drop them even when they turn away from him. That God is the one who loves, seeks, and saves us is manifest in Jesus Christ. All this can be summed up by saying that God is the Covenant-God, which for me is the most essential thing that we can say about him. Because he is this, he has created man to be with him. What it means that he is the Covenant-God becomes manifest in Jesus Christ, in whom the covenant is actualized. And because he is Covenant-God, he also wills to be present with us and with the world, and to give us strength and the courage to live.

But up to this point, everything is too much set in sequence; in reality things are much more intertwined. The God whose *presence* I experience is the *Other* who *loves* me. That is to say that we can speak about the one God only in a threefold way, i.e. trinitarianly. He is the Other who has revealed his presence and himself in Jesus Christ and who gives himself to me, to us, so that we experience his presence and believe in him. To say the same thing once more: i encounter (and that is the Spirit) God (i.e., the Other, the Creator) in the man Jesus Christ (i.e., the Son). It is evident that herewith I am approaching the doctrine of the trinity — but it is not the same thing. I cannot believe in a trinitarian God as though there were in him a triad: God the Father, God the Son, and God the Holy Spirit. The Son Jesus Christ is not God, but a man who is so fully one with God that I encounter God in him; and the Spirit is not an entity alongside God the Father, but is God himself who shares himself with me, the power of his presence, the power of his holy love. Therefore I cannot speak of a trinity in God. But I must speak about him trinitarianly in the sense that I have described above: that I need three terms to speak about the encounter with him.

sense that I have described above: that I need three terms to speak about the encounter with him.

> The doctrine of the trinity is not explicitly formulated by any ecclesiastical council. The fact that it does not appear in the Bible says nothing in and of itself; the question is only whether the various forms in which testimony is borne in the New Testament to God, to Jesus Christ, and to the Spirit necessarily had to lead to this doctrine. The thinking-through of the relationship between God, Jesus Christ, and the Spirit has been accompanied by much strife. The terminology of "one essence (substance) and three persons" stems from Tertullian (about A.D. 200). Afterward this formula makes its way into church history; in this process however, the terms "essence" and "person" are given differing content by various theologians. Their meaning is never unequivocally and precisely established by any official ecclesiastical authority. In any case the Latin word "persona" did not have the meaning of our "person."

> It is generally recognized in our time that the trinitarian formula is incomprehensible for people today. Hence it is frequently replaced, or at least is interpreted with the words "one God in three modes of being." But what does "mode of being" mean here? Is it something fundamentally different from what we mean when we say of a man that he is a parent, lover, friend, and doctor? Do we intend then to indicate only that God is a living and not a static God?

> The doctrine of the trinity is understood among theologians in such diverse ways and among non-theologians is so fully or solely accepted as a formula or is so misunderstood as a kind of trio of Gods, that I regard it as nothing lost if we drop this doctrine, which is formed by theological reflection on the basis of the God who reveals himself. Indeed, that has also become necessary for me as a consequence of my objection to the traditional doctrine of the incarnation. In church history the doctrine of the trinity also has developed after and as a further consequence of the doctrine of Jesus' being God.

XIV. LIFE AS GOD'S ALLY

In the preceding chapter we started out from the personal experience of faith in order to gain a view of what is meant by "the Holy Spirit." As we now go further into the work of the Spirit, I propose at first to direct attention to the individual man. This order is not obligatory. We could also begin with the church as the community which is formed by the Spirit. That would even have a certain advantage. This community after all is already there before the individual believer. It certainly is true in the Netherlands that most Christians have grown up and become believers in this community. On the other hand, the community does not exist apart from or alongside the individuals who are her members. As long as this connection of the individual believer and the community of believers is not lost sight of, it does not too much matter where we begin.

Faith

We believe in God because we are grasped by the power of his presence. The confession that faith is the work of the Spirit is another way of expressing the truth that it rests upon an experience with God. That can either say everything or nothing. Nothing, if by this we mean only an inner sense of the overwhelming and the transcendent. Everything, if we actually mean the experience of the presence of God; of God who is the great Ally of man, and who wills to be his Ally even when man rejects him; who therefore has given himself as a guarantee that his covenant with man will prevail. That he is this God has been made manifest in what he has done in the biblical history of Israel and of Jesus Christ. This must be related to us. Hence it is not enough to say that faith is based upon the experience of an encounter with God. It is impossible without this experience. But the experience must be accompanied by a knowledge of who this God is, knowledge of his revealing and saving activity. Hence in order to come to faith, a man is always dependent on other men who tell him of this activity, and hand it down to him. This handing-down can have many different forms. It can occur through the writings left by the biblical authors or by later great believers before us. It can also occur by means of oral transmission by our contemporaries, parents, friends, teachers, or preachers, in sermon, instruction, and conversation. It does not lie within human power that in and through this handing-down even God himself becomes manifest in his active love and that it becomes an experience of being addressed and grasped by God. Men cannot transmit faith; they can only transmit the content of faith. But this too is an indispensable element in faith. This again indicates how much the work of the Spirit in the individual depends on his work in the church and hangs together with it.

Thus faith is a knowledge of God in the most total and existential sense of the word. And because it is a knowledge of *God*, of this God who sustains and loves us, this knowing at the same time always denotes a recognition of him as our God, a submission to him — in short, faith.

1. That believing in the sense which we mean here is something different from "regarding as likely" is so obvious that I mention it only as a reminder.

2. There is a certain tendency to set "believe in" and "believe that" in contrast to each other. In this view "believe in" is the same as a trust in God that is based upon an immediate contact, and "believe that" is what we do with respect to so-called saving truths. I regard this placing in contrast or even alongside each other as an error. I believe *in* God, who has formed a covenant with me, but this then also means that I believe *that* he is my Covenant-God, *that* he has become manifest in Jesus Christ.

3. Closely related to this is another distinction that is made, that between faith as action, as when we say, "I believe," and as a designation for the content of belief, as in "the Christian faith." But I regard even this distinction, which of course we can make in conceptual terms, as of no consequence. Belief has a content, and it is impossible really to know this special content and to express it without believing in it. The "act" of believing and its content go together. In theological jargon: the *fides qua* as act of faith (literally: belief with which [I believe]) and the *fides quae* as its content (literally: the belief which [I believe]) so fully form a single whole that in my view the whole terminology is superfluous.

The question is often posed whether a person can do anything about whether he believes. We have talked about a being addressed by God and a being grasped by the power of his presence. This much is clear: a man can so isolate himself that he does not allow this power admittance to himself. Perhaps this is the sin against the Holy Spirit: that a man so armors himself that he can no longer be reached by love, that he is no longer able either to give or to receive love. But even then God has the last word: he can irresistibly break through even such armor. But the real question is a different one: it is whether every person encounters God in his life. And here I am not thinking primarily of those people who live outside the realm of Christendom and church — and there are many of these, even in our christianized society — but of those who want to believe and appear unable to do so. Is it possible for a person to seek God without finding him, to call on him without his answering? Certainly there are times in the lives of most Christians when God seems to hide himself from them. I believe that we are not obliged simply to connect this with sin. If we believe in the freedom of the Spirit, we shall also have to accept it when God withdraws and hides himself. There is also such a thing as a sighing in his absence and a waiting for him and keeping oneself ready for him. And beyond that I simply do not know. I only know that God is the Ally of every man and that he abandons no man. And perhaps it is indeed true, as Pascal said, that longing and seeking for God are possible only because he has already laid hold upon man and man has already "experienced," in whatever way, his love. In any case these reflections suggest that we must be careful with the idea of "experience", and that being addressed by God perhaps can occur in a level of our existence of which we are not at all or only vaguely conscious.

On the other hand, I regard the question whether faith is exclusively a gift of God, or whether man must do something for it, as a false question that is based upon a baleful way of thinking of competition between God and man. What is involved is a love-relationship in which God has the initiative. But the power of love activates the recipient of love. This holds true even of the love of a human person; so much the more, then, when God is the lover. Hence I am unhappy also with the often used figure that faith is nothing but the stretching out of an empty hand to have it filled. The intention is clear; people want to interdict the idea that we can earn salvation. But if one actually thinks from the perspective of the covenant, in terms of the love-relationship between God and man, such a misapprehension cannot arise. We cannot earn even the love of a fellowman.

Believing in God means believing in him who as Covenant-God has bound himself in free love with man and does not desert him, even when man is unfaithful to him. In the consciousness of our own shortcoming and unfaithfulness we know that if God continues to hold us fast, he does so in spite of ourselves, by his forgiving us. Hence faith is always an amazed and grateful acceptance of God's forgiveness. But that is only the half of what must be said here. And now I refer back to an earlier chapter, where man was described as that creature that God wants as his covenant-ally. God's aim is the mutual alliance with man. He is concerned with the man who turns to him, his covenant-man. That is also what is essentially new about Jesus Christ: the covenant-man, and thus the covenant's actually becoming two-sided. Atonement/reconciliation is more than forgiveness. It is the actualizing of the covenant, and that means man's turning to God. For God's coming to man — this is his way from all eternity, his very nature.

It is true of this turning of man that again it is altogether God's doing and at the same time man's own free action. We men, in our human freedom, turn to God because his love has become too powerful for us.

> In dogmatics, and especially in that of the Protestant churches, the terms justification and sanctification have always played a major role. Generally speaking, the understanding of justification is that God regards man as just, acquits him, does not impute his guilt to him. This is actually another word for what we earlier called forgiveness. Sanctification usually indicates that God places man in a life of fellowship with himself in such a way that man's life is thereby transformed; he begins to function as covenant-man, to use the term that we have made central. Thus justification and sanctification indicate the two poles of the covenant relationship. The former of these two words points to God, who wants to be our Covenant-God (and, considering what we are like, forgiveness is necessary if this is to be), and the latter points to us men who may live as God's covenant-men.

Turning toward God

Is it possible to describe how this turning to God occurs, or, said in another way, can we describe how a person becomes a Christian? And directly connected with this is another question; can we describe what it means and involves to be a Christian, to live as God's covenant-ally? As a matter of fact, these are not two different question; it is at the most a matter of different accents. For it is true of most people that they do not turn to God once for all and then go on to live the rest of their lives in commitment to him, but they must turn to him again and ever again. Moreover, it is not true that we first become Christians and then thereafter begin to live as Christians, as though the two were separated from each other in time.

Any and every description here is inadequate and actually impossible. You also cannot describe what happens to a person when he or she "falls in love." And in a certain sense, turning to God is a little bit the same as a "falling in love" with God. That will be different for each person, depending on that person's nature. Hence we can only repeat what has already been said above, on p. 5.For what we are aiming at here is what is generally identified as conversion or regeneration. Both words refer to the same thing, and they appear not to be defined in contrast to each other. In regeneration the emphasis is placed more upon the fact that God himself in his holy presence draws man to himself and awakens him to a new life in communion with God himself. On the other hand, conversion rather involves the human side: a discomfort with oneself and a turning of oneself to God.

Alongside the word "conversion" I should like to place the word "reversal." The former is the translation of the Greek word that literally denotes a change of attitude and thinking, while the latter is a translation of the Hebrew term that is derived from the verb "to turn around." For both are involved, the acquiring of a new frame of mind, so that a man begins to think about things in a new way, and a decision of the will, so that he turns to God. In turning to God, after all, the whole man is involved, with his feeling, thinking, and willing.

In any case it is not possible to give a blueprint of how conversion, which is another term for becoming a Christian, comes about. It *can* be a sudden experience, as was the case, for example, with Paul, Augustine, or Luther, but it does not *have* to be such. Perhaps it is significant that the images most often used in the Bible to indicate the covenantal relationship of God and man are those of the husband-wife and the parent-child relationship. In that between husband and wife there is frequently a particular event at a particular moment whereby they realize that they want to be united for life; a child, on the other hand, grows up in the nurturing love of its parents.

It is obvious that this turning to God involves a turning away from an existence in which one lives, as it were, with his back to God. This living with one's back turned toward God is the same thing as what we called (in chapter V) man's being a sinner. We recall that therein the issue was not an analysis of what it is to be human, but an utterance of faith. We cannot speak about sin in a meaningful way exclusively on the basis of introspection. Perhaps a distinction could be made between a consciousness of guilt and an acknowledgment of sin. The former can arise out of an confrontation with ourselves, with our "better self." There is no reason to speak about this as such with contempt. But acknowledgment of one's own sin is possible only through encounter with the living God, and is thus the work of the Spirit. Therefore also no acknowledgment of one's own sin is possible without repentance. And both together are given with our conversion, which is a turning around and a change in our thinking, away from our stance of rejecting God and toward him.

Hence it is extremely dubious as a matter of method when in pastoral work or preaching one tries first to convince a man of his guilt in order thus to bring him to faith.

The new life

And again we come back to the question whether it is possible to describe this new life as God's ally. It will be as varied as we human beings are different in nature, talents, and circumstances of life. Only one thing can be said about it in general: in one way or another it will bear a resemblance to the life of Jesus. Jesus was the perfect man-of-God, he was fully God's covenant-man. Our life as men of God, therefore, however it may be, will be conformed to his life, will be modeled after his. I deliberately use the passive form here, because the issue here again is the work of God's love which, so to speak, lifts us above ourselves. Even on the human plane a person functions differently and better in an environment where he is conscious of being accepted and when people expect something of him. But these words are too weak. We are after all talking about a vital fellowship with God, whereby we are re-shaped and transformed into new persons, just as we also change in a vital fellowship with another person, a friend or a spouse. And, to maintain this comparison still further: this transformation is a process that is never finished. If in a marriage or a friendship we are no longer being shaped and molded by each other, if we no longer let ourselves be shaped by each other, it is no longer a living, vital relationship, but routine. And now the same thing can be said again in such a way that the human action is better kept in view. Then life as God's ally can be described as following Christ. Even in this the initiative does not rest with man. We follow him because we are drawn along by him, by his Spirit. But we, we ourselves, follow and go along with him and strive in our lives to be recognizable as his disciples. Hence it is not possible to work out in terms of content what form discipleship in general must have. This form is dependent on the situation. For discipleship is not the same thing as an attempt to copy Jesus. The form of it will be different for a person in the Netherlands from that of one in Russia, South Africa, or India, and different for a person in the twentieth century from that of one in the first or the sixteenth century. But whatever form the discipleship shall have, and whether it now lies more on the directly interpersonal level or more on the social or political level, in any case it will be characterized by the marks of love and service. For this is the essence of Jesus: that he committed himself wholly to the service of his fellowman, because he was wholly in God's service; that he did not seek himself and his own happiness, but in love gave himself wholly to God, and therefore also to others. We do not attain this "wholly," but perhaps therein we can begin to resemble him a little bit. That this discipleship to Jesus then is also a discipleship to God, a reflection of God, is, I hope, evident from earlier chapters (see especially chapter III).

This new life can also, seen from another perspective, be described as a life lived out of gratitude. If we know of God's love, of his forgiveness in which, in spite of everything, he wills to be our God, then there can be no question of our failing to live, in self-evident gratitude, as forgiven persons, held fast by him, as his allies. It is obvious that this manner of speaking also is justified. Yet I am somewhat fearful of it; the struggle and the conquest of self that it costs us to follow Jesus appears therein to be pushed aside. It is not all so self-evident, and it is not all so automatic. We must also very soberly do our best and learn not to place ourselves at the center of things.

"Good works"

Does it make a difference whether a person is a Christian? Is he thereby a better person? This question is often being posed in the church, but also and especially outside the church. In general, the most prominent criticism directed by outsiders against Christianity is that things are no more human and humane in the church than in the world, and the Christians cannot be distinguished from other people. We may not dismiss this criticism merely by saying that it is not Christianity's business to make better people, morally speaking, and that Christians are sinners like everybody else, differing from others only in that they know what the others do not know, that they are in God's hands. It is true that being a disciple of Christ involves more than ethics, but it does have an ethical side. If it is true that the knowledge that we are accepted by God is a power in our lives, then that must also be evident. And love and service, which we have called characteristic marks of the new life, the life of a Christian, are not something inward, but are features of behavior.

Now in dealing with the question cited above in more specific terms, I do not do this as a possible answer to non-Christians. We shall have to take to heart their criticism as a judgment upon our Christianity. I have not the slightest need to prove — even if I could — that believers are "better" people than non-believers. Whenever the church in the past has taken this path, it has always led to a reprehensible triumphalism. But if Christians pose this question in self-criticism, it cannot merely be pushed aside. In order to answer it, however, we must give attention to two things. First, the question should not inquire whether a Christian is a better man that a non-Christian, but at most whether he is a better man than he would be if he were not a Christian. And further, the question must not be posed with respect to ourselves alone. For the new life in love and service means an orientation away from ourselves, and toward God and our neighbor. If I now put myself under the magnifying glass, so to speak, in order to see how it is with me, I negate what I am inquiring about.

But if we now look away from ourselves to our fellow Christians, it surely is true that everyone knows people whose Christianity is evident: from their manifest readiness to help others, from the way in which they take the side of those in society who are deprived, from their modesty and self-denial — which has nothing to do with self-disparagement, from their attitude of forgiveness, or even from their wise humor and their acceptance of life. We all know of "good works," not our own but of others, which they themselves as a rule do not even recognize. Not with myself but with my fellow Christians in mind I dare to say that through their relationship with God people can become "better" people and that, thanks be to God, this also can be and often is outwardly visible. Moreover, that there are non-Christians who do "good works" and who live just as freely and joyfully as Christians do — happily so! After all, man, every man, is from God; so why should it not be possible that even without knowing it one might act as God's ally, and do the work that God intends?

Suffering for Christ's sake

With reference to being disciples of Christ, we usually think of the suffering that the Christian in the world may expect. The New Testament and the history of the early church are full of this theme. In the highly religious but anti-Christian world of that time, living as a Christian often brought with it persecution. This is no longer true, at least in Western Europe. Our society, in spite of its being secularized and the injustice that exists in it, is christianized and tolerant. A Christian will have to assume a critical stance even in relation to this society. It is a judgment upon the seriousness of our discipleship that for the most part we feel altogether at home in this society or can so fully detach ourselves from it that we are not too much burdened by it. But even if we do not adopt either of these positions, there still is no thought of persecution and hardly even of opposition to Christians. And yet — there are people who with unflagging faithfulness labor in the service of the kingdom of God, even when their labor is unfruitful. People who for the sake of Christ with great abandonment stand in the breach for humanity and justice, even when others become fretful about it. People who devote much time and attention to the ordinary, unspectacular church work, and who in spite of all discouragement cheerfully press on. People who no longer know what words they can bear witness to Jesus Christ's salvation so that their words will have resonance, and who yet continue ever anew to attempt that witness. People also who are bowed down under the burden of the superficiality, the divisions, the folly, and the polemics in the church, without being able to see a way to rise above these. Perhaps it is too strong an expression here to speak of suffering for Christ's sake, but all this does lie in that direction.

> The New Testament call this "oppression." It "oppresses" many Christians that the ministry to which they are called, to bear witness to Christ, often is unfruitful, and perhaps still more that they often cannot find any sensible form for this ministry in a climate of polite, oblivious indifference.

Christian attitude to life

The distinction between a Christian's actions and his inner attitude is artificial. Hence in the preceding the two are intertwined. If now attention is briefly somewhat more directed toward the way in which faith affects the way a person lives, his attitude toward life, his habit, it is true that this involves an inner temperament, but this will also be discernible to others. Thus we have spoken of an inner peace, joy, and acceptance of life that can radiate from a Christian. Of course this has a great deal to do with one's nature and character. In contrast with our actions, in this respect it is much less possible to effect this by striving, except perhaps by the practice of prayer.

1. In the belief that God in his love accepts us, we can get rid of our guilt. Reconciliation after all implies that God does not hold our guilt against us. Hence we can leave it behind us; we need not drag it along with us as a steadily increasing burden. Forgiveness — real forgiveness even among men — is a tremendous liberation. Here it is at once evident how the "inward" and the "outward" are connected. For if we have once experienced this liberation from God's hand personally, it is really inconceivable that we should withhold it from a fellowman who has incurred guilt in relation to us.

2. As we said above, suffering for Christ's sake is indeed too great a claim. But everyone has to deal with ordinary human suffering in his everyday life. The Christian will deal with it in a particular way. The epistle to the Hebrews says that Christ learned obedience through his suffering. Following after him, men can

grow by their sufferings. Any suffering can become for us a training school in our being Christians. This does not mean that it must be given by God and that we therefore must submit to it. Too much suffering is caused by human fault, our own and that of others, to allow that affirmation. It does mean that sometimes it is only in suffering that there emerges what resides within a person, that suffering can be an occasion for proving ourselves as Christians. How this verification will appear will vary quite noticeably for each person. But it is not merely a false cry to say that even in our suffering God is present and that his presence lends strength.

Included in this universal human suffering, in my opinion, is fear of death. This will have to be discussed further in a later chapter. But in any case the certainty of God's love will help a person to deal with this fear. This, however, does not give us the right to make "being able to die well" a kind of test for our faith or for the faith of others. There are too many other factors — for example of a vital and physical nature — that play a role to allow that kind of interpretation.

3. And then there is the feeling of the meaninglessness of life, to which many people in our time are subject, and that not as a tortured question but rather as a self-evident fact about which there is no need for any further reflection. It is not true that a Christian is automatically set free from being assailed by this feeling. But it is true that this feeling is ever again refuted by the knowledge and experience of God's presence. For if our life and that of the whole world is in his hand, then it cannot be meaningless, and then all the confusion in our own lives and in history must have a meaning in him. Man is called to a covenantal fellowship with him, to a growing unity with him; this is the meaning of man's life, whether he knows it or not (yet). The world is destined to become God's kingdom; this is the meaning of the world, even though she herself does not (yet) know that. Believing that existence has a meaning, while we still see little or nothing of that meaning, believing in God's intention for our lives and for the lives of our fellowmen and for the world — this says that a Christian is a person who has hope. He hopes, expects that God will after all actualize his intention. Believing in the meaning of existence because we believe in God is the same as hoping, as building upon something that is not yet present.

This chapter must be read together with the preceding one. Then it is clear that here throughout we actually have been talking about the Holy Spirit. For living as a Christian is the same thing as living in God's presence. And that is the same as the Holy Spirit. But this chapter also must be read together with the ones that follow, the one on prayer and especially the one on the church. The church, after all, is not a separate entity alongside and in addition to Christians. But even when this chapter is set in context with the next chapter and the next, it still is not a well-rounded whole. Any description of what it means to live as a Christian — in other words, what the work of the Spirit in the individual person is — has something arbitrary about it. Whichever way the description goes, some will always have the impression that it could also have been done differently. Hence I am aware that in this chapter I have only brought out certain aspects of the subject, while other, equally important facets have been neglected. For the covenant-relationship with God and discipleship to Christ are as wide-ranging and as many-sided as human life itself.

XV. ADDRESSING GOD

The first chapter of this book had as its title "Addressed by God." This chapter is the complement to that one. Being addressed and addressing: this expresses the reciprocal nature of the covenant relationship between God and man. Man's experience of being addressed by God comes first. Thereby he has become aware that God stands in a particular relationship with him — a love-relationship, as we have called it. And "relationship" signigies the to-and-fro character of a real mutuality. Man, addressed by God, is conscious of being called to respond to him with his life. In the preceding chapter we gave an indication in broad outline of what it means to give this response or, as we called it there, to live as God's ally. But one essential aspect still was not discussed there, namely that in any case it also includes man's addressing God. That is the subject in this chapter.

In the beginning of the book it was said that being addressed by God constrains man to speak about him (page 3). This can occur in an account of faith, in a theological treatment, in confession, in testimony, in a sermon. It also constrains man to think about God. This we call "meditation." But along with this thinking and this speaking *about* God there is also a speaking *to* God. If a man lives as God's covenant-man in fellowship with him, this always includes speaking to him. For just as speaking with each other establishes and maintains fellowship between men, so also does this hold true for God and man. God "speaks" to man and man speaks to God. This speaking to God is called prayer. Praying is the human side of the "conversation" that maintains fellowship between God and man.

The basic form of an actual conversation of one man with another is that they address each other; they say "you" to each other. The same also holds true for the "conversation" between God and man. The basic form of prayer is simply to address him, to say "you," or "thou" to him. Actually everything that a person can say further in prayer to God is included in this. For in this saying "you" man does not leave behind him his life and the situation in which he is saying this. On the contrary, therein he relates to God precisely what concerns him; in his saying "you" he brings it before him. If we turn to God from our being happy or joyful and say "you" to him, this becomes an expression of our gratitude. If out of our grief or distress we say it, then our saying "you" becomes a cry for help. If it is said out of our consciousness of our own shortcoming and guilt, then it becomes a plea for forgiveness. And if a man shares in the suffering of a fellowman, or if he feels oppressed by the madly whirling world, then "you" becomes the most concentrated form of intercession. Sometimes we will want to use the specific words — spoken aloud or inwardly — to say in the presence of God what is included in this "you"-saying, but that is not strictly necessary. By our turning to God in the special situation of the moment and calling on him in it, we have, in fact, placed before him our happiness, our distress, or the distress of others, and handed it over to him.

Prayer as not self-evident

In the first chapter we spoke about the self-evidence of God. To whatever extent and whenever God is self-evident to us, that is, when he speaks to us for himself, our praying also is a self-evident matter. For what is more self-evident and more natural than that a man who has experienced God's voice coming to him and who is aware of his covenant relationship with him now also in turn addresses God, and says "you" to him?

> In this light, certain objections which are frequently raised against praying and especially against prayers of petition appear not actually to hold water. Why, it is asked, should a man pray to God for something? After all, God knows, without man's asking for it, what he needs and what is good for him. And besides, God surely will not let himself be influenced by a man's praying! If God were only the Almighty, Omniscient, Unmovable, and Unchangeable, there would indeed be no sense in asking him for anything; and certainly not if he were an impersonal Power, the First Cause, or Being itself. Then any thinking or addressing would be meaningless. But he is a God-of-men, a God who wants to have men as his covenant-partners. Therefore he does react to men's deeds and omissions (page 14), and he does will to let himself be influenced by them. Here it is obvious how closely related is our thinking about prayer with the view of God that we have.

Yet for many people praying is not at all such a self-evident matter in our time. This is partly because in this matter they are thinking of forms that did not present the slightest difficulty to their parents and grandparents, but that for us no longer fit into our manner of life. I am thinking, for example, of the stipulated morning and evening prayers, of kneeling before going to sleep, and particularly of daily prayers with the whole family. It is not merely that we are too busy for all this and that we lack the necessary simplicity and childlikeness (which is something different from childishness). Often a feeling of inward embarrassment toward ourselves or toward others, plays a role, too. But it seems to me that it is not necessary to preserve these forms for dealing with God that functioned in another time. Those who can still deal with God in these forms by all means should not give them up. Those who no longer can do so must not feel guilty because of their inability, but should rather seek for other forms. It may be that simply saying "you," or at least a much briefer and more succinct way of praying, in which we place before God the matters that concern us at a given moment, is a form that comes more easily for people toay. Would not all sorts of what used to be called, somewhat slightingly, "a little prayer" actually have been essentially the same?

But the real difficulties with praying lie elsewhere. They have to do not so much with giving thanks or confessing guilt, but with asking for something, with petitions. This is due to the fact that we have arrived at a different stance in the world. We have already spoken about this in the first chapter: the more nature has become for us predictable and subject to our control, and history has become the result of analyzing forces and human decisions, the less can we believe that God arranges everything that happens in nature and in history, even down to the last detail, from case to case. Therefore we cannot honestly ask in our prayers that he will do this.

But even if formal prayer and explicit requests have become difficult for us, we still can in inward honesty place before God the causes that are near to our hearts, perhaps simply by telling him about them, and perhaps by saying "you" to him, out of our concern. In this "you" then our petition for his help is, so to speak, included, enfolded. Sometimes I think that men and women today pray in this way more often than we realize, and that we pray for more than we can, strictly speaking, justify. But perhaps all of us are in our praying beyond and ahead of our understanding. For this reason also it is so difficult to speak about prayer. It is so easy to say either too much or too little, and one can hardly make it exactly right.

What we may pray for

But this does not relieve us of the responsibility of forming a clear idea of what we can request in prayer with a good conscience. It is not permissible to ask, without discrimination, for everything that we simply hope or wish for, although we may indeed "discuss" everything with God, or tell him about it. Perhaps we can ultimately ask for only two things, in full confidence that God will also grant them. First, we can ask that his will may be done. Not in the sense of our submitting to "whatever God ordains," which often is not much more than adjusting to the inevitable. But God's will is that the world be set right. Said in another way: his will is the Kingdom. Praying that God's will may be done is praying in the direction of the Kingdom, asking for what is in harmony with the Kingdom that is coming (see chapter XX). If it is aimed at this, then the petition can be as concrete as one may wish. Then we may pray for peace in the Middle East, for the liberation of political prisoners, and for the elimination of discrimination. However, this means that we cannot pray in the direction of the Kingdom without also working toward the Kingdom. Praying that God's will may be done has far-reaching ethical, social, and political consequences.

But it is not only God's will that the totality of the world shall reach its goal of fulfillment. He also wills that the life of the individual person shall be whole and sound and shall achieve its destiny (see chapter XVI). In this direction, again, we can ask for quite concrete—and even material—things, such as meaningful work, human friendship, or victory over despair or frustration. But praying for these still may not reduce our responsibility for our own actions: this is so obvious that it hardly needs to be stated.

And in the second place, we can ask for the Holy Spirit, again for ourselves as well as for others. In this we are not asking for something, but for the presence of God, that he will draw us and others to himself, will give strength and comfort, will show us the way in the ordinary course of life and in the special decisions that a person must sometimes make. Again, of course, this petition does not relieve one of the obligation to exert oneself and to use one's sound reason.

But there is still more to say about the connection between the Spirit and prayer. We pray, as we said, in the direction of the Kingdom, in the direction of the goal that God has designed for the world and for man, and in that context we can ask for quite specific things. But the history of humanity and of individual human life is usually not transparent to us, and we often do not know what lies in the direction of the goal that God intends for us. Moreover, how often have people thought that they knew, while a later generation or even they themselves at a later time were convinced that they had been mistaken! That could keep us from praying for specific things in the direction of the Kingdom and in the direction of the fulfillment of our own lives and the lives of others — and then taking concrete action in harmony with such prayer — if we could not believe that the Spirit comes to our aid in our praying. For in our communion with God the Spirit trains us, so that in the course of our lives we learn more and more to see what is God's will for the world, for our fellowmen, and for ourselves. And besides, the Spirit redirects our prayers, if they are not in harmony with the Kingdom. In fact, this is only another way of saying that God hears and accepts our misdirected prayers, which in spite of our intention do not tend in the direction of what he wills.

> The above must not be so exaggerated as to suggest that it is no longer we who pray, but only the Spirit within us. Paul says it differently: the Spirit comes to help us in our weakness (Rom. 8:26). If man himself were excluded from this process, the mututal relationship and reciprocality of God and man would be abolished.

However, there are also very definite boundaries set for our petitions. We may not pray for what God has left, on the basis of his covenant relationship with man, to the freedom of us men (thus, for example, I have been wondering for years whether we may rightly pray for the unity of the churches in the Netherlands). Further, we may not pray that God will interrupt the course of nature for our sake. After all, it is precisely through the order and regularity of nature that God has given a certain security to human life on earth, so that it is livable. Just imagine that we could not depend on the sun's rising the next morning, or that the "law" of gravity should suddenly, altogether arbitrarily, no longer hold. And what is obvious in such trivial examples is also applicable in matters which are less transparent for us, such as the natural course of an illness or of natural phenomena such as earthquakes and droughts. Indeed, is it not precisely The great praying people of the Bible, the psalmists, and the author of the book of Job, were acquainted with it. Praying can also be a calling to God in which we grope and search for him, or even reproach him. We may even express before him our rebellion against him.

Just as on the human plane we will ask another person for something that, given his nature and capacities, he is willing and able to give us, so we may ask God only for what is in harmony with his nature, as we men know it. This is the meaning of our praying "in Jesus' name." Jesus taught us to say "Father" to God, and to pray in his name is meant to remind us who this God is to whom we are praying. And further, the expression, "in Jesus' name," is meant to remind us that our praying and petitioning must be in harmony with Jesus. He has, after all, set an example for us of what God wants of and for man. This includes, among other things, that we cannot pray self-centeredly, concerned only with our own well-being, without at the same time involving our fellowman as well. Is it not, for example, a dubious thing for us here in the Netherlands to dare to pray for our daily bread while people elsewhere are lacking the most basic necessities of life?

Answered prayers

The frequently posed question as to whether praying accomplishes anything and has meaning is actually a wrong question. In our encounter with another person who is dear to us we do not ask whether our speaking with him or her has meaning; the encounter itself comes about precisely in the reciprocal speaking and being spoken to. Thus also the speaking-to-God belongs essentially in the encounter-event of God and man, and its meaning lies in this encounter-event itself.

Yet the figure of addressing and being addressed may not be carried too far. Most people very seldom have the experience that their speaking to God is concretely answered. Hence I also hesitate to say, as is often done, that we must let our speaking to God be followed by a listening for him. It usually happens that there is precious little to hear. Yet, as we said earlier, faith is founded on something like an encounter-experience, an experience of having been addressed by God. God's speaking to us has preceded our speaking, and, we hope, it will also follow it — as surely as the fellowship with God is not only something that a man believes, but also something that he experiences, even if only occasionally. But this experience is never something that is within our power. Very often it will appear that our prayer remains unanswered. This is probably the greatest hindrance to our prayers: the fear that we are praying into empty air, the feeling that the heavens are closed. This hindrance is nothing new. The great praying people of the Bible, the psalmists, and the author of the book of Job, were acquainted with it. Praying can also be a calling to God in which we grope and search for him, or even reproach him. We may even express before him our rebellion against him.

But even when the experience itself is lacking, and when we feel that God is absent, there is the awareness that in spite of everything God hears us when we pray, because he has bound himself to us. There is no such thing as unheard prayer.

But this is not the same as saying that all prayers are answered, that God will do or will grant to us what we ask. It goes without saying that we cannot bend him to our will with our praying; in no way is he ever subject to our manipulation. We should never even try to manipulate him, just as we should never try to do this with our fellowmen. For that would be a lack of respect for the other person, and on such lack of respect any personal relationship is shattered. And we have already said that an answer to our prayers cannot happen in such a way as to disrupt the coherence of human life, of history, and of nature.

A human being cannot perceive how God guides the life of the individual or history in its totality to its destiny. The ultimate future of man and the world is not delivered into human power. It is God's work, but human action — and prayer too is a kind of action — is not thereby negated; in one way or another it is taken up into God's work, and is used by him, though I do not know how. Every prayer that is offered in the direction of the future and with an eye to this future, even when it includes petitions for very specific and merely temporal things (daily bread for those who lack it) is a factor in the consummation which God will bring about. Could you not therefore say that such prayers urge him on toward the consummation, and thus — because in whatever way he will, God takes account of them — collaborate in the consummation?

It may appear that I am too easily dismissing the matter when I speak in this way of answered prayer. But just as God's being Lord over the world is not obvious and cannot be seen, but must be believed, so also we cannot see or prove that he lets himself be influenced by human prayers and grants them. We can only believe it.

> And if then a prayer for healing is in fact followed by healing? May we not even then speak of answered prayer? I believe that this is in fact the case. Otherwise we would again begin to think of a divine intervention in the natural process of the illness. It is medically calculable whether, for example, a certain penicillin product will work on a bacterium. Of course there are many things that physicians do not (yet) know, and they themselves are often surprised. But that still is no reason particularly to attribute to God what the physicians cannot explain or cannot calculate in advance, and just then to speak of an answered prayer.

> But, we ask further, isn't it absurd to pray for healing for ourselves or for someone else, and then when what we pray for actually happens, not to call this an answer to prayer? But the absurdity lies in our prayer for healing. Do we not ask for healing only when we see this as a concrete possibility for which we can hope? And does not this prayer fall silent in case of an incurable illness or at a deathbed, so that we no longer ask for healing but for the presence and help of the Spirit? Perhaps therefore it would be more honest if we did not ask God for healing, but came to him with our concern, our fear, and our hope and laid them before him, telling him about them. And in case of a healing then perhaps we should not speak about an answer to prayer, but rather should once again express our joy and our gratitude to him.

> Or are these distinctions too tortured and over-subtle in an actual life-situation? I do not know.

We can speak of the answering of prayer in still another respect. Prayer not only influences God, but also the person who prays. Where it is something that happens between God and man, that is not surprising. Prayer has a transforming effect upon the person who prays, by strengthening him, by prompting him to action, and above all by its liberating influence upon him. In God's presence he can lay down the matters that trouble and oppress him, so that he does not have to bear the whole lot of them himself. One can shrug this off by saying that it is a purely psychological thing, and that any "quiet time," and calm self-searching, any yoga exercise, can have a similar psychological effect. Indeed, here again it cannot be proved that this influence upon the person who prays is the responsive action of the Spirit. Even of the working of the Spirit we must say that it can only be believed; and, I would want to add, experienced.

Conclusion

It is not merely a hypothetical danger that all the foregoing reflections may take away from praying all the spontaneity and natural naivete. But I fear that a great many people have already lost this spontaneity. It cannot be regained by pretending that all these questions and hindrances do not exist, but by examining them. There is a childlikeness that precedes all questions, but there is also a childlikeness that can be rediscovered when one has gone through all the questions.

In this chapter we have addressed ourselves to the prayer of the individual person. We could also have treated prayer later, in the context of what we say about the church. There is, furthermore, no compelling theological reason for dealing with it in this place. But most people have more difficulty with personal prayer than with the praying that is done in the meeting of the congregation. This is because, on the one hand, tradition is more strongly maintained there, so that the traditional forms of prayer in the liturgy still function. On the other hand, the community also provides for the individual something to hold to; the responsibility for his own prayer is carried in part by the prayers of others. Therefore I have focused the discussion upon personal prayer, for which the individual believer himself must answer. As a matter of fact, most of what is said above holds true precisely in the same way for the prayer of the community.

XVI. THE FUTURE OF OUR LIVES

The essential nature of man is that he may be God's covenant-ally. This nature is not something that is simply available to him; it is the destiny that is given to him by God. For while man is God's ally by virtue of God's initiative, he must ratify this covenantal relationship from his own side. He only lives in that direction; it is still future. Of course not merely future. A person can know out of his own experience what a life as God's covenant-person is. If that were not so, the two preceding chapters would not have been written. But throughout those chapters we had to be careful not to claim too much and thus not to be speaking in conflict with reality. The full realization of our being man with God always lies ahead of us. This gives to the life of Christians an openness and forward-looking orientation, toward the future. And, as we said earlier, that makes their life worthwhile and gives meaning to it.

Death as our future

We are on the way to our destiny, and thus to the future — as long as we live. But our life has a boundary. Every person, whether he is aware of his destiny as a covenant-person or not, is on the way toward death. For every human life here upon earth has an end; someday it will have run its course and will be past. Death is the limit of our life; this is really the only thing we can say about death. We can, looking ahead, experience our death, but we do not really experience death itself, but our earthly life as a life that is characterized by death, limited, finite, mortal.

These last words must be taken with utmost seriousness. It was earlier said (p. 34) that the whole person, body and soul, is human and non-divine. He is wholly creature and as such is limited and perishable. For centuries people have believed that man had an immortal soul, which at death is separated from the body that perishes. We must abandon this idea; it is based upon an image of man that is no longer ours. For by "soul" we do not understand a part of man that can be detached from the whole. We see man as a unity, and in this view his soul (whatever may be our precise understanding of what that means) is not only bound up with his corporeal being, but is wholly interwoven with it. Hence when a man dies, he dies entirely, body and soul.

Moreover, we can no longer accept the notion that death is the punishment for sin, a notion that is found throughout all of church history. We know that long before men existed, death was already present; it is given along with life itself.

Even if man should not sin, he would be a finite creature and his life would have an end, just as it has a beginning. Death is natural and belongs to the life that is given by God.

The story of the so-called fall in Genesis 3 appears to be in conflict with this. In that story death is indeed connected with sin, a view that is also found in the New Testament, specifically in Paul's writings. In chapter V we have called the belief in creation a believing extrapolation of the experience which man has had with his Covenant-God. Then in chapter VII we pointed out that the story of Paradise and the fall must not read as a historical description of how everything came to be as it is now, but that we must understand it as a profound illumination of the human condition, in which we are told how things stand for actual, historical man before God. For the biblical writer it is an inexplicable anomaly that man, every man, sins. But the other fundamental disruptions in the human condition also, death, laborious toil, the ambivalent relationship between man and woman, according to him actually should not have to be so. Thus here we are not given any objective information about some primeval age or another, but we are invited to recognize in this description the human situation of all of us.

> For the great majority of the Old Testament writers, the bad thing about death was that thereby the bond between God and man was definitively severed. Thereby the concepts of life and death acquire a surplus-value. Life is a great good, for it is the time in which a man or the people of Israel can be together with God, and conversely, death is to be feared, because in it man is cut off from God. It is in this light that we must see the connection between death and sin that is set forth in Genesis: through the sin, man on his part breaks the bond with God; through death, now, God from his side, also breaks the bond.

God as our future

As we have said, death is the ultimate horizon of our life. Someday there will come a time when I, as I know myself as a man here upon earth, shall no longer be, a time when everything here will simply go on, but I shall no longer have a part in it. And then? The question seems meaningless. For if in death we shall no longer be, if there is no more time left for us, how then with respect to ourselves could we speak of a "then," of a time after death? Looking from the perspective of life toward death, we cannot think beyond it, and the only thing that we can say is that for us "then" there will be nothing more. But if we are no longer there, God will still be there. This assurance is bound up in our belief in God, in all that we know of him and have experienced of him. This too must be taken seriously. The God who will be there when I no longer am is the Covenant-God, whose very nature it is that he wills to be together with man. And man is always a particular man; he has a face. The God in whom I believe is the God who wills to be with me, who has laid a claim upon me and who wills to have me as his covenant-man or covenant-woman. Even after my death he will still be the same. If this is so, it cannot but be true that even in and beyond my death he will still be my God, and that even then he will still will to have me as his ally. For him I am not interchangeable with another.

In light of this awareness what was said above about death must be further qualified. It is true that for man-by-himself death is the end, but man-by-himself is an abstraction that does not exist. He is always man-with-God. Moreover, we may not say that here at the boundary of life it is only God who is concerned and not man. For God-by-himself also is an abstraction. We know only of a God who has allied himself with man. Hence in the confession that the Covenant-God will still be there even after our death there is the confidence that after our death we shall still be held fast by him and thus even for us there will still be something after death.

There is still another consideration that prompts the same insight. There are quite a lot of Christians who say that for them it is unimportant what happens to them after death, if they may only believe that God achieves his purpose for the world. But the issue is not what we are satisfied with, but what God is satisfied with. Only very imperfectly do we realize in our lives our covenant-destiny. And if God really is like we have come to know him, he cannot be content with man as he is on this side of death. He has started on the way with us; he has revealed himself and his will to us and has transformed our lives by the power of his presence. May we not then also expect that he will achieve his aim with us, that he will cause his covenant to become reality in full reciprocity? Not on the basis of what we desire, but on the basis of what we know of God's will, I cannot believe that death is the end of it all.

> Some have thought that the fact that no one can fully accept, in his feelings, his own death indicates that, consciously or unconsciously, he is aware of a life after death. I cannot judge whether distress over death actually is given with our humanness. But assuming that there is in fact a universal human longing for a "hereafter," that still could not give us the assurance that there is a reality that corresponds to this longing. On the contrary, it would rather have to make us apprehensive that "life after death" is nothing more than wishful thinking. We cannot base the expectation of a future beyond death on what we know of man, but only on our faith in God.

Jesus Christ as the firstfruits

What we have said finds its confirmation in Jesus Christ. He is the only true covenant-partner of God, the only man who has lived out his destiny. In him we see what the full realization of being human is. In him we also see how far the rest of us are from that realization. And above all, in him it has become manifest that God does not grow weary of his covenant-partner and that he does not allow the bond between himself and his covenant-partner to be broken by death. Jesus, too, like every man, died, body and soul, because he too was subject to all the limitations that are given with our being human. But death was not the final word. The conviction that after his death he still is alive belongs to the center of the Christian faith. The believers in the Old Testament times already knew that God willed not death but life. The resurrection is the indubitable sign of that.

But if we may speak here of a sign, this implies that Jesus' resurrection is not an isolated event. As surely as he arose, so also we shall arise. He was not raised as the only one, but as the firstfruits, to use Paul's language (I Cor. 15:20). For Jesus is not merely a man, but *the* man, in whom, on the basis of God's election, all men are comprehended (see above, p. 68). Therefore all men are also included in his resurrection. Jesus Christ represents us in his obedience. He also represents us in his resurrection-life; we shall also share in it.

Here the question is immediately posed whether this sharing in Christ's resurrection-life is only future. Is it something that awaits us after our death, or is it a reality now? We are, after all, dead to sin, as Paul says, and transplanted into a new life; and that is something so unbelievable that it is like being born again, like a new creation. This new life is a life of following Jesus, a life that comes more and more to resemble his. And this gives an answer to the question that was posed. Our new covenant-life is a life that is becoming like the earthly life of Jesus. The full resurrection-life, conforming to that of the exalted Lord, still awaits us. Stated even more strongly: it is precisely the new life now that gives us a vision of that life. For only as we experience what it is to live as God's ally in his presence do we realize also that it is no more than a hesitant and imperfect beginning and thus begin to long for the full achievement of it. Said in another way: it is only the experience of communion with God through the Spirit that arouses our longing for unbroken communion with him. This is what the New Testament means when it calls the Spirit the "earnest" of our hope.

The new life that we already know even now is not the same as the future resurrection-life, but it cannot be detached from that. And again we look to Jesus Christ. His resurrection did not nullify or negate his earlier life; on the contrary, we have understood it as the exposition and ratification of his life (p. 61). If we may believe in our conforming to him, this will also hold true for our resurrection-life. This conclusion is confirmed by the fact that the words "life" or "eternal life" are used in the New Testament, and especially by Paul and John, for the present as well as for the future life. The person who believes now already has (eternal) life; he is transposed into a new order of existence, in which, as it were, he has already left death behind him. Even now his earthly life is a "life after death," lived in a relationship with God which cannot be nullified even by the end of his earthly existence. And what the future beyond this earthly life can bring him is the perfecting of it and the unveiling of what now can only be believed and hoped for, but not yet seen. Thus the great contrast in the New Testament is not that between life and death in the ordinary sense of the terms, but that between belief and unbelief.

> In the New Testament the words "death" and "life" have a biological meaning, and they also point to a quality of life. For that matter, the same is true also in our own usage; we say, for example, that someone only began to live after he married. On the other hand, the New Testament does not say that the resurrection has already occurred. The noun refers exclusively to a future event, and the verbs "to arise" and "to raise" are used primarily in the future sense. In this connection it must be remembered that John forms an exception to this rule; he attaches such great weight to eternal life in the present that he is hardly interested at all in a future resurrection.

Life after death

Out of the present time, in which the gracious power of the Covenant-God is experienced, faith comes to the confession that he is the Creator (chapter III). And just as the logic of faith prompts us to extend the line backward, this logic also prompts us to extend the line forward, toward the future. This holds true for the individual as well as for the totality of things. Just as God is the Creator of the world, so also will he perfect it; and just as he is the Creator of my life, so also will he bring my life to its consummation. But we do not know what this perfection will look like; this, after all, lies beyond all that we now know or understand.

Hence one could say that here, at this ultimate boundary, we must fall silent, that it is sufficient for a person to know that it is not nothingness that awaits him there, but God. When we now try to say something to suggest the content of the life after death, we do not give a description of something that surpasses our capacity to imagine, but we are only pointing, by means of images, in symbolic language, in the direction in which, we hope and trust, the future of eternal life lies.

In the words "eternal life" indeed there is already some content implied. Eternity is something that pertains to God alone; it is a symbol which, without describing, declares that (not how!) the eternal God has to do with us in our earthly time and yet at the same time transcends it, goes beyond it (above, p. 18). Without plunging into philosophical reflections, we can say that "eternal life" indicates that in some way or another our life after death is drawn into God's time-order. Similarly, the childish-sounding words about our going "to heaven" declare that we shall be together with God, in this case with a figure of a spatial kind. Heaven is after all the figure for God's transcendence in which he is with us here on earth (p. 18). The fact that life after death surpasses any conception is clearly indicated when it is characterized as "glorification." "Glory" also is once again something that actually belongs to God alone. It is like a blinding light that human eyes cannot bear. And when a man is glorified, he is, so to speak, drawn into this impenetrable light and thereby he receives a share in God's glory. Glorification points toward a transposing of human life into a "glorius" new form of being human in God's presence.

> The word "glory" is appropriated from the Old Testament. There it means, literally, "weight," and then that which gives weight to a person, or renders him imposing (from this then the transition to the meaning of "honor"). Said of God, it is the power of his appearing, when he reveals himself, and then especially the blinding brilliance that shines forth from him (Ex. 24:15; Ezek. 1:27, 28). Not until the time of salvation will this glory, that is, God himself in the power of his deity, dwell upon earth, and man be permitted to hold it. In Jesus Christ this is fulfilled, and still not yet fulfilled. In him God's glory has come to dwell among us, and through the Spirit men also can reflect this glory. Yet the full disclosure of God's glory, as well as man's participation in it, is reserved for the future. Thus in the New Testament also the word continues to hold the eschatological significance which it had in the (later parts of the) Old Testament.

Thus all these references to life after death point to our relationship with God. We do not know what it will be like, but we cannot conceive of it other than being a perfect state of communion with him. This also lies in the very nature of the matter, for precisely that which is experienced through the Spirit even now by way of fellowship with God gives us the assured expectation that beyond death this will be brought to perfection, and that then there will be a communion with God and a knowledge of him that will be more direct and complete than it is now. Hence we also can understand Paul's speaking of a seeing "face to face" and the common reference in dogmatics to a "beatific vision" of God, although that figure perhaps appears somewhat too static and too specifically esthetic for us.

If we cannot conceive of the resurrection life other than as an unfolding and perfecting of what we have seen and experienced in this life as our destiny, this includes also the full realization of our relationship with our fellowmen. The Bible also uses figures that point to this: a banquet, a wedding, a festival. Hence I do not understand why the question whether in the hereafter we shall see and recognize the people whom we have loved is usually swept under the table as altogether too naive — often with the remark that the blessedness of being with God will blot out all else. But if we may hope that our humanness will, in whatever way, be saved and brought to its full destiny, why then may we not also hope that the same holds true for our human love which is an integral part of our humanness? And if we may hope that our relationship with God will prevail beyond death, why not then our relationship also with those whom we love, which on the interpersonal human plane is the portrayal and reflection of that relationship with God?

Resurrection and judgment

The foregoing could give the impression that the line is being too easily drawn from our earthly life to the life beyond death. Hence the image of the resurrection is important. It reminds us that death signifies an end for us and that a new creative act of God is required, just as inscrutable as that of his original creation, if there is to be any life beyond death. The image of resurrection is intended also to express the idea that the whole person is involved in this matter. I myself die and, thanks to God's faithfulness, I myself await the resurrection life. I do not know what this "I myself" is, and therefore I likewise do not know wherein the identity of this "I myself" now and then will consist. But I believe that I shall have the same "face" in God's presence.

And then the idea of the judgment. First of all, this too is a figure, a reference to something that we anticipate because it issues from all that we now know of God. We have come to know him as the God who says "no" to the life that turns away from him, "no" to our selfishness and greed, "no" to all our lovelessness and inhumanity. He judges and rejects all this, because all this is, to use John's terminology, death. But he also sets human life right — and this is also included in the term "to judge." Or, to use another figure: like a physician he cuts away what is dead, and this cutting away is perhaps a very painful operation for man; and perhaps more must be cut away in the case of one man than in the case of another. But, to maintain this same image, the purpose in this is that the person actually shall be healthy, really and fully alive. For real and full life is perfect communion with God, it is resurrection life.

It follows from the foregoing that I can do nothing with the idea of a hell. And by this I mean not only the idea of hell as the "place" where after death people are punished and tortured in terrible ways, but also hell as a designation for being finally dead for all eternity, that is, being separated from God, and thus as rendering eternal man's turning away from God in this life. It is said that the idea of judgment with its alternative of heaven or hell underscores our human responsibility; our decision for or against God has eternal import. But the entire message of Christ is precisely that we are not held fast by our guilt. To believe in Christ means to believe in the boundless love and faithfulness of God, and to believe also in his creative omnipotence whereby he sets aright the misused human life even beyond death. For only thus does God receive his own rightful due, by setting men right.

1. The Apostles' Creed speaks of a resurrection of the flesh. This expression can easily arouse misunderstanding. The words are intended to reject the idea of a soul that is in itself immortal, to counter the depreciation of the physical side of being human, and to affirm the resurrection of the whole person, the man himself. Whether the resurrection life also includes a new, glorified bodily state, as Paul surmised, is in my opinion of no importance for faith; we will do well not to speculate about that (see also p. 61).

2. It is demonstrated by experience that belief in reward and punishment, heaven and hell, is not necessary to maintain morality. Paul's opinion in I Cor. 15:32, that if a person does not believe in the resurrection he then will live dissolutely, appears as a general rule not to hold true.

3. According to the Bible, resurrection and judgment of the individual person will not take place immediately after death, but only at the end of time, at the so-called return of Christ. This idea is meaningful in the sense that it gives expression to the interconnection of the individual life with that of all men. Our life is embedded in the totality of history, and therefore only with the end of history will it find its actual manifestation and transformation. But this again is figurative language and not information that tells something about the time and duration of time after death. Therefore I consider the question of what will happen to us in the "time" between our death and the end of history not only to be unanswerable but in essence wrong. We cannot know whether there will be a time in between — in the sense that "time" has in our earthly life.

Summary

The hope of a personal life after death is not a central concern in our times. As a reaction against an earlier overemphasis on the "hereafter" this is both understandable and healthy. For by emphasizing the "hereafter" the value of life here and now often was implicitly denied. Man today is, on the contrary, conscious that this earthly life is the life that God has given and that it is his intention for his will to be done by men in this life and on this earth. What will come "hereafter" is not our concern; to orient ourselves to that draws us away from what must be done here and now.

This line of thinking is so strongly rooted in present-day thinking that many believers feel themselves directly addressed by it. And indeed, the life after death cannot be the center of gravity for faith; that center lies rather in the relationship with God. Generations of Old Testament believers knew of the love and faithfulness of the Covenant-God without hoping for a life with him after death. This must cause us to think, for it is an indication that the convenantal communion with God does not stand or fall with the hope of a personal future.

Yet, curiously enough, in this chapter it has become evident that all that we said earlier about God, about Jesus Christ, and about life through the Spirit tends, with an inner logic of faith that appears to me unavoidable, toward this hope. In this chapter, indeed, we have only thought through to their consequence the lines which had already been drawn. All the preceding discussion issued in this chapter, so that, seen from this perspective, without this chapter the previous ones actually were not complete.

Hence we may cherish this hope. Through it, life here and now can become worthwhile. The assurance that at the end it is God — and thus not nothing but everything — that awaits us, can make our existence, in spite of all its frustrations, sorrow, and difficulties, a great adventure, moving toward the future. But it is not that we *must* hope, but that we *may*. Here again it is true that Christianity is not a number of doctrinal truths that must be believed. It may be that the logic of faith which is persuasive for many is not so for many other believers. It may also be true that this logic is indeed for some compelling for faith-reasoning, but the heart cannot grasp it. Similarly, it may be that the heart wants to hope, but the understanding cannot grasp it. That is not of essential importance. What is of such importance is only the living covenantal communion with God and the doing of his will here and now in covenantal relationship with him, even if the believer cannot believe in a personal life after death. For even those who, in the words of I Peter (1:3), are born again to a living hope, know that their future rests not on their hope but solely on God's covenant.

XVII. THE CHURCH

The church as fellowship in Christ

Personal belief in Christ and fellowship belong together. This has been true from the very first. The first believers did not first come to faith and then thereafter join themselves together. It is essential for faith that it is oriented to fellowship and it creates fellowship. It was the immediate encounter with the risen Lord whereby the disciples became Christians and which at the same time brought them together into a Christian fellowship. And where Jesus Christ is proclaimed as the crucified and risen one, ever again new persons are grasped by God's presence and are incorporated into this fellowship. Where the Holy Spirit — that is, God's overpowering love in Christ — makes people into believers, fellowship is formed. Christian fellowship is no more derivable from man alone than is faith itself.

This does not mean that it develops apart from man. It is after all persons who constitute this fellowship and who desire it. Here the same thing as was said about faith holds true, namely that it is both the gift of God and the will of man, and both totally, without diminution of one by the other. So also the Christian fellowship is a gift of the Spirit, but it does not develop apart from the will of men.

> The question whether Jesus himself "founded" the church is one that is still constantly being debated, which is implicitly answered in the negative in what is said above. It is true that during his lifetime Jesus formed a community with his closest followers, and it was natural for this community to continue after his death, at least when through his resurrection it became evident that following Jesus had not been a mistake. But we may first speak of the church where people believe in Jesus' message and in his cross and resurrection and where they desire to transmit this belief to others.

This fellowship is experienced. It is not an idea, and moreover it is not merely an inner feeling, but it is experienced in its functioning. One could say that this fellowship must happen again and again. It happens in that those who believe in Christ strengthen each other in their faith; in that they come together to offer thanks to God and to celebrate their salvation; and in that they help and support each other in their daily lives in all sorts of ways.

I deliberately refer to what is called "ecclesia" in the New Testament and what we call church or congregation as Christ's fellowship, for the inward bond of unity of Christians in their belief in Christ and in service to each other is essential to it.

Further, it is not sufficient for us to say that we believe in this fellowship. Fellowship, or community, is something that is really experienced — or it is no fellowship. For example, only because for Paul this mutual bond was a reality could he write about the community as he did in his epistles. And this bond was evident to outsiders as well. They could see that Christians helped each other and that they assembled to do certain things together. It is significant also that the same word, "church," is used for the local congregation and for all Christians together. The fellowship is in principle worldwide. In New Testament times this was expressed in the fact that a group of Christians here would help a group elsewhere, that they conveyed greetings to each other, and that they sympathized with each other. But the reciprocal bond becomes a reality first of all where Christians are directly and personally engaged with each other in matters of the faith. A local church is not the whole church, but it is fully church. Said even more strongly: it is precisely in the immediate association in the local fellowship that the church can be most intensely experienced.

> The Greek word "ecclesia" also appears in non-religious language, and there it signifies an assembly (of the people; see Acts 19:32). On this basis some theologians think that the assembling of Christians in worship is the basic form of the "ecclesia." But regardless of how important the worship service may have been in the early church, it is primarily in that context that the New Testament speaks of the "ecclesia," but in the context of the experience of mutual love and mutual service.

This Christian fellowship is indeed an experienced reality, but it is not perfect, and it has never been perfect. And I am not thinking primarily of those people who act so manifestly in conflict with the spirit of this fellowship (and this spirit is the spirit of Christ, the Holy Spirit) that they commit treason against the mutual bond and thus place themselves outside the fellowship. The community's expelling them then is an unavoidable consequence. Moreover, there will always be people who do not clearly and obviously place themselves outside the fellowship, but who do so more subtly, by their inner attitude. Now it is in the very nature of every community of persons that it includes members who do not really belong to it. The larger the community is, the more unavoidable that is. But this is not what I mean when I say that the Christian fellowship is not perfect. Even in the fellowship of the disciples of Jesus Christ there is a great deal that should not be there: human vanity, lack of consideration for others, deep-seated differences of opinion, childish bickering. One need only read the epistles of Paul to see how much strife and conflict raged in this very community about which the same Paul could write in such lofty terms. Paul was not thinking from the perspective of an ideal concept of the church that existed only in his imagination, but from the perspective of the experience of an imperfect Christian community that actually existed and that created a yearning for a fuller, unbroken bond of unity in which the spirit of Christ alone, and nothing else, would rule. Only when we have experienced something of this fellowship, in which Christians help each other and stand together for their task, do we know that it is less of a fellowship than it should be and can be. The church is on the way to being itself, and it has been so since the very beginning.

The gifts of the Spirit

We began this chapter by pointing out that the church is a community which is formed and maintained by the Spirit. That is nothing but an empty boast unless it is immediately added that it is *people* who together form this fellowship. As is the case with every human community, so also with this one it is true that there are tasks and functions that must be fulfilled if the community itself is to be able to function. And it is people that must perform these tasks. But in this case these people are disciples of Christ who are impelled by their faith — or, better said, by the power of God's love — to place themselves at the service of the Christian community. It is the Holy Spirit — the same Spirit who makes these persons into believers — who equips and enables them for this service. Once again it is Paul who above all has clearly seen that the structure of the church must be defined by the gifts which the Spirit gives to the members. In the preceding chapter we pointed out that a person can live as a Christian only by the presence of God, that is, by the Spirit. Faith, love (and thus fellowship also), and hope are awakened by the Spirit. This same working power of God also gives to the believers certain gifts. Thus there are in the community some who have the special gift of preaching, other who have the gift of perceiving what action is required by the community in a particular situation, and still others who have the gift of providing pastoral help to their fellow believers and supporting them in material need, or of teaching them, or of giving leadership to the community life or to special assemblies. Paul indeed mentions still other gifts which evidently functioned in the communities that he knew, such as the gift of performing wonders, or of healing the sick, or of speaking in tongues. According to him, everyone has a special gift (see, for example, I Cor. 7:7), and all these various gifts serve, each in its own way, for building up the community that is at issue, it is not surprising that Paul regarded speaking in tongues as not very important. Glossolalia after all goes beyond the understanding and conscious will of man and is incomprehensible for others, and thus it is less able than other gifts to contribute to the establishing of the community (cf. I Cor. 14:1-19).

Because all the various gifts are given for the service to the community, it would necessarily be unthinkable for them to be in competition with each other. Not everyone can do everything, not everyone has all the gifts; where the believers together form the community, they are dependent upon each other. Paul's figurative language is suggestive: the community is like a human body, with its diverse members and sensory organs. When every believer actually thus places his gift at the service of the whole, or, differently stated, when each one allows himself in the use of his gift to be guided by love for others, the church is built up to be a body, Christ's body.

Gifts of the Spirit, or, to use the biblical term, charismata, are not the same thing as the natural talents of a person. But it likewise is not true that the two have nothing to do with each other. When a person comes into the magnetic field of God's love, it can happen that his natural abilities are thereby activated and placed in service. Then he appears to be able to do things and to have capacities which perhaps he never even suspected of himself. Therefore also it is not correct to think of charismata primarily in terms of exceptional or ecstatic phenomena. Anyone who is able, though perhaps very stammeringly and tentatively, actually to comfort a fellowman in distress experiences this as a gift from God, a gift of his Spirit, for which he can only be heartily grateful. Or anyone who has the gift of helping, by means of a question or a comment, to get a conversation of a group of Christians back on track, when it is in danger of getting lost in inanities or in misunderstanding, will himself be surprised at this, and it will make him very modest; he knows that perhaps the next time it will not succeed. For the Spirit is not the possession of man, and in the gifts that he gives we still remain dependent upon God. However, as we have already said, since in these gifts we are also dealing with the natural endowment of a person, we can also speak of exercising gifts. Pastoral ability and techniques of dialogue, to stay with the two examples just cited, can in fact be learned, to a certain extent. But in spite of this, there is also the experience that with all one's natural ability and with all the possible training, one is lifted above and beyond oneself by God.

Hence a charisma, in the biblical sense of the word, is not something that is objectively demonstrable. There is no definable dividing line between a natural talent and a special gift of the Spirit. Christ's community, which is aware of the power of God's presence, will speak of a charisma where outsiders see nothing but innate abilities or possibly parapsychological talents.

It follows from all the above that the various gifts that function in the community for its edification cannot be precisely determined once and for all. Even the summaries of them which Paul gave are not systematic; he lists them more or less as they occur to him (cf. I Cor. 12 and Rom. 12:6-8). Hence there is no reason to assume that his summaries are complete. Why, for example, should the artistic ability with which poets serve the Christian community not also be a charisma of the Spirit? It is equally unreasonable to assume that in other times other gifts could not also come forward. Might we not pray in our time that to some there might be given the charisma of imagination to see new forms for the upbuilding and the structure of the Christian fellowship? Or the charisma of being able to listen, to understand, and to interpret what another is saying? That would even be in line with the gift of interpreting tongues, about which Paul speaks.

> I am aware that I have not devoted any attention to the ecstatic, charismatic phenomenon of speaking in tongues. I cannot say anything sensible on this subject, for without wishing to deny it, I must say that this lies completely outside all that I have ever experienced or shared. But on the basis of the New Testament I may say that this ecstatic element may not be allowed to occupy a central place. From what is handed down to us about Jesus we do not get the impression that he was an ecstatic.

> It is another matter with the gift of prophecy, which is repeatedly mentioned in the New Testament. This was a non-ecstatic charisma which was highly regarded in the earliest community. It can best be described as an actualizing of salvation, the interpretation and proclamation of God's saving intention for the present time and for the future.

Twofold service

Because the church is the fellowship of those who recognize that they are God's covenant-partners (recall chapter XIV), the community as a whole also is God's partner, his covenant-people. This also implies that the church lives in discipleship to Christ. As the only perfect covenant-ally, Jesus Christ, with respect to the time that lies behind him, is the summation and representative of Israel, and with respect to the time ahead of him, he is that for all humanity. The church is that part of humanity that accepts this representation and therefore also means to live as represented by him. And that is the same thing as being his disciples. In terms of content, this amounts to a life in service to God and to humanity.

But as essential as this twofold service is, we still must not speak about it too immediately and exclusively. It is true that God's chief concern is not the church but the world. But at the same time we may say that he is truly concerned with the church. God, who in his very nature is Covenant-God, is after all concerned with men as his covenant-people. And this is, in spite of all the imperfection and provisionality, the community that wills to be reflected in Jesus Christ and that knows and believes that God is its covenant-ally and that he wants it to be his covenant-people. Even the fact that the church itself is only on the way to becoming itself does not diminish that fact.

But once that is said, it must immediately be added that this covenant-people stands in the service of God and of the world. Or, actually, the two may not be so loosely connected. To be in God's service, to do his will, means a being-there for the world; and service to men, doing for them what they need, means that doing what God wills, and is thus service to God, worship (Translator's note: In the Dutch there is a play on words here. The word translated "worship" is, literally, "God's service," and thus a combination of the two words earlier combined in the form translated as "service to God.").

It is impossible here even to give an approximate description of what all this service to men in service to God includes. In any case it is the same thing as doing everything that contributes to the salvation and blessing of the world. And the world's salvation is to live as God wills for it to live. Therefore the most fundamental service that the church can offer to men is to tell them who God is and to say to them that they may live as his men under his gracious lordship. In this "telling" I include more than just proclamation, instruction, and personal testimony. In our time it frequently can better take place in group or personal conversations; and presumably there are a great many other forms, such as, for example, film or theater. Here it goes without saying that this "telling" becomes unbelievable if it is not matched by the quality of life of the person who does the telling.

But service for the blessing of mankind also includes concern for its (continuing) existence, concern for humanity's welfare, working for peace, taking a stand against injustice and oppression. These are not the ultimate values, and they do not constitute full salvation and real peace with God. But Jesus too concerned himself with penultimate things, as Bonhoeffer called them. The physical healings that he performed were not the ultimate salvation, but they were indications that pointed toward it. The community, too, in discipleship to him, may and must concern itself with the healing of what is sick. In our changed time, this healing then will certainly have also a political and social form.

We can summarize this entire service or ministry under the concept of "mission." The community is, in service to God, sent to the world in order to be of service to the world. And this mission is not an optional pursuit, a hobby, of a few, but is committed to the entire fellowship with all its members. In this connection again it holds true that not everyone can and must do everything. In this respect also the members will complement each other, and there will be groups of Christians who will devote themselves, in the name of others, to a particular aspect of this service to the world. Here then once again we may think of the various gifts, the charismata, that God gives. It is true that these are spoken of in the New Testament only with respect to the building-up of the community. But because the community cannot be detached from its mission, we may also extend the line that Paul drew to include the community's ministry to mankind. And the mission is not only committed to the entire church, but it also extends to the entire world. It is genuinely "ecumenical." The near neighbor, people close at hand, are included just as surely as are people far away, and our post-Christian fellowmen just as surely as the pre-Christian ones.

And then the other side, service to God for the sake of the world: the community performs this service by living and acting as God's covenant-people (that is its worship; see the translator's note above, p. 117), and by doing this vicariously for all humanity. The world cannot (yet) worship God, cannot (yet) bring its needs and its hopes before him, cannot (yet) recognize his lordship over it; it does not (yet) know peace, and it does not (yet) live in the freedom of God's reconciliation. Meanwhile, with all its imperfection, the Christian community does this provisionally for the world, in its place. As we have summarized the service to the world with the key word "mission," so here we could speak of "pro-existence."

Service to men and service to God, mission and pro-existence, together constitute the priesthood of the believers. For this is the quintessence of being a priest: that one appears before God on behalf of men, and that one represents God, as it were, before men. Thus also the community in its mission to the world may represent God in Christ, because it reflects him on the human plane, however partially and imperfectly, and in its worship it may represent the world before him.

> The idea of the universal priesthood is taken primarily from I Peter 2:5,9. There the two aspects which we have identified also appear; the believers as a holy priesthood bring spiritual sacrifices to God, and they proclaim to the world his mighty acts.

> The priesthood of all believers received a strong emphasis in the Reformation with a clearly polemical thrust aimed at the Catholic hierarchy. This explains why even now this concept frequently has an individualistic content: every believer is a priest, that is, everyone has direct access to God. In our times the concept is even so sharply narrowed that it often signifies not much more than everyone's having his say. But I do not believe that it is right to think first of all of the individual, nor of the personal relationship with God. The believers together form a "spiritual house" and a "holy nation" and are, as such, a holy priesthood, in the sense that is indicated above. Of course it is also true that this priesthood consists of believers, and that thus every believer is called to be "priest." But it is asking too much of the individual if therein he is detached from the community. Here again it holds true that it is not necessary for everyone to do everything.

The marks of the church

Summing up what has been said up to this point, we can speak of three identifying marks of the church: that it really is a community, that it stands in service to God, and that it performs its service for the world. But then the question is posed whether this description of the church does not float entirely above the reality. Have we not come out again with an idea of the church instead of the actual church? I would want to add here what I said earlier with respect to Paul. The church which we have described is not an idea, but it is an ideal. And we speak about it in this way because we have experienced, seen, and noted something of this "ideal." Perhaps not in the "official" church and the activities which it has organized. Perhaps we have experienced the Christian community in a youth or student fellowship, in a Bible study or discussion group, or in a work-group of people who came together for a specific task in service to God. And perhaps — why not? — in the worship service or an assembly of the "official" parish. But a momentary experience is not enough. If it was an experience of an actual relationship, then it brought with it a responsibility and a concern for each other. And this too is not merely an ideal, but also a reality that we have experienced now and then.

And the church that subsists in its being in service to God for the blessing and salvation of the world — this too is an ideal, but yet also a reality that we have experienced; and perhaps once again not primarily in the "official" church, but in groups that strive for the blessing and well-being of others. And then once more: why not also in the "official" church, as it is — sometimes — thrown open to the need of the world, as it — sometimes — dares to protest against injustice, as it — sometimes — through its preaching, through its re-telling, actually transmits the gospel, the good news of God's ultimate salvation?

If we go by these identifying marks of the church, it follows that a group of Christians in or even outside the "official" church can really be church. Not the whole church, but a genuine manifestation of the church; but this only (1) when it is aware of being related to, and exhibits this relationship with, the world-wide Christian fellowship; (2) when it is conscious that the service that it renders can only be a part of the service that is committed to this world-wide fellowship by God, so that is also remains dependent upon others, and (3) when it does not cut itself off, does not become an in-group in which not everyone can find a place. Such a group then will be able, at least in principle, to observe the Lord's Supper together.

What we know "officially" as church is that only in a very partial way, and sometimes we have the impression that it is only barely so. For even though it recognizes and confesses that it is a community that belongs to God and that it exists only in order that his will may be done on earth, in actuality all too often it leaves us out in the cold, we cannot experience any fellowship in it, and it does not allow God's lordship again and again to be a reality. When all this is the case, it can hardly be any comfort to say that it is still on the way to being itself. In any case, no one needs to tell us that it is not the kingdom of God, and not even a provisional portrayal of the kingdom. We surely see that for ourselves. We may not expect perfection of the church. But it is church only when it is a fellowship that is in service to God and to the world; if it is so little in that service that nothing of it can be perceived or experienced, then it is no church. Hence the three characteristic marks mentioned above have a critical, judging function in relation to all existing forms of the church, in relation to all that calls itself church.

> I regard the terminology of the visible and the invisible church as misleading. Because the church is an experienceable community which performs a twofold service, it is by definition visible. But it is true that this visible community has a side that is a matter of faith. That it is the Spirit that forms and maintains this community, and that it serves God, and that it really is working for the salvation and blessing of the world, all this can be said only from the perspective of faith.

> Since the Council of Constantinople in 381, the characteristic marks and criteria of the church have been listed as its unity, holiness, catholicity, and apostolicity. Insofar as these concepts point to certain aspects of the church, I am glad to adopt them. We ourselves have said above that the church as a community is one in the reciprocal relation of its members. It can also make good sense to call it holy, catholic, and apostolic, although these adjectives are not used of the church in the New Testament. It is "holy," because it is sanctified and belongs to the sphere of God's holiness; God has called it together and laid claim to it. It is "catholic," because it is comprehensive and inclusive. It is intended for all men, of whatever race, tribe, status, or color of skin, and it does not *a priori* exclude anyone; moreover, it does not tie itself to one particular aspect of saving truth, but is inclusive with respect to content as well. And it is "apostolic," because it is oriented to Christ and knows of him solely through the apostles' witness to him; it believes the apostolic testimony concerning Christ and hands on that testimony to others.

> The churches of the Reformation did not deny these *notae* (characteristic marks), but they did in fact place ahead of them the marks of the pure preaching of the gospel and the right observance of the sacraments. And these are indeed also important functions of the church.

> But both the Catholic and the Reformation marks appear to me not to get to the heart of the matter. The church that can be described in these terms is, to my way of thinking, too static and too much an end in itself.

Office and church order

It is not possible for us to subscribe directly to what the New Testament identifies as office, because this word does not appear there. In a sense, then, we shall ourselves have to give content to the term. Office has to do with certain functions which must be fulfilled so that the church as a community can function in its twofold service. Stated still more precisely: it is these functions that hold the community to its discipleship to Christ by holding it to him.

Earlier in this chapter we spoke about the diverse gifts that the Spirit gives to believers for the building-up of the community, so that it can actually function as community. The members with their various charismata are at the service of each other, and they affect each other in relation to Jesus Christ and in his commission for them in service to the Kingdom. Thus there is obviously no conflict between charisma and office. Certain charismata can be institutionalized in an office. In the case of the charisma, the accent is placed on the free gift of the Spirit, given to certain persons for the service of the whole company, and in the case of the office the accent lies on the functions which must be fulfilled for the sake of the whole company. Those who are charismatically gifted naturally come to the fore, and office-holders are named or elected. However, what is involved is nothing more than a difference of accent. For in the purely charismatic structure of the Pauline communities they also recognized the special gifts of those who performed specific services for the church, even though this recognition appeared more in practice than in a public official declaration. And in the ministerial structure, which from the second generation of Christians onward became the dominant pattern, those were chosen as ministers of whom it was assumed that they had received the charisma for the ministry. Whether a certain man actually has the gift for a particular ministry cannot be determined by the community with certainty. It undoubtedly happens that the community is mistaken in this judgment. But, as we said earlier, a charisma does not necessarily involve something outside the talents or the innate gifts of the person. It can be determined with a certain degree of probability whether a person, considered in ordinary human perspective, is suited for a particular ministry (cf. I Tim. 3:1-13). And this can be an indication of God's charisma. Thus a particular charisma is, as it were, the spiritual inner side of the ministry.

From the above, the following conclusions can be drawn:

1. The ministry does not arise out of the community, for it is God who through his Spirit equips people for particular ministerial functions in the community. Then it likewise is not primarily the function of the ministers to represent the community, but to build it up. Their work is more oriented within the community than outside it. When this is forgotten, almost inevitably the office contributes to the narrowing of the universal priesthood, of which of course the ministers too form a part. Thus they do not stand alongside or over against the community, but altogether within it.

2. But furthermore, we cannot simply say that the ministries are given and established by God. He gives persons who have received the charisma to perform particular services and functions in the community. We do not label all these services as ministries, but only those which bring to the community's memory Christ's salvation and which define the community in terms of that salvation. The official structure brings order in the community by regulating the charismatic ministries. This is a human arrangement, but that by no means suggests a condemnation of it. Only if everything is done in order can everyone have what is his due in the community, and the community can optimally fulfill its service to God and to the world.

3. The official structure must provide opportunity for others also, in addition to the ministers, to use the gifts that are given to them. It is not only the ministers who have the charisma of presenting Christ's salvation, and there are also other gifts of the Spirit besides those that are regarded as offices. The ministry serves the community in order to build it up. It may not be used in such a way that it oppresses the community, or in such a way that it stands in the way of the universal priesthood of a mature church more than it promotes that priesthood. Church order is what determines which ministries there shall be in the church and defines the function of each ministry. What has just been said about the official structure applies here too: church order too is a completely human arrangement. It orders the life and work of the church, both inwardly and outwardly. Therefore it cannot be fixed once and for all, but it is governed in part by the constantly changing world in which the church must perform its ministry. For although the Christian community is nor formed or guaranteed by whatever form of church order, it is foolishness to suppose that it could ever exist outside such a form.

guaranteed by whatever form of church order, it is foolishness to suppose that it could ever exist outside such a form.

On the basis of this reflection I refer once more to what was said earlier, that a group of Christians that is actually a fellowship in service to God and to the world can be a full manifestation of the church, and that therefore in such a community — in principle — the forgiveness of sin can be pronounced, the blessing can be given, the Lord's Supper can be celebrated, and baptism can be administered. It may be that the church order does not allow all this. If in such a case the violation of this order actually would be a hindrance to the proper functioning of the whole church, this freedom must be foregone. But it must be kept prominently in view that church order exists solely in order that the Christian community in its worldwide scope can fulfill its service as well as possible, and that it may not lead a life of its own alone. Tis is the criterion by which every existing church order must be measured. Therefore sometimes, precisely for the sake of the Christian community, an existing order will have to be violated, in the hope that thereby a better one will be created.

The one worldwide fellowship

I have not spoken about the problem of the many churches and the one church. The emergence of the various separated churches can be described historically, but it is in fact an anomaly, and from the perspective of the nature of the church it is just as unexplainable as is sin from the perspective of the nature of man. If one takes as a starting point the critical concept of the church that I have tried to develop in this chapter, then the various churches — insofar as they really are churches — with their various church orders and their various ministries are one Christian community. For if it is true that church order and office are human and thus are relative, they cannot destroy the unity. Here also it holds true that the various churches can indeed be fully valid manifestations of the worldwide church, but that no one church can do everything. Every church is dependent on the others. Only in relationship with each other can they all together, in mutual service, completely perform the service to God and to the world to which they are called. And might we not in this connection also extend Paul's line and say that every church has its own special charisma for the edifying of the one body? In light of all the preceding, it is self-evident that this body will be visible in the reciprocal relationship of the churches and can be experienced. But in this respect also it once again becomes manifest that the church is only on the way to being itself.

XVIII. PORTRAYAL

AND CELEBRATION OF SALVATION

A. Baptism

The sacred drama

Becoming a Christian is conversion, a turning away from the old life and entering upon a new life, rebirth, letting God's forgiveness in Christ's death and resurrection be true for oneself, following after Christ and beginning to resemble him. All this happens when a person comes into the magnetic field of God's love and when thereby his life, as it were, is swept clean. And when this happens to him, he is thereby incorporated into the community of those to whom the same thing has happened. This is the kernel and the summation of chapters XIV and XVII. And now all this can be said precisely so of baptism. Through baptism man is involved in Christ's death and resurrection, he is born again and transplanted into a new life and is added to Christ's community.

This parallelism resides in the very nature of the case. Baptism is after all the initiation, the inauguration of the life as a Christian. In it is pictured and portrayed what happens when a person is taken captive by God in Christ.

The Christian community has had baptism from the very first; there has never been a church that did not practice baptism. In this practice the believers have followed Jesus Christ, who let himself be baptized by John. Yet the baptism of the church was not the same as John's baptism. John had called men to repent because the Kingdom of God was about to dawn; by letting themselves be baptized as a sign of their repentance, they would escape the coming judgment and gain a share in the Kingdom. When the young Christian community took over baptism, these aspects were indeed retained, but through Christ's death and resurrection everything came to stand in a new light. For now baptism was altogether connected with Christ's saving work and was seen as incorporation into his community.

There is no complete doctrine of baptism to be found in the New Testament, not even in Paul, who speaks about it explicitly several times and repeatedly makes more indirect references to it. This in itself does not signify anything, for in the preceding chapters it has repeatedly become evident that the Bible does not offer any systematic doctrine, but only the building stones for such. But here it is another matter, for what baptism is and what it signifies cannot actually be expressed in words. The distinctive thing about it is that it is an action, something done, a sacred drama. Words are indeed employed in it, but these words are fitted into the action. And in this sacred drama things happen that simply cannot be entirely captured in words.

What baptism is is known only to those who have participated in this sacred drama, and if indeed we nevertheless must speak about it, this can only be done in an oblique allusory way, with the help of images, figures of speech, just as the New Testament does. There baptism is pictured as the old man's being buried, as a washing away of the filth of sin, as being clothed with Christ as with a new garment, as being born again, as a sealing for the future, or as a mark that stamps one as God's possession. All this is figurative language. But this figurative language points to the reality of God's action in Jesus Christ that is actualized for the person being baptized. That God in that action also takes possession of this particular person is portrayed in the sacred drama of baptism. Or, we must actually say, this first happens in this drama. For the alternative, so frequently posed, that either baptism is a symbol and an assurance of something that is already a reality or that something new happens in it is in principle a false alternative. Of course it is a symbolic action, a portrayal of the liberation of the person from the powers that draw him away from God, but in this action that is enacted, something new also happens with this person. It is as with a socio- or psychodrama. In it a situation is only acted out, but thereby something effectively happens with the players, something in them is changed. Thus also baptism is a play that does something to the players.

Similarly, the other alternative in which baptism is seen either as a human confession or God's action is likewise a false alternative. Baptism is a play that from beginning to end is acted out by men -- but these men are touched by God's love. This holds true for the community in whose midst the baptism is administered, it holds true for the person who baptizes (and in most churches this is, in keeping with their church-order, as a rule a minister), and it holds true for the person who comes to let himself be baptized. And in and through this drama the person is placed in the force-field of God's presence, and he is as it were carried along in a movement that will extend over his entire life. A person who comes forward to be baptized thereby declares that he wants to belong to Christ and his community, and thereby he confesses his faith. But he can make this confession only because the Covenant-God has already taken his will captive. And in baptism he receives new power for his further life as God's ally, and thus it is God who acts in this event.

Thus the Spirit -- that is, after all, the God who acts -- works before, in, and after baptism. This last in particular must not be forgotten. For baptism is the inauguration drama, the play of the initiation into the life that is oriented to God, the bath of regeneration, as it is once called in the Bible in an expressive image (Titus 3:5). This means that it is no more than a beginning, entrance into a new manner of existence which will have to take shape in the on-going life. It sets the person on a new way which he must continue to tread as a disciple of Christ in the power of God's love. Therefore baptism can never be detached from ethics. Hence it also is not surprising that in the New Testament it is discussed almost exclusively in that context. It will have to be ratified in the life that follows. The original strength for this is given in baptism. That is what happens in this sacred drama.

It cannot be said that Jesus "instituted" baptism. He no more instituted baptism than he "founded" the church. But just as the church lies in the extension of Jesus' fellowship with his disciples, so also baptism lies in the extension of Jesus' baptism by John. Hence it is also understandable that the gospel of Matthew speaks of a commission to baptize given by the risen Lord. The power of God's action, which was made manifest in the resurrection -- or, to say the same thing in another way, the spirit of Christ which first became fully effective in the resurrection -- prompted the adoption of the ancient rite of baptism and filled it with the whole reality of God's reconciling action in Christ.

The person who is baptized

When I thus called the baptismal event a sacred drama in which the person being baptized is set on the way of a new life, I was thinking of the person being baptized who consciously plays a role in this drama. It is in fact a curiously passive role. The person is baptized, he undergoes the bath of regeneration, he is clothed with a new life. It cannot be otherwise. Here something is done to a person. But it must be added that he lets all this happen to him, he chooses to have it happen to him. If the Holy Spirit is at work in the sacred drama of men, if the power that resides in this drama is to produce some effect upon the subject, then he must, as passive participant, be able consciously to share in this drama. He must know what is enacted in baptism, what baptism is all about. Thus it will have to be preceded by a certain amount of instruction. It seems right to me, then, that at baptism the subject confesses his faith, in words however simple, just as it was already the custom in the church very early. It is self-evident that this original faith then later, in the community into which he is incorporated, must become more

By seeing baptism thus as a sacred drama, in which something happens precisely because it is a solemn, ritually prescribed drama, the question can arise whether its effect is not of a purely psychological kind. This idea is all the more obvious because the comparison with a psychodrama is used by way of explanation. In a certain sense the same thing is true here as what was said in an earlier chapter about the connection between charisma and natural ability. Of course the consciously experienced baptismal event has a psychological effect, because a certain pattern of anticipation is connected with it; however, this does not deny that in this psychological effect God is drawing man to himself and giving him strength for a life as God's covenant-partner. Insofar as the effect of baptism is experienced, of course this is a psychological phenomonon; that in it man encounters God and receives a share in the Spirit of Christ is only to be believed, as it has been believed from the beginning of the church all through the centuries.

From all that has been said it will be evident that I regard the baptism of infants as not the most suitable form. I do not base this view on the fact that there are no clear indications that in New Testament times infants were ever baptized along with their parents. But according to the New Testament baptism is something other and something more than a confirmation of God's grace in Christ, more than a trustworthy sign that he has laid his hand upon this particular person who is baptized. Paul in particular speaks about it in much more realistic fashion: sins are washed away, the baptized is reborn and is set on a new way. The spirit does this, but it does not go beyond the consciousness and the will of the person involved. God's presence is indeed a power that becomes too strong for man and overpowers him, but this overpowering includes man's acknowledging that he has been won over. Otherwise it becomes mere magic. Baptism does not operate primarily upon the intellect of the person baptized, but if it is to have an effect upon him, he must be able to experience it and to know what is involved in it. Now it is true that those who argue in favor of infant baptism strongly emphasize that it must later be understood by the person baptized; according to them there is alson an essential connection between baptism and faith. And indeed, if in later life baptism is understood and confirmed (perhaps in a fixed form, such as in public confession and confirmation as a member) then it can exert its influences subsequently. But this brings with it an intellectualizing. For then it is not the event of the action itself that is effective (that would be mere magic), but only the understanding of it; not the submission to baptism, but only the knowledge of what it signifies. Hence it is not, in my opinion, the most proper and most biblically responsible form, to enact the sacred drama of baptism unless the actor upon whom the action is wrought, i.e., the person baptized, knows something about it.

This does not mean, however, that we must wait until this person has reached maturity in his faith. Baptism is, after all, the beginning of a way that does not end until death and even a young child can consciously desire to belong to Christ and his community. In any case I would want to plead for a very flexible policy about the age for baptism.

Since Augustine, connection is often made in the church's doctrine between infant baptism and original sin. It is evident that this presupposes an understanding of sin, or of original sin, that is in conflict with the view which we have developed above (chapters VI and VII).

Rules for the drama

If baptism is a portrayal of initiation into the new life (liberation from sin, and rebirth) and of incorporation into the community, and if this portrayal carries within itself the power to effect this, then the way in which it is performed must also correspond to this meaning. But our baptismal rites hardly do this. This extreme soberness is certainly understandable and defensible as a reaction against a baptismal liturgy that had become incomprehensibly, excessively ornate, and magically interpreted. Yet it is a hindrance to full participation in and experience of baptism as sacred drama. Without obliging us to enter into all sorts of liturgical issues, the following considerations deserve some attention.

1. Baptism must be enacted in the community, and the community is not merely a spectator, but also a fellow-participant. It is continuously maintained in existence by the addition of new members to it through baptism. Therefore it must declare that it is happy and grateful to God, who provides for its propagation. Thus its "role" must be one of prayer, thanksgiving, and praise.

2. Whether baptism is performed by sprinkling or by immersion is not an issue of ultimate importance. But if in baptism the washing of regeneration, in which sins are washed away, is acted out, then this is no longer to be recognized in our ritual, and it is necessary to seek for a better form for it.

3. And why could we not enact the being clothed with the new man and the being sealed as God's possession for the future hope, as this was already very early done in the church, namely by putting a white robe on the person who is baptized and by making the sign of the cross on his forehead with oil, as a mark and seal?

Of course our soul and our salvation do not depend on such things. But if baptism could be more clearly experienced as a sacred drama in which a reality is enacted, that could be a counterbalance to the preponderant intellectualism in our church, and perhaps the event of baptism could regain in the life of the community and of the person baptized the important place which it obviously had, according to the New Testament and the church fathers, in the early church.

B. The meetings of the community

Worship services as a visible form of the church

It is not my intention here to deal in detail with the church service of worship. However, it is not possible to omit it completely; it is too central an element in the life of the church to allow that. Of course it is not the only element or even the most essential one. There is in the life of the church a double movement, almost like a kind of breathing in and breathing out; the community comes together for worship and then goes out into the world for its service there. If it is forgotten that this second movement also is an essential part of being church, the life of its members is divided into a life on Sunday and a life through the week. If the church is concentrated too exclusively on worship, moreover, the danger of its becoming a clergymen's church can hardly be avoided. But here now we shall deal with the movement of coming together. In any case this aspect of the church's life has this advantage, that in it the church as a fellowship, a community, is more visible and demonstrable.

I propose only in a few lines to indicate where, in my opinion, the main point in worship lies. Just as in baptism the initiation and incorporation of the individual into the Christian community is acted out, so in the service of worship the life of this community in its encounter with God is acted out. In the preceding chapter we listed three essential marks of being the church: the relationship with God, the reciprocal relationship, and the relationship with the world. All three must be given their just due in worship. However, the relationship of the community with God is primary. What is involved is, after all, the enactment of the encounter with him. That it actually results in this encounter cannot be guaranteed by any liturgical structure. Therefore the community will pray for God's presence. But it will do this in the constant expectation that God will be with it; it knows after all that he is its Ally. But although God's presence cannot be compelled, the community can let itself be kept to God in Christ, in the reading of the Scripture and in its exposition. Therein it is reminded of its salvation, and this salvation is actualized and re-presented to the community. And the community's response and reaction to this salvation will have to be expressed. This occurs in its hymnic praise and adoration of God and in its prayers. In this the community is acting as God's partner and his "counterpart."

In the second place, it must become manifest in the worship service that the community is a living fellowship in reciprocal bonds of obligation. This fellowship-character resides in the very fact of being together, in listening, singing, and praying together. Moreover, in the experience it becomes manifest that the believers here can comfort, admonish, encourage, and strengthen each other. It can also be expressed in the fact that in the community's prayers, special personal joys or distresses of the members can be brought before God. And further, the gathering together is the symbolic portrayal of the fact that the members also intend to stand by and support each other in a material way.

Finally, in the church's coming together the third essential mark also must take shape, namely the fact that it serves the world. This happens in a more implicit way, in that it praises and worships God on behalf of the world, and in a more explicit way, in the fact that in its petitions it lays before God the needs of the world, and in the fact that in his presence, the community reflects together upon where and how it is called to be of service to the world. An offering for a special purpose can be the formal sign of its readiness also to offer actual help.

Some questions

What has been said above prompts some critical questions about the practice of worship as we generally know it.

1. Is it made clear enough in our services that what is involved in them is the community's encounter with God? The most expressive portrayal of this encounter is, I believe, the back-and-forth exchange between the leader and the community. This back-and-forth, however, usually is reduced to a few fixed responses of the congregation. But why could not the prayers, for example, thought through and prepared in advance, be voiced by members of the congregation, so that in this part of the service the minister can take a less prominent place?

2. All that we know of the early church indicates that the entire worship service there was a corporate event, in which now one, now another, spoke. It is true that the congregation that assembled then was only a small one and the danger of disorder and confusion was not an imaginary one. But still the question must be considered whether in our time the whole congregation could not play a greater role even in the preaching. In this connection I am not thinking primarily of discussion or conversation. These belong more in the context of a study group than in that of a service of worship where God's salvation must be given expression and actualized. For this undertaking the knowledge of the preacher as specialist undoubtedly is necessary. But is not the knowledge also of the member of the congregation necessary, the one who often is better informed about the various areas of the world's life in which the actualization must occur? Would it not therefore be good if the sermon were not only prepared by members of the congregation together with the minister -- something that is already happening in increasing measure -- but also developed, as it were, in the meeting itself by several persons? This too is being tried here and there.

3. As we said above, in the worship service the mutual relationship among the members is portrayed and celebrated. But is justice done to this concept in actual practice? Should not our worship services be conducted in a more personal (I would almost say a more homey) way? In the last analysis in the community that comes together is also the "family" of the Lord" (in the epistle to the Ephesians the Christians are called members of God's household!).

4. The community is the fellowship that is formed by the Spirit. Shouldn't that be evident, among other ways, in the fact that in its meetings there should be room for spontaneity? Disorder does not serve to build up the community, but neither is the community served by the strict regulation to which we are accustomed, in which nothing unforeseen and unexpected can ever happen.

In any case it is evident that if the community wishes actually to portray in its meetings the encounter with God, this requires a mature community, and education and training to produce this maturity.

C. The Lord's Supper

New Testament data

The most highly concentrated portrayal of salvation takes place in the Lord's Supper. In contrast to baptism, here the community is imitating Christ and doing what he did. We saw earlier that having a meal with other persons must have played a striking role in Jesus' conduct. We are told about this again and again in the gospel narratives (p. 62). The significant thing about this was, on the one hand, Jesus' fellowship and solidarity with those who were religious and social outsiders. But in addition, the banquet was a fixed symbol for the kingdom of God. The meals that Jesus held then were intended also to be a prefiguring of the time of full salvation and a sign that the coming kingdom is now already present in the world in him. This is also clearly the point of the story of the miraculous feeding, which we find in all four gospels, though in different versions. It is striking that this story, in the very choice of words used (taking bread, giving thanks, breaking, giving), is clearly intended to remind us of the Lord's Supper. Indeed, the same also holds true of the form in which Luke describes the meal that Christ had with the travelers to Emmaus (Luke 24: 30).

All these meals form the context, the framework, in which the Lord's Supper must be viewed. In this connection a special place is held by Jesus' last supper with his disciples, because Jesus then explicitly "instituted" the Supper for the church. For in contrast to baptism, here we can speak of an actual institution by Jesus. We are told this four times in the New Testament (Mark 14:22-25; Matt. 26:26-29; Luke 22:14-20; and I Cor. 11:23-25). Now it is worthy of note that no two of these accounts are precisely alike and that even the words with which Jesus gave the bread and the wine to his disciples are handed down in differing versions. This is only to be explained by the fact that there were differing words of institution in circulation and that the early church placed no particular weight upon the exact choice of words. But the same theological ideas are found in the four narratives.

1. The Lord's Supper signifies a remembrance of Jesus, and especially of his suffering and his death. The main idea is not his death as such, but its saving significance for the believers. This remembrance is also at the same time more than a remembrance. The eating of the bread and the drinking from the cup proclaim Jesus Christ who has given his life for the world. It is not only the accompanying sermon that makes the Supper a proclamation, but the action of the Supper is already that in itself.

2. In another respect also we can speak here of more than a remembrance. Memory looks back to the past, but when the community observes the Supper, Jesus Christ is with the community, as surely and as really as he was in the midst of his disciples at the last supper. The bread and the wine are the visible representation of Christ himself.

3. In this special Supper instituted by Jesus the bond between God and his community is again and again confirmed. Both Paul and the three gospel writers

indicate that through Jesus' death the covenant has become effective in a new way.

4. Finally, according to all four traditions this Supper points to the future, to the time of full salvation, when God's Lordship will be wholly and universally actualized. The three gospel writers explicitly mention the coming fulfillment of the kingdom of God, while in the words of Paul this future perspective also is voiced ("until he come").

Thus the words of institution at the last supper confirm what is also manifest in Jesus' many other meals that are related: that the Lord's Supper is oriented to the future and that joy over the salvation already given and yet to be expected is the dominant note.

While the most prominent theological perspectives in the New Testament texts are clear, there still remain a great many unresolved questions, which however are more of scholarly interest than of importance for faith. The most prominent problems are:

1. We cannot reconstruct Jesus' words of institution. Paul is the earliest source for these words, but his accout too is the product of an earlier process of tradition.

2. We shall never be able to determine with certainty whether the last supper occurred on the evening of the Jewish Passover meal (thus the symoptic gospels), or on the preceding evening (thus John). Although much has been written about this, it does not make much difference as far as content is concerned. For on the one hand, even the evening before the Passover meal must have stood in the light of the coming festival; and on the other hand, curiously enough, in the New Testament accounts of the institution the Passover plays no theological role. The breaking and offering of bread, the expression of gratitude to God, and the blessing over the cup are still a constantly maintained tradition among believing Jews at every banquet and festive meal. We find no trace in the texts of the recollection of the Exodus, which was and is the main part of the Passover meal with its elaborate ritual. The establishing of the covenant, on the other hand, to which the texts do refer, does not come up in the Jewish Passover, but is celebrated in another feast, later in the year.

3. Various Greek manuscripts are lacking Luke 22:19b, 20, so that there is a question whether the longer or the shorter text is the more original. At present, New Testament scholars are more inclined toward the former, but there is no unanimity on this.

4. In Mark and Matthew the orientation to the future joyous banquet in the kingdom of God is dominant, while in Paul the commemoration of the Lord's death is more central. For this and other reasons the hypothesis is suggested that originally there were two different types of celebration of the Supper, one exchatological one, and one in which Christ's atoning suffering stood at the center. If this was indeed true, still in any case these two types very early grew together.

The question which has, however, played the greatest role in church history, and which has been the cause of passionate conflict, is how Christ's presence is to be conceived of and what is the meaning of the little word "is" in the words of institution. This question, however, does not lie in the terrain of the New Testament, because the entire inquiry is alien to the New Testament. Medieval theologians have tried to give an answer with the help of the philosophical apparatus that was available to them. But if we try to work with such concepts as elements, substance,and accidents, we entangle ourselves in the most impossible intellectual difficulties. Christ's presence is not a static presence, but it aims at his encounter with the believers, there in the Supper. And Christ, who encounters man, is the Spirit (see chapter XIII).

His Spirit is with us when we celebrate his Supper, and it is particularly the bread and the wine which in the Supper represent his presence, because in the last supper Jesus gave these a special emphasis and thereby made them bearers of this special meaning.

The observance of the Supper

The Lord's Supper can only be observed in joy. How could it be otherwise, when the community therein recalls the salvation that it has received through Christ, when it is privileged to celebrate this meal together with him, and when it thereby is permitted to look ahead to the Kingdom of God? Actually, "look ahead" is too weak a term. The fellowship with each other and with God in Christ which is experienced in this Supper is a foreshadowing and even a foretaste of the perfect fellowship for which we may hope in the final consummation. But this also means that this meal is not itself already the fulfillment. When we observe the Lord's Supper, we still have both feet planted on this earth, and are not transported to the celestial regions. The Supper is given to us for the "interim," for the time when Jesus is no longer physically present on the earth and the fulfillment, the consummation, of salvation is not yet present. In this "interim" we are spiritually strengthened by this meal. This "we" is in the first place the corporate "we" of the community, although we who observe this meal together also come into our own personally.

When we speak of the observance of the Supper thus, the critical thought must arise that in practice it frequently is true that neither an actual meal nor an actual celebration takes place. This could very well be one of the main reasons that many Christians do not know what to make of the Lord's Supper and that much of what is traditionally said about it sounds high-flown and hardly real to their ears. I do not believe that a richer liturgy or one that is more adapted to the tradition of the first centuries could effect much change in this regard. I think that the solution must be sought in another direction. The Lord's Supper is meant to portray our salvation essentially in the fact that the same thing is done as Jesus did with his disciples, namely to have a meal with actual eating and drinking. This is also the way the first Christians celebrated it, but it is likely that the so-called love feast (*agape*) and the Lord's Supper were very quickly separated from each other. Thereafter the latter came more and more to be a stylized sacred action. If we want to let the festal and fellowship-creating character of the Lord's Supper be expressed, we would have to celebrate it again imbedded within an actual meal. Within that meal, the, the fixed liturgical moments which declare that this meal points to a reality above itself can find their place: the recollection of Jesus Christ (the so-called anamnesis), the thanksgiving, the prayer for the coming of the kingdom, intercession for each other, for the worldwide church, and for the world, the invocation of the Spirit (the so-called epiclesis), that is, the prayer that Christ will be among us in and with his Supper.

One of the ancient elements in the liturgy of the Supper is the bringing of the sacrifice, or offering. In the course of time it has had a highly diverse content. At present, for example, in some churches a role is played by the idea that Christ's sacrifice on Golgotha is brought to God's remembrance, or that we, as it is said, enter into Christ's sacrifice. Or, again, that we bring to God the sacrifice of our worship or even the sacrifice of our life. However, I am uneasy about any liturgical action that can give the impression that in the Lord's Supper we offer anything, in whatever form, to God. In relation to him we are totally and entirely the recipients and not the givers.

The only form of sacrifice that appears to me compatible with this Supper is that in which, through a symbolic action, our (material) care for and service to each other, to the whole church, and particularly to the world take shape. John the evangelist does not say anything in his gospel about the institution of the Lord's Supper. Where the other evangelists relate this, he gives the narrative of the foot-washing (13:1-20). Indeed, in his entire description of Jesus' last meal he places great emphasis upon Jesus' service. This service-character is generally neglected in our observances.

The circumstances often will not allow the observance of the Lord's Supper in an ordinary common meal. But even then the observance can be more personal and the fellowship-character can be more strongly expressed than frequently is done. And even then it would have to be done more naturally and less ceremoniously — which does not mean with less reverence and dignity. For example, we should be able during the observance to speak with each other. We should be able to wish peace to each other and to "greet each other with the holy kiss," as it appears to have been the custom in the New Testament churches, although, with our more reserved nature we would more easily do this by shaking hands with each other. But however it is done, in one way or another we must simply give outward expression to the fact that here the Christian community is actually celebrating the fellowship of its members with each other and with Christ.

If we thus rescue the Lord's Supper from its too rigid formality, so that in the observance there is something to experience, it also makes sense to allow children to participate in it, as soon as they want to do so and can understand that this is a meal of the disciples of Jesus Christ, who are doing the same thing as he did in his last meal. And when a child can understand that, it will also have reached the age when it can share the drama of baptism and consciously accept it. Therefore there is no reason, in my judgment, to set aside the established sequence of baptism and participation in the Lord's Supper that prevails in most churches.

I have deliberately avoided the term "sacrament." This word was introduced by Tertullian into theological language, with the meaning of "salvation mystery." Later on it acquired our narrower meaning of sacrament, and only at the very end of the middle ages were the seven sacraments established as necessary for salvation. The Reformation then limited them to two, baptism and the Lord's Supper, in the conviction that these were the only ones that Jesus Christ himself had given to the church. However, I see no reason to identify these two actions together with the concept of "sacrament." They are not the only "means of salvation" in which salvation is portrayed, represented, and imparted. This also occurs, for example, in the reading of scripture, in preaching, and in catechesis. And as for the specific institution by Jesus Christ, this does not apply in the case of baptism anyway.

The Supper and the unity of the church

In conclusion, a comment about the Lord's Supper and the divided state of the churches. There is an essential, indissoluble connection between this meal and the unity of the Christian community. The very earliest interpretation of the Supper that we have, that of Paul in I Cor. 10:17, points in this direction. The alternative, which used to be stated frequently, that the common observance either is the fruit of already existing unity or it accomplishes this unity, is regarded in our time by an increasing number of Christians as a false alternative. The Supper is an expression of mutual bonds of unity, but at the same time it also serves to form and to strengthen these bonds. This is true even of an ordinary meal with guests; how much more so then in this meal where Christ is, so to speak, the host. Where the unity in Christ is experienced as a reality that cuts across church boundaries, the Supper may therefore, I believe, be celebrated together. It may be that various church orders do not permit this — although they often allow more freedom in this regard than is commonly thought. Yet for the sake of the unity of the whole body of Christ the violoation of fixed rules may be called for here. I am not thinking primarily of the delegates to ecumenical conferences. These people are together as representatives of their churches, and therefore for them questions pertaining to church order must necessarily play a role. I have in mind rather the "unofficial" groups and work fellowships, about which I have already spoken in the preceding chapter. In this connection it is of primary importance that such groups be aware of being a manifestation of the one Christian community and that they let this be evident in one way or another in their observance of the Supper, for example by observing it together with a local congregation wherever this is in any way possible. In any case their observance must never be a private undertaking or a kind of demonstration. For the Lord's Supper is given tothe entire church of Christ.

XIX. ISRAEL AND THE CHURCH

In the eighth chapter, on Israel, we restricted ourselves to the Old Testament, but when we thereafter treated Jesus, we were in fact still engaged with Israel; not only in the sense that Jesus can only be understood in the perspective of the past history of his people, but also in the sense that in him this history continues and he forms a part of it. His life and activity fell almost entirely within the Jewish people and were directed toward bringing salvation to this nation. But this still does not put it strongly enough. He is himself the salvation. As the man who is given by God and is wholly filled with God, he is the summation of all Israel and he, representing Israel, in his perfect obedience has now caused the covenant between God and this people, in all its mutuality, to become a reality. In this sense he is the realization, the fulfillment of the covenant -- and fulfillment of the covenant means salvation.

We have constantly spoken about Jesus as the Christ. But when we here so emphatically affirm that he forms a part of the history of Israel, we should call him first of all "Messiah." These two words have literally the same meaning; "Christos" is the Greek translation of the Hebrew "messiah," which in the later Old Testament writers and in Judaism was a designation and an honorific title for the one who would bring God's salvation to Israel. This expectation is realized in Jesus; he is the Messiah of Israel. And as Israel's Messiah he is also the Christ of the nations. For the fulfillment of Israel's expectation of salvation brings with it the universalizing of this salvation. But what is involved here is more than merely playing with words. For although the two terms literally have the same meaning, they have a different implication, because the role of Jesus for Israel is different from that for the other nations. For his own people, as their Messiah, he fulfills the covenant-destiny of this people; thereby this covenant now has become effectual in a new way and Israel is confronted with its Covenant-God in a new way. And for the Gentiles, as the Christ, Jesus is the revelation of the God whom they have not known up until now.

But in the chapter on the church we seem to have lost sight of Israel. That now must be remedied. In doing this we must maintain that the church has its origin in the resurrection of Christ; this becomes evident in the fact that we could describe the church as the Christian fellowship. Thus in relationship to Old Testament Israel it is in any case a new beginning. It is not merely the continuation of earlier

Israel, nor was the church already present in Israel in a concealed way. But it is true that Israel continues to live on in this church. Moreover, there are still Jews and in our time there is even a state that calls itself Israel. We cannot place a full stop, with Jesus Christ, after the history of the chosen people of the Old Testament.

> The terms Israel, Jewish people, and Jew have become ambiguous. In the following I use the words "Israel" and "Jewish people" interchangeably as designations for the totality of the Jews, regardless of whether they live in the land of Israel or not, and regardless of whether they adhere to the Jewish faith. Then there still remains the difficulty of determining what it is that makes a Jew a Jew. The only definition that actually can be given is that a Jew is a Jew who knows that he is a Jew. At first glance this appears to be a tautology. In essence, however, it intends to say that the tradition, the awareness of sharing in a history and a destiny, is crucial for being a Jew.

Israel in the church

It is a strange irony of history that for the church in our time the place of Israel in the church has become a problem, while in the primitive church it was the place of the Gentiles that was the problem. The first Christian communities in Palestine were composed of Jews. Historically we know little about them. About the Christians outside of Jerusalem we are lacking the data, and about the community in Jerusalem Luke does indeed tell a few things, but it is difficult to discern what is historically reliable in this. In any case we may assume as certain that these Jews who believed in Christ continued to participate in the Jewish religious life. They formed a kind of Jewish sect, or perhaps rather a particular school or denomination in the Judaism of their time. There is nothing to indicate that these Christian Jews regarded themselves as the only true continuation of Israel in contrast to their other compatriots. It was rather that they had a message that was addressed to all Israel.

The problem of the Gentile Christians presumably first arose outside Palestine. The core of the communities even there must have consisted originally of Jews, but Gentiles also came very quickly to share the faith, and the question had to be answered as to what was the status of these Gentile Christians. In the beginning it was very difficult for the Jews to accept them on the basis of equality and to have table fellowhship with them unless these Gentile Christians first had been circumcised, as a sign that they too belonged to Israel's God and his covenant. This shows up specifically in Paul's letter to the Galatians. But the situation changed very quickly. The Jewish Christian communities disappeared and the church became a church almost exclusively composed of Gentile Christians. The only Jews in it now appear to be no more than some sort of curious exceptions. Yet this Gentile Christian church too is essentially related to Israel. As long as it is church, it is connected with Jesus Christ, with him who first of all is Israel's Messiah. On the basis of this fact the following may be said:

1. In Jesus Christ Israel continues to live in the church, even if there should no longer be a single Jewish Christian. For Christ represents Israel. Therefore the church, whether it will it or not, is never free of the Jew. At the moment when

Christians break the bond with Israel, they deny their Lord.

2. In Jesus God has arrived at his goal for his covenant with Israel, and thereby this covenant is, as it were, thrown open to others, the non-Jews. they too now have acquired a share in it. Thus these others are, in the most literal sense of the term, those who have come in alongside, the "pro-elytes." In the New Testament two figures of great attractive power are used to express this: the Gentile Christians are like wild branches that are grafted onto the tree of Israel, or they are like aliens who are made naturalized citizens. It is good to give full weight to these figures in a church made up predominantly of Gentile Christians. They can save these Gentile Christians from self-exaltation. It is not true, as is often half unconsciously suggested, that there must *also* be a place in the church for Jews, but conversely, that there is *also* a place for non-Jews.

3. Only because the church is the Messiah-believing part of Israel plus the proselyte Gentiles, in its totality it has a share in the past convenantal history of God and Israel, and the sacred writings of this people have become the church's books also. The church has its beginning, as we said, in the resurrection of Christ. But the entire history of Old Testament Israel is the Church's pre-history, even insofar as it is, empirically speaking, a church of the Gentiles. This holds true not only for the patriarchs, for Moses, David, the great prophets, and the many proofs of God's convenantal faithfulness; Israel's constantly renewed apostasy and manifold failures also belong to this pre-history of the church. This is not surprising, for also in the church's own history we see more signs of God's preserving love than of the church's own obedience.

4. Although the Gentile Christians are the proselytes, those who were added, they are not a kind of second-rank Christians. In the church the Jew does not have any advantage over the non-Jew. In Christ their separation is nullified. This is the first and most fundamental sign that the reconciliation with God also brings along with it reconciliation on the human plane. Biblically speaking there is only one basic distinction between people, that between Jews and non-Jews. Because even this distinction does not hinder the unity of the church, the differences that, biblically seen, are only secondary certainly cannot do it. The unity of Jewish Christians and Gentile Christians is a model for the unity of the church. Therefore the question of separate congregations of Jewish Christians is an issue that concerns the entire church. The so-called German Christians in Hitler's Germany were not the only ones to propagate such congregations: there are also Jewish Christians who argue for such. But the rightness of this separation must be contested, in principle and theologically. The elimination of the fundamental distinction between Jews and Gentiles by Christ must assume a visible shape in their forming together a single community. This does not rule out the recognition that in particular cases a certain association of Jewish Christians can be meaningful. These Christians, because of their minority position, sometimes are confronted with very specific problems that can be better dealt with pastorally in their own group. In such a group their own Jewish cultural values also can more easily be preserved. For just as in New Testament times a Gentile did not have to become a Jew in order to be a Christian, so also in our time we shall have to insist that a Jew as Jew can be a Christian — while still on the other hand being Jewish may not be regarded as of essential import. Analogously, the non-western Christian in the church also need not abandon his own culture, though he may not become locked into this culture. For this person too the position of the Jew in the church is a model.

It is a quite common practice for Christians to call the church the new or the true or the spiritual Israel. In a certain sense this is in line with the idea that the church has acquired a share in the Old Testament covenantal history. But these labels are dangerous. They suggest either that the church is the direct continuation of the chosen people of the Old Testament, or that it has replaced that people. Neither of these is true. Moreover, and for me still more nore significant, they smack of an impermissible ecclesiastical triumphalism. Indeed, the name Israel is not even applied to the church in the New Testament; this happens for the first time only in a Christian writing at the end of the second century.

Israel outside the church

But it is not Israel within the church that is the real problem for Christians, but Israel outside the church, that is, that overwhelming majority of Jews who cannot acknowledge Jesus as their Messiah. Indeed, it seems inconceivable that the very people who through their centuries-long relationship with God were prepared for his action in Christ have rejected this divine action, while many Gentiles, of whom this would much less have been expected, have accepted Christ. At least this is the way Paul felt, and in his letter to the Romans he tried to find an answer to the question that tormented him, as to how it is possible that Israel, in spite of its advantages, resisted its own salvation. In this connection he is convinced that God's dealing with Israel since Christ's coming cannot be in conflict with his earlier covenantal actions. It is impossible that God could go back on his word. From this insight Paul comes, in a laborious train of thought, to the assurance of faith that God has not rejected his people and that he ultimately will lead them to their destiny. For the gifts of his electing grace and the call to his people remain in effect. Paul sees this confirmed, by way of example, in himself and in the individuals from Israel who believe in Jesus Christ. His words must not be taken to mean that only these few, this "remnant," are Israel, while the others, those who are "hardened," are outside. For him, those who are obedient are the representatives of *all* Israel, the visible guarantee that one day the entire people of God will attain salvation.

Paul leaves no doubt that Israel's rejection of Christ is sin and disobedience. He uses the harsh words "fall" and "hardening" to describe that rejection. But even this disobedience does not take place outside God's saving will; his grace is still at work even in it, and even thus Israel still is an instrument in his hand. For because Israel has rejected Jesus Christ, salvation has come to the Gentiles. God has used the hardening of the Jews to draw the non-Jews to himself. Yet this is not the last thing to be said about Israel. For someday, when "the fulness of the Gentiles" has attained salvation, Israel too will repent. This is the way of salvation that God is taking, that while via the Jews (although it is via their fall) the Gentiles have come to salvation, one day via the fulness of the Gentiles Israel too will attain its destiny.

Thus God has, so to speak, reversed the order of salvation. Once salvation had to come to the Gentiles through Israel. In an unsuspected way God has accomplished this through fall and rejection. Now, however, in a reverse way, salvation must come from the Gentiles to Israel, so that then, through the conversion of "all Israel," the time of salvation in its fulness will break through, and all God's promises will be fulfilled; for when Israel accepts Christ, that will be, for the world, "life from the dead" (Rom. 11:15), the full realization of salvation.

Other New Testament writers also have thought about the Jewish people in its rejection of Jesus, even after his resurrection, and not all of them arrived at one and the same conclusion. Thus for example Matthew, a Christian Jew of the second generation, appears to have written off his people. Thus Paul's view is not the only one in the Bible. But the interpretation that he gives is so much in line with the way in which the prophets spoke about Israel's unfaithfulness and God's faithfulness, and it is so fully grounded in basic biblical ideas, that we cannot, as I see it, escape the convincing force of his argument. This does not mean that I want to take over in our time everything that he says without further ado. For example, I dare not speak of disobedience and hardening of the Jewish people. The church has been so guilty through the centuries in relation to this people that Christians are the last ones who may accuse the Jews of disobedience. Further, in our time we can no longer say that the Jews reject Christ. Most of them, both the pious and the secularized Jews, live completely outside the sphere of Christianity; they never have been actually confronted by Christ and therefore cannot consciously reject him. Here I pass over in silence the question whether the church has not perhaps become so estranged from its Old Testament origins, in the course of time, that in the Christ whom the church preaches, God's free and obedient covenant-partner can hardly be recognized.

But even if we avoid the word "guilt," we Christians cannot, any more than Paul, surrender the conviction that Israel is called to accept Christ and that this is its destiny that is God-given. This means that we shall not be able to concede that the Jewish understanding of "law and prophets" is more adequate than that of the church. Christians undoubtedly can learn much from Jewish theologians, but they will not be able to take over the Jewish interpretations in their entirety. We believe that any exposition of the Old Testament writings that is not open to the message of Christ and cannot lead into it is in one way or another off the mark.

But this does not minimize the fact that on the basis of all that we know of God's dealing with Israel, and on the basis of our own experience with God we are just as much convinced as was Paul that God has not abandoned the Jewish people. This conviction of belief is confirmed by the fact that Israel still exists, in spite of the vagaries of history, in spite of the many persecutions to which it has been exposed, and in spite of all sorts of forces that have worked in the direction of assimilation. This continuing existence can also be explained in other ways and is not a compelling proof of God's preservation. Yet it can be for us a confirmation of our belief in God's faithfulness.

Does this now imply that even in the future the Jews cannot disappear as a specific community, that is, that they cannot be absorbed into the other peoples, nor can be rooted out? Indeed, I believe that just as God's church will continue to exist, in some form or another, so also this people will be preserved -- at least until it recognizes its Messiah in Jesus and follows him. And who can say whether this will happen only at the end of time? However, we must not venture too much in predictions of the future; for God's action in history cannot be mapped out in advance, but at most can only be indicated in some measure afterward.

> In the preceding I have deliberately refrained from calling the Jewish people still God's chosen people for all time. We can say that on the basis of his election God still continues to have a special bond with Israel, that it is still his beloved, as Paul expresses it. But this is not the same as saying, that it is still the chosen

people. Men can so detach themselves from God's purpose that he can no longer use them and he then sets them aside, that is, he rejects them (see chapter IV). When Paul compares the Jews who have not believed in Christ to branches that have been cut off, he is thinking along these lines. But we must not forget that such a rejection is not for him an irrevocable final sentence. However, we will do well not to presume to know too much about this. The relationship between God and Israel is not our business, and we shall have to leave it to God to determine to what extent this people is doing the work of God even in our own time.

It is not enough to say that Israel is still sustained and preserved by God. It must be added that Israel also has a future. God once set out on a way with this people, and he will not abandon it before he has achieved his aim with it. And because his covenant-will is stronger than all else, we may trust and believe that Israel will come to its destiny, in which it will find full salvation in fellowship with God. And as Christians we can conceive of this only thus: that Israel as a corporate whole will one day recognize that Jesus has fulfilled the covenant for it as well and that only in this recognition can it fully actualize its own covenantal relationship with God.

But if Israel will come to this recognition, it is dependent upon the church for this. The church is, after all, the community of all who believe in Christ and tell others about him. Therefore it is only through this Christian community, which now consists primarily of Gentile Christians, that Israel can be confronted by Jesus and invited to accept its destiny in Christ. It is evident that that places a great responsibility upon Christians. It is their calling to make manifest, in their words, their manner and their actions, in their joy and gratitude, the salvation that is given to them in Christ, in order that thereby all men, and Israel in particular, shall attain this salvation for themselves as well. On this point again we find ourselves compelled to follow Paul, who said that the Gentile Christians would have to make Israel jealous. If we look around us with our eyes open, it is not necessary to dwell upon the point of how far we are, at the moment, from that state of things.

The return

We still must speak about the return of many Jews to the country, which we have witnessed in our own time. What is involved here is an interpretation, from the perspective of faith, of a bit of highly controversial contemporary history. Therefore we shall not be able here to speak with too much certainty, because we are no prophets who can make clear and transparent, from God's perspective, these ambiguous historical events.

The Old Testament witnesses see a connection between the election of their people and the land of Palestine — or perhaps in this connection we must rather call it Canaan. According to them, this land is the place that God gave to Israel in order there to fulfill their destiny as his covenant-people. Just as they understood the calling of their people as grace, so also did they regard the possibility of dwelling in the land. Hence they regarded the expulsion from the land as a sign of God's turning away from them and his judgment; nd for them the final salvation also was bound up with the land. Let us nto too readily say that we can no longer accept a theology that is so bound up with the land. Let us not too readily say that we can no longer accept a theology that is so bound to a specific spot on the earth.

Because the God in whom we believe deals with men of flesh and blood who live at a particular place in this earth, our faith, if it is not simply to evaporate, should be able also to have a geographical aspect.

But there is a difference before and since Christ's coming. Before he came, God's revealing action was directed in particular to this one people, although even then it had a universal dimension. Through Christ salvation is relieved of every restriction and has become, so to speak, accessible for all men. In this respect the distinction between Jews and non-Jews has disappeared. But this is not in conflict with the conviction of faith that the Jewish people, even in their rejection of Christ, continue to be preserved by God. This people has its true encounter with Christ still ahead of it, and until then, it maintains its own wa alongside the Christian community. And on this way this special land is, as it were, the security deposit of God's faithfulness. The bond with the land remains in effect, by God's provision, so long as this people may exist in its particularity. This particularity is something temporary, provisional, which will come to an end when Israel has realized its destiny in Christ. Hence the return can indeed be a sign of God's faithfulness, but it also belongs to the provisionality of Israel's continued separate existence. I do not know whether it is a fulfillment of divine promises and the beginning of a new saving action by God with the people and with the world. I only see, from the factuality of the historical event, that this people is not a petrified fossil, as the historian Toynbee thought, but that it is still alive and that it once again has been given a new possibility of fulfilling its calling. But it is no more than a possibility, which it can use for good or for evil. And perhaps it is connected with Israel's special position before God that the way in which Israel uses this possibility can bring blessing or bane to the whole world. But I shall leave off here; otherwise we should be overstepping the boundaries set for our faith-reflection and end up in salvation-historical speculations. In any case the return can be for faith a visible indication that God is still engaged with this people and that he provides a future for it, and this is reason enough to be thankful for the return. For just as he preserves this people and gives it a future, he also preserves and provides a future for us and for the whole world.

This last insight then raises the question whether we still can speak of a special position of Israel. Is that not in conflict with what we said earlier about the opening up of salvation by Christ? To answer this question we must refer back to the "particularist" election of Israel before Christ, of which the Old Testament speaks. In this election this people was set apart from the other peoples and was the recipient of God's love in a special way; but precisely in this special relationship it represented the other peoples (chapter VIII). In Israel it became manifest how God is the Ally of all. Precisely in God's special devotion and attention it was a mirror of the world. Similarly, all that is said in this chapter about Israel applies to all men. If we still speak of a special place of contemporary Israel, this special character lies in the fact that what applies to all applies to this people par excellence; its "advantages" are advantages that are available to the whole world, and its destiny is the destiny of every man. Israel is preserved and sustained by God's love, and therein it is the sign of God's care and faithfulness for all. With Paul we dare to hope that God will lead all Israel to its ultimate salvation; and similarly we have the boldness to trust that God will set in order the whole world, the whole of mankind.

XX. THE FUTURE OF THE WORLD

The symbol of the Kingdom

There are two different questions which cannot be reduced to each other: that of the future of the individual human life and that of the future of humanity and of history. In both questions, however, the issue is the meaning of our existence. In chapter XVI we saw that our personal life does not end in nothingness, but that it is saved, preserved, and fulfilled in its relationship with God and with our fellowmen. But we do not live only in the direct personal relationship of man with God and man with fellowman. We also have our place in the larger, more impersonal associations and structures of work, of society, of culture. We are a part of the total history of mankind upon earth. The question of the meaning of that history is not answered by pointing to the eternal destiny of ourselves and of all men one by one.

We are more aware than were earlier generations of our share in the responsibility for the struggle for right and justice on earth, for peace among nations, for the welfare of humanity, and for the protection of nature. This means that concern about personal and individual salvation has shifted more into the background and the question of the future of this world has acquired for many a previously unknown urgency. For in this question, what is involved is not what will happen in distant times, but the history in which we are set and the decisions that we must now make in that history.

For many Christians in our time and particularly for those who are socially and politically engaged, the expectation of the Kingdom of God has become the quintessence of their faith. They will often find it difficult to describe in terms of content precisely what they mean by this. In any case it is for them the most comprehensive framework for the world and history, the supreme symbol of the future. and of the hope and the faith that the world will be set right.

It is not strictly necessary to identify the ultimate universal future in terms of this figure. In the Old Testament the view that God is not the King of Israel alone, but of the whole world, and that in the future he will fully unfold his royal power, does not appear until the time of the exile. And in the New Testament the idea of the Kingdom assumes a central place only in the synoptic gospels, while the term is used by Paul only a few times, and in the rest of the writings hardly at all. Yet the fact that the entire proclamation of Jesus can be summed up as the announcement of the Kingdom is reason enough to give this concept a central place. Moreover, this symbol is particularly suitable as a designation for the all-encompassing hope for the future, because we connect with it political as well as social and indeed universal ideas. In the first place, the political idea of God's kingship is expressed in it. The Kingdom points to the expectation that God will fully reveal his lordship over all that is, and will so fully exercise that lordship that there will no longer be anything that resists his will. In the second place, there are included in this concept, for us, certain expectations that fall in the social category. It has to do with peace, with right and justice, with rehabilitation of society's weak and despised persons. And finally, it also has for us a universal sound. God's Kingdom will encompass existence in all its dimensions, the life of the nations and of mankind, history and nature alike.

The basis of the expectation of the Kingdom

Just as the expectation that man is saved and preserved beyond death by God is based upon belief in the love and faithfulness of his Covenant-ally, so also the expectation that history and all existence will be perfected by God is based upon belief in his sovereign power that conquers all resistance. The Christian hope that the world has a future is not a conclusion that is drawn from the course of history, but is given with faith in God. We have had the experience with him that he is stronger than the powers that threaten to detach us from him -- and this holds true not only for personal afflictions and assaults, but also for the drawing power of our intellectual and cultural climate with its idolatry of prosperity and its enslavement to technology. Therefore we believe in his sovereignty and omnipotence (pp. 16-17), and we are convinced that he is the master of all powers that seem to control history. And therefore we dare to trust that he will bring this history to a good end.

This was Israel's confession, too. In the great events of its history, the exodus from Egypt, the occupation of Canaan, the establishment of the Davidic monarchy, the exile and the return from exile, it had experienced the power of God, a power that appeared to be stronger than the great world empires. And these experiences gave the people courage for the future. If God had proved himself so almighty, he could not fail to exhibit this omnipotence in the future also. The experience of God's kingship in the past and the present gave assurance of his total victory in the future. Israel's expectation that God's lordship over the whole world would be made manifest was the explication and the extension into the future of Israel's corporate experience of God in its history.

> Israel's faith always had a future dimension. This was already present in the early experience that Yahweh had delivered his people from Egypt and had gone before them, to lead them to the promised land. Thereafter the expectation of the future assumed the form that Israel trusted that God would destroy all enemies of his covenant-people. The prophets, because of Israel's disobedience, no longer expected the political stability of the nation. In this way the expectation lost its narrowly nationalistic color; it embraced in its vision the Gentiles as well, and in increasing measure it acquired features that transcend ordinary earthly reality. And while in earlier times the fulfillment was expected in the imminent future, as time went on the fulfillment was more and more shifted to a distant or indefinite future. Finally, in apocalyptic, a genre of literature of which the latter half of the book of Daniel is the only representative in the Old Testament, the totality of all

history and the entire cosmos is viewed. Apocalyptic language is foreign to us, and the descriptions often appear fantastic to us, but if we look through and beyond this language, we see how grandiose the future perspective has become. Contrary to all logic -- the book of Daniel was written in a time of severe persecution -- the total victory of God is maintained. However, this victory, which will be the great, all-decisive turning-point of history, as pure future lies outside this aeon, outside the world-order, the dispension in which we now live.

The belief in God's lordship over history that is expressed in the Old Testament has been confirmed and made sure for us in Jesus Christ. In this connection then we must pay special attention to those aspects of his activity which do not lie primarily on the inter-personal human plane -- although I am aware that the distinction between these aspects of his conduct that are oriented to the individual person and those that are oriented to society and universal human existence is relatively artificial. In Jesus' driving out of the demons and in his miracles, and then particularly in his so-called nature-miracles such as the stilling of the storm, but also in the curious words that he saw Satan fall from heaven (Luke 10:18), Jesus' power from God over the anti-godly forces in nature and in history is manifested. It is not important whether this utterance actually comes from the "historical Jesus" and whether he actually did all the "signs" that are attributed to him. If they are stories of the early community, it is evident from them that in any case the first believers experienced in Jesus Christ God's lordship. And this is all the more true concerning the resurrection. Though it could appear in the crucifixion as though the world is ultimately stronger than God's will, the resurrection definitely reveals the contrary. In the resurrection God gives to Jesus Christ and to all that he represents a new future. And what he represents is the Kingdom of God.

The Kingdom as the end and goal of history

The Kingdom as the complete manifestation of God's lordship that permeates all dimensions of existence signifies a complete inversion of the world that we know. For the world as it is, with all its injustice and violence, is not as God wants it to be. This total inversion is not a human possibility in history. All efforts that have ever been expended to build a perfect society have always run aground on human inadequacy. What can be seen in the course of history gives us no reason to believe in a gradual development. There is nothing to indicate that the world is becoming better and better until it turns into the Kingdom, so to speak. This does not imply a one-sided historical pessimism. Great and good things have been done in the past and the present, and in many respects progress certainly has been made. Conditions of society have been improved in many places, in many countries consciences have become more sensitive, the feeling of social responsibility for all humanity has increased, and there is significant progress in health care, to name only a few examples. But alongside these, in this century we have also experienced the demonic power of evil in a scope which we would have thought no longer possible. Technological development has opened up great possibilities for good, but it has also made possible efficient gas chambers and the atomic bomb. Every new revolution has set right some injustice and created more new injustice, and every new struggle for freedom has brought with it new slavery and unfreedom.

But it is not only what we see around us that refutes, as I see it, the hope of an immanent development of history into the Kingdom. It is also refuted by the cross and the resurrection. The crucifixion is the continuing reminder of human resistance against God; it shows that the world does not want to accept God's lordship. And the resurrection, the only point in history in which this lordship has been wholly and entirely expressed, is an utterly unprecedented event, the absolutely new, which is not an extension of our human possibilities. Thus the biblical-apocalyptic insight that the consummation of history will likewise be the end of history is confirmed both by empirical experience and by the resurrection faith. The Kingdom of God points to a new situation beyond our historical, earthly reality.

The expectation of the Kingdom as the end, or, better said, beyond the end of history, is a warning against all naive and therefore short-winded belief in progress, that overlooks the fundamental ambiguity of all historical events and makes light of the resistance against God on the part of the hostile forces in humanity. But the Kingdom is not only the end, but also the consummation of history. That is, God will bring world history, which is in his hand, to a good end, to its destiny. And its destiny is, in the words that Jesus taught his disciples to pray, that God's will shall be done, not only in personal life, but also "on earth," that is, in earthly society, with its structures and ordinances. God does not will that the earth should be lost, but that it should become his Kingdom. And because this is the will of him whom we have come to know as the king of the earth, we may be confident that he will accomplish his will.

The debate over whether men here on earth can help to build the Kingdom or whether it is solely an incomprehensible work of God appears to me to be unfruitful. That God's lordship is made manifest and prevails lies solely in God's hands; it is, after all, a matter of *his* lordship. But as long as history continues, his lordship occurs in and through human actions. The Kingdom, seen as a reality beyond the end of history, is God's deed alone. But the Kingdom seen as the goal and destiny of history does allow human action its proper place. Men can act in the direction of the Kingdom.

Such action is not limited to those who do this in conscious discipleship to Christ or in a conscious relationship to God, although these can draw strength and a sense of direction from these conscious ties. But where it involves a political action — and of course the term "political" must not be understood here in the narrow sense — every action that brings greater justice upon earth, that works for an increasing humanizing of society, and that is engaged on behalf of the preservation of humanity may be seen in the light of God's Kingdom as an actualization of God's lordship on earth. So long as history continues, this actualization will have a partial and fragmented, and often an ambiguous, character. Did the Constantinian empire, the Enlightenment, the French Revolution, and the Russian Revolution serve the Kingdom of God, or precisely the opposite? It is obvious that any judgment that we make here can only be a relative one. This side of the consummation, human action is, in its ultimate meaning, inscrutable. The symbol of the so-called judgment is intended to remind us of this fact. It says to us that only "at the end" will the worth, in God's eyes, of all human deeds be unveiled and made manifest.

For the sake of conceptual clarity I have here used the Kingdom, somewhat arbitrarily, only as a symbol of the final consummation. However, in view of the fact that it is also the goal and destiny of history, in a certain sense it is also present in history. Indeed, this is obvious. What is involved in the Kingdom is God's royal lordship, and God is ruling even now (Jesus Christ and his resurrection demonstrate that), although he will fully manifest this only in the future. In harmony with this, Jesus sometimes spoke about the Kingdom in figures that suggest a small beginning in the present, which in the future will grow into something mighty. Similarly, according to Matthew and Luke he identified his driving out of the demons as the dawning of the Kingdom.

Some apocalyptic, biblical images

1. The idea of the *return of the Lord* has occupied a major place in the church at some times, and it still holds such a place among some groups. The New Testament and, in harmony with it, the Apostles' Creed do not speak of a return, but of a coming. This is understandable, because the idea in the Bible with respect to this "coming" is a coming in full manifestation and glory. The coming of Christ refers to the same reality as the coming of the Kingdom. Now the latter says more to us today, first of all because it is less easily misunderstood as being a realistic description, and in the second place because the symbol of the Kingdom suggests the political and social dimension. But in this Kingdom it will be as it was in the activity of Jesus Christ: his concern for the poor, for sinners and tax collectors, and his taking his place alongside those who suffered under the imperfection of this world show the direction in which we must look when we think of the Kingdom. And this not only in the sense that the "poor" and "those who mourn" will be personally satisfied and comforted (though that too!), but also in the sense that they can only truly be satisfied and comforted in a new, transformed world. Thus the imagery of the coming of Christ in glory, the coming of him who let God's will be done here on earth, gives content to the imagery of the Kingdom.

Bound up with Christ's coming (again) is the idea that the final judgment will be accomplished by him. If we analyze this figure of speech, it says on the one hand that God, in whose light human deeds will be made manifest, is as we have come to know him in Christ, and on the other hand that Christ is the norm of history by which all human actions will be measured.

2. In the apocalyptic thought-pattern, *cosmic catastrophes* that will precede the coming of the Kingdom have a fixed place. Now in our times the ultimate expectation of the future has once again acquired a cosmic dimension. For we hope not only that history will be set right, but that nature also, which by man's fault is out of joint, will in some way or another be set right once again. The Old Testament images of a glorified nature, in which inconceivable fruitfulness and peace in the animal kingdom are dominant, have acquired for us a deep symbolic meaning. Moreover, the insights of modern natural sciences as well as the nightmares of an atomic disaster have made the idea of a total destruction of the earth more believable than was the case one or two centuries ago. But this does not mean that we can adopt the conception of cosmic catastrophes that announce the coming of the Kingdom. We do not know what will happen in the end-time of history, and even the biblical writers did not know. We expect the Kingdom as the consummation of history. That is, we hope for a future and for God's ultimate salvation of our earth. But whether this will happen through the annihiliation of humanity and the world lies outside the range of our knowledge.

3. Further, we cannot simply adopt the idea of the *thousand-year king-dom*, which appears in the Bible only on the periphery, in Rev. 20:1-6, not even if we detach it from its mythological clothing. The idea in this is the expectation that in the end-time, still within history, here on our earth a blessed time will dawn in which Christ will rule in company with his believers. But here again it is true that no one can foresee the course of history. Yet the conception of the so-called millennium contains a profound truth of faith, namely that the future, so to speak, lays claim upon history and sheds its light in history in advance. For in history, not necessarily as its last stage but again and again, here and there, there exists the possibility of a "thousand-year kingdom," something like a provisional, advance fulfillment, even though this will constantly be threatened by Satan's breaking loose again (Rev. 20:7).

In this same area also lies the truth-content of the idea of the *antichrist*, who is to appear before God's victory has perfectly prevailed. This symbol of personified evil points to a concentration and exaltation of all anti-Christian forces in history. However, we cannot know whether such a concentration of evil will occur at the end. Just as there can be times in history of something like a provisional fulfillment, so there are also apocalyptic times when evil grows to satanic proportions. Faith knows then that the future does not belong to this evil but to God. This is what the figure of the antichrist says in mythological language.

A new heaven and a new earth

As we have already said, the hope of the kingdom is based upon what we know of God. We make an extension of the experiences of history, out of the past in which we have come to know God's royal power — and I am thinking primarily of the exodus and of Jesus Christ — toward the future. It cannot be otherwise than that he will bring to a good end what he has begun in history. The Kingdom of God is our design for the future on the basis of the past. This does not mean that our hope is only a projection of ourselves. God himself projects himself and his Kingdom, so to speak, on the screen of the future.

Of course we cannot give any detailed description of the Kingdom of God. Just as we were able to speak only in figurative language about life after death, because it is a life beyond our earthly time and space, so also is the same true of the Kingdom that we expect beyond history. Again, this does not mean that these are "only" figures of speech, for these images are taken from what we know of God. The actuality of the Kingdom will not be different; it will only be more and greater than we now can hope.

Alongside all that has already been said in this chapter by way of content about the Kingdom, for me one of the most expressive images offered to us in the Bible is that of a new heaven and a new earth where righteousness dwells. "Heaven and earth" is a way of saying "everything that is." Everything will become new, different, and good. It is obvious that we must not think in this connection of the universe in the sense of modern natural sciences. The universe has become infinitely greater for us than it was for our parents and grandparents, and certainly for the biblical writers. The Kingdom is the expectation of all that has to do with, and has any connection with, the earth.

Faith has nothing to say about what lies beyond this range. Righteousness will prevail on this new, transformed earth. That is, everything will be set right before God and thus will itself come into its own: things, society, people; the last-named above all, of course; in the society which we know, people allow each other so precious little to receive their just due. But things, nature, and the animals are included, too. As the poet of the book of Job says, God also made the utterly unnecessary and, for man, useless animals, such as the wild donkey and the locust, and even the monsters Behemoth and Leviathan. God obviously takes pleasure in his creation; it is more than just the stage for humanity. Then may not this creation also be taken up into the expectation of the future? Of course this is not a description, but only a dream, but dreams about God are not necessarily a delusion.

And then there is the figure that says the same thing with a somewhat different accent, that God in his Kingdom will wipe away all tears, that there will be no more death or grief or pain, but also no hunger, no thirst, no strife, and no injustice. Particularly in this picture of God's future the political-social and the personal element are intertwined. From our perspective it is impossible to see how life after death as transfiguration of personal human existence and the Kingdom as consummation of history are related. When we try to interweave these two expectations, we become entangled in all sorts of rational difficulties or speculative fantasies. But I am convinced that God sees them as one and that someday, when we no longer "see in enigmas" — and even this is once again the language of dreams and figures — this connection will be revealed to us too.

In the foregoing we have spoken more than once about the Kingdom in terms of unveiling and becoming manifest. We expect of the future the becoming manifest of the still concealed meaning of history, the becoming manifest of the ways mankind has taken, which of these ways have led toward the Kingdom, and which were blind alleys and wrong roads; and we expect above all the becoming manifest of God's lordship, which now is already believed but is not yet irrefutably visible. But it is enough to speak only of unveiling. The Kingdom is more than a becoming manifest of what already is; it is also fulfillment and consummation. Therefore it is not true simply that in Jesus Christ God's decisive action has already occurred. In this connection the figure is often used of a war in which the decisive battle is already won, so that it is only a matter of time until the enemy finally concedes his defeat. I am glad to adopt this figure, but it must function in two directions. It is true that the enemy has suffered a crushing defeat, and this knowledge can be a great comfort and encouragement. But there is not much yet to be observed of this defeat; the war is still going on, the fighting is still raging, men are dying, and there is still privation and hunger. And the peace will not only make manifest that "actually" the war had already ended with the decisive battle, but it will also bring the end of the distresses of war and a new, infinitely better life.

How long yet?

When we described the Kingdom as the consequence of our belief in God, we drew a line from our present time to the future. But there is also a line running in the other direction, from the future to our present. Thereby the future becomes normative for our ethos. The Kingdom that we expect and that runs counter to our society with its orders and structures becomes the norm and the mainspring of our (political) action in history. We said above that the ultimate value of all our deeds will become manifest only at the end, at the "last judgment." But although our action in history has an ultimate ambiguity, the belief that the Kingdom is the norm for our conduct means that we have a standard that enables us to do with a good conscience what we think must be done. For the Kingdom is the doing of God's will, the will of the Covenant-God who is revealed to us in Jesus Christ as fully as he can be revealed to men in history.

The Christian ethic is not an interim ethic, as it is said to be; not a kind of provisional ethic that applies during the "interim" between the resurrection and the coming of the Kingdom; but it is a Kingdom-ethic, an ethic that represents the Kingdom insofar as this is possible this side of the consummation.

But precisely when we see the present in the light of the future, we become aware of the discrepancy between the Kingdom and the world in which we live. No gratitude for the salvation that God has given us in Christ and no experience of God's presence now may make us forget this discrepancy. On the contrary, precisely on the basis of this gratitude and this experience we shall suffer over the suffering of the world, we look forward to the coming of the Kingdom, and we hope that we shall not have to wait too long for it. For the expectation of the Kingdom of God, if it really is expectation, cannot fail to hope for the fulfillment as quickly as possible, tomorrow, the next day, in our time, if possible. Therefore there will also be a zealous striving for the Kingdom. I do not know whether our actions can hasten the coming of the Kingdom. But we may be convinced that in any case the Kingdom will come, in God's own time, and that in the process, in a way that we cannot perceive, our actions also will play a role, and therein will find their fulfillment.